WOMEN AND TRAFFICKING:

A SOCIO-LEGAL PERSPECTIVES

WOMEN AND TRAFFICKING: A SOCIO-LEGAL PERSPECTIVES

DR. MD ARIF WADOOD

KALPAZ

Published by

Kalpaz Publications
C-30, Satyawati Nagar,
Delhi – 110052
Ph.: 011-47034999, 9811692060
www.kalpazpublications.com
E-mail: kalpaz@hotmail.com

Distribution Network
www.gyanbooks.com
India, USA, Canada, UK, Australia, France

ISBN: 978-93-5722-664-6 (PB)
First Published, 2024

Printed at: Gyan Press, Delhi.

WOMEN AND TRAFFICKING: A SOCIO-LEGAL PERSPECTIVES

Author: DR. MD ARIF WADOOD

Dedicated to My Most Loving Parents

Late Abdul Wadood

&

Shakera Khatoon

“Who have made me what I am and
Given me all that I have”

Contents

Foreword

Throughout the world, trafficking has been identified as the third largest source of profit for organized crime followed by arms and drugs generating billions of dollars annually. Trafficking is a complex term which includes not only trafficking in women and children alone but it occurs for other purposes too; for instance, cheap labour, prostitution, organ trade, drug couriers, arms smuggling etc. Moreover, it becomes more challenging due to its variations throughout the world and India is not an exception. It is under this backdrop, the book on **"Women and Trafficking: A Socio-Legal Perspectives"** by Dr. Md Arif Wadood has rightly pointed out that, young girls are trafficked to major cities and towns for the purpose of commercial sexual exploitation, the most common and glaring being for prostitution. It becomes more complex when trafficking for prostitution is seen as a traditional and cultural practice by communities in India such as Bedias, Sanyasi, Devadasi and Jogin traditions are still prevalent in 21st century with the tacit support of family and society. The book provides a comprehensive analysis of the socio-legal along with historical, cultural and economic factors are underlying cause of trafficking in India.

The author navigates the challenges and opportunities of social and legal reforms and restructuring of trafficking laws in contemporary India. The major focus of the book is to show the involvement of women in this profession. The author argues with empirical data that 80% of Bedia women introduced into the profession by their parents due to mother's profession or tradition/social custom. While only 20% women were introduced into this profession by their relatives or their family members due to poverty. The author has rightly said that, in the prevailing climate of Bedia community have been traditionally practicing prostitution and such type the community profession is a big challenge for the Government as well as several organizations who have been working in protection of human rights of CSWs. Firstly, because of involvement of huge political and criminal nexus, women have become a commodity in this game and even they are not in a position to demand for their dignity and struggle for their rights. Secondly, to identify red light areas are now diminishing and no longer remain a concept for sexual exploitation. Thirdly, they are not able to come under one umbrella so they have no platform to come forward to demand for their rights and it is very sad that the government has no effective rehabilitation programmes.

The author in this book has rightly pointed out that, trafficking for commercial sexual exploitation is an organized crime that violates women's basic human rights to live with dignity and their bodily integrity. This book analyses the socio-legal issues of trafficking and provides a chance to actively participate in the process of transforming anti trafficking laws, to protect the traffic victims from exploitation and to fight the problem of trafficking for commercial sexual exploitation. The author has clearly mentioned ways and means to address the problem of trafficking through legislation, law enforcement, adjudication of cases and shelter homes for the well-being of trafficked victims in general and women in particular for the future of India.

This book will be of enormous interest to all those who are interested to address the problem of trafficking and prudent in shaping the future policy makers to improve the situation of women who are the victims of trafficking. The author appeals to government and local body to take efforts to evolve an effective remedial measure to protect the women's dignity and their bodily integrity in order to bring them in mainstream development.

Prof. (Dr.) Nuzhat Parveen Khan,

Presently Professor and Former Dean, Faculty of Law
Jamia Millia Islamia, Central University New Delhi
Former Chairperson, ICC. Jamia Millia Islamia, New Delhi
Former Dean School of Law
Bennett University, The Times of India Group

Foreword

I am delighted to write this foreword for Dr. Md Arif Wadood's book **"Women and Trafficking: A Socio-Legal Perspectives"**. The book is an attempt to understand, analyse and evaluate the effectiveness of legislation concerning 'trafficking for Commercial Sexual Exploitation' in India. Trafficking of women has been emerged as one of the major problems for India because of the fragile social and economic conditions which forced many women to become victims of trafficking, prostitution and other forms of violence. Often poverty, vulnerability of women and children, lack of access to education, health care and lack of livelihood options are some of the underlying cause of trafficking. The author argues that, the matter becomes more complex when trafficking for prostitution is seen as a traditional and cultural practice by communities such as Bedia, Devadasi, Jogin etc. traditions are still prevalent in some part of India and have the tacit support of family and society.

The author addresses socio-legal problems related to trafficking of women and if there would be no legal support further aggravates the situation of women who are the victims of trafficking. However, the author has clearly point out that, there has been an appropriate law against these sorts of crime but due to certain anomalies in the laws and lack of implementation make the trafficking laws unable to protect women from being victimised. In order to provides a complete understanding of trafficking of women, the author has clearly pointed out that the conceptual understanding in the spheres of prevention, protection and prosecution are not sufficient to address this complex problem in a holistic manner.

This book is an invaluable resource for scholars, lawyers, sociologists and others seeking in depth understanding of the intricacies of immoral trafficking for commercial sexual exploitation of women in contemporary India. The book will be of enormous interest to all those who are interested to address the problem of trafficking and prudent in shaping the future policy makers to adopt four ways to improve the situation of women who are the victims of trafficking through legislation, law enforcement, adjudication of cases and shelter homes. Furthermore, the author appeals to government and local body to take efforts to evolve an effective remedial measure to protect womanhood from disgrace.

Prof. (Dr.) Ghulam Yazdani
Dean
Faculty of Law
Jamia Millia Islamia
New Delhi, India

Preface

I feel proud and happy in presenting this book to the readers who are interested in the socio-legal aspect of human trafficking. Human trafficking is an organized crime that violates basic rights to live with dignity and bodily integrity. It is one of the heinous illegal trades globally after arms and drugs. Today India became a source, transit and destination for both in country and cross border trafficking due to many reasons like geographical location, population, economy etc. Furthermore, it becomes more challenging due to its variations. Often, poverty, vulnerability of women and children, little or no access to education and health care and lack of livelihood options are some of the underlying cause of trafficking.

Various empirical data shows that, young girls are trafficked to major cities and towns for the purpose of commercial sexual exploitation, the most common and glaring being for prostitution. However, the matter becomes more complex when trafficking for prostitution is seen as a traditional and cultural practice by communities such as Bedias, Sansi, Devadasi and Jogin tradition, which are still prevalent in some part of India and have the tacit support of family and society. Hence, we need to think in a holistic approach to deal the problem of trafficking among women of such communities like Bedia and other. Since it has been observed that, economic viability of the women among the such continues to determine their status in the community. In fact, they are held in high esteem till the time they are economically productive. However, putting it clearly, the female sex in this community has been reduced to objects or commodities with a mere monetary value which needs to be address so that they each woman in the Bedia community can live their life in a dignified manner.

Furthermore, such commercialization of women's body is not only a serious crime but also an abuse of women's dignity that results in physical, social, mental damage to millions of women every year. Many women all over the world find themselves treated unequally with respect to bodily safety and integrity and in many cases these hardships are caused by their being women and in many cases laws and institutions perpetuate these inequalities. Consider an example of the existing systems concerning "trafficking of women for commercial sexual exploitation" in the spheres of prevention, protection and prosecution are not sufficient to address this complex problem in a holistic and human rights-based manner. Since, the conceptual understanding that regulates "anti-trafficking legislation" so far has equated "trafficking with prostitution". It has; therefore, limit the scope of tackling various forms of trafficking. Therefore, it unable to deal with the vulnerability of the victims and the process that put them in circumstances of "abuse as victims of commercial sexual exploitation (CSE)". Furthermore, it imposes the burden of abuse on the victims only and abstains from talking the abuser as well as perpetrator. It has been found that majority of the countries legislation dealing with trafficking are designed in such a way to address prostitution and not trafficking. Still trafficking is not considered a serious crime and considered it as a minor offence as it is equated with prostitution.

In order to address issues related to trafficking of women, my empirical study shows about the involvement of Bedia and Non-Bedia women in this profession and found that that 80% of Bedia women introduced into the profession by their parents due to mother's profession or tradition/social custom. While only 20% women were introduced into this profession by their relatives or their family members due to poverty. Therefore, in the prevailing climate of Bedia community who have been traditionally practicing prostitution so my appeal to government and local body to take efforts to evolve an effective remedial measure so that they may use womanhood from disgrace. Moreover, it can be argue that such type the community profession is a big challenge for the Government as well as several organizations who have been working in protection human rights of CSWs among Bedia community; firstly, because of involvement of huge political and criminal nexus, women have become a commodity in this game and even they are not in a position to demand for their dignity and struggle for their rights, secondly, to identify red light areas in Agra division are now diminishing and no longer remain a concept for sexual exploitation, thirdly, they are not able to come under one umbrella so they have no platform to come forward to demand for their rights and it is very sad that the government has no effective rehabilitation programmes.

Today, trafficking of women emerged as one of the major problems for India because of the fragile social and economic conditions which forced many women to become victims of trafficking, prostitution and other forms of violence. Moreover, if there would be no legal support provided then it further aggravates the situation. Although, there are laws against these sorts of crime but lack of implementation due to various reasons make the laws unable to protect women from being victimized. As a result, trafficking within the territory and across the border is gradually increasing.

The present book entitled as "Women and Trafficking: A Socio-Legal Perspectives" are helpful in understanding the laws of the land related to trafficking and the process of its implementation should be reviewed to improve the situation of women. This kind of socio-legal studies explore the ways and means to improve trafficking laws, protect the traffic victims from exploitation and to fight the problem of trafficking for commercial sexual exploitation. Furthermore, this book is always helpful for scholars, researchers, students and policy makers since it shows us a different picture of what our priorities should be in the matter of trafficking. Therefore, I have tried my best to give a complete understanding of the problem of trafficking of women for scholars, researchers, students. Moreover, I have also suggested policy makers to adopt four ways and means to improve the situation of women through legislation, law enforcement, adjudication of cases and shelter homes if we want to move policy choice in the right direction. More importantly, this book may prove prudent in shaping the future policy for trafficking which may contribute to large extent for the well-being of trafficked victims in general and Bedia women in particular.

I have great pleasure in acknowledging my gratitude to all those persons who have helped me in a substantial manner for completing this book. My professors, colleagues and friends from the teaching community provided the guidance, books and useful suggestions at various junctures. I am particularly thankful to my supervisor, mentor and guide Prof. Nuzhat Parveen Khan for helping me for preparing the manuscript of the book. I am also thankful to Prof. Ghulam Yazdani. Prof. Eqbal Hussain, Prof. Faizanur Rahman, Prof. Mohammad Asad Malik, Prof. Qazi Mohammad Usman Prof. Humayun Akhtar Nazmi, Prof. Mumtaz Ahmad and Prof. Mohammad Sohrab for their guidance and support.

Finally, I must admit that, I would never have been able to bring out this book without the help of my wife Dr. Ghazala Rizvi for her intellectual and moral support. I am also thankful to my brother Prof. Md Arshad and my friend Dr. Shamseer Alam for their unwavering support in completing this work. My thanks are also due to Dr. Amit Garg, Director of Kalpaz Publications, Gyan Books Pvt. Ltd. for accepting and publishing my work.

New Delhi **Dr. Md Arif Wadood**

List of Acronyms

AIDS - Acquired Immune Deficiency Syndrome
BNWLA - Bangladesh National Women Lawyers' Association
CEDAW - Convention on the Elimination of all Forms of Discrimination against Women, 1979
CRC - Convention on the Rights of the Children, 1989
CrPC - Criminal Procedure Code
CSE - Commercial Sexual Exploitation
CSW - Commercial Sex Workers
HIV - Human Immunodeficiency Virus
HIV - Human Immune Virus
ILO - International Labour Organisation
INGO - International Non-Governmental Organisation
IPC - Indian Penal Code
IT(P) Act - Immoral Traffic (Prevention) Act
MOWCA - Ministry of Women and Children Affairs
NGO - Non-Governmental Organisation
NHRC - National Human Rights Commission
NPA - National Plan of Action
SAARC - South Asian Association for Regional Cooperation
SEACT - Sexual Exploitation and Abuse of Children including Trafficking
STI - Sexually Transmitted Infections
UN - United Nations
UNICEF - United Nations International Children Emergency Fund
VAW - Violence Against Women
WHO - World Health Organisation

Chapter - 1

Understanding Trafficking of Women in India

This chapter is an attempt to explore immoral trafficking for commercial sexual exploitation among women. Trafficking of women as an organised crime that violates their basic human rights and makes them to live like an animal. Indeed, it has been observed that, young girls are trafficked to major cities and towns for the purpose of "commercial sexual exploitation", the most common and glaring being for prostitution. Moreover, trafficking becomes a vicious crime which involves worst forms of human rights abuses including emotional, physical and sexual violence with bleak possibilities of rescue or reintegration with their families.

Today, India becomes a "source, destination and transit for both in country and cross border trafficking". Moreover, the problem of trafficking of women for commercial sexual exploitation is more challenging due to its myriad complexities and variations throughout the world and India is not an exception. It has been often found that, poverty, vulnerability of women and children, little or no access to education and health care and lack of livelihood options are some of the underlying cause of "trafficking". However, the matter becomes more complex when trafficking for prostitution is seen as a traditional and cultural practice by communities such as Bedias, Sansi, Devadasi and Jogin tradition, which are still prevalent in some part of India and have the tacit support of family and society.

Furthermore, it is estimated that, "human trafficking has been identified as the third largest source of profit for organised crime, followed by arms and drug, has been generating billions of dollars annually at the global level".[1] According to United Nations Protocol, "trafficking is defined as any activity leading to recruitment, transportation, harboring or receipt of persons by means of threat or use of force or a position of vulnerability or of the giving or receiving of payments or benefits to achieve the consent of a person having control over another person, for the purpose of exploitation which include sexual exploitation, forced labour or services, slavery or practices similar to slavery, servitude or the removal of organs."[2]

It makes clear that, trafficking in persons is a complex term which includes not only trafficking in women and children alone but it occur for other purposes too; for instance, "cheap labour, prostitution, organ trade, drug couriers, arms smuggling etc.".[3] In order to understand trafficking properly, it is vital to take into account the other forms of movement of persons within and across borders, such as 'migration and smuggling'. Migration is the movement of persons from one country to another, by legal or illegal means. It can be voluntary (with consent) or involuntary (without consent). Involuntary or forced migration includes the displacement of persons (due to natural disasters) and trafficking.[4] It has been observed that, "international migration is regarded as a diverse international business with a vast budget, and is believed to provide hundreds of thousands of jobs worldwide".[5] But, "the business is run by institutionalised networks with complex profit and loss accounts, as well as agents and individuals, each of whom stands to gain commercially".[6] Moreover, it has been often found that, "people might migrate to seek opportunities (primarily economic) to support their dependents or to escape domestic violence".[7]

Besides migration, "smuggling in persons consists of the transport of persons, with their consent, to another country through illegal means to other country".[8] In this way, trafficking in persons resembles the smuggling of migrants, which is the subject of a separate protocol (Protocol against the Smuggling of Migrants by Land, Sea and Air), but there are several important differences.[9] Moreover, it often undertaken in dangerous or degrading conditions, involves migrants who have consented to the smuggling. Trafficking victims, on the other hand, have either never consented or, if they did so initially, their consent has been rendered meaningless by the coercive, deceptive or abusive actions of the traffickers. "Another major difference is that smuggling ends with the arrival of the migrants at their destination, whereas trafficking involves the ongoing exploitation of the victims in some manner to generate illicit profits for the traffickers".[10]

"Finally, smuggling is always trans-national, unlike trafficking. The victims of trafficking can be either taken to another country or simply moved from one place to another within the same country".[11] It has also been observed that, "trafficking and smuggling in migrants are facets of trans-national organised crime that have often been called the dark side of globalization".[12] The opening of markets and borders due to globalisation has facilitated the movement and transport of people across countries, which means a larger number of immigrants. This has necessitated stricter visa regulations (especially for women and children), which, in turn, have led to a rise in the number of illegal immigrants moving in search of unorganised employment. As a result, globalisation has brought about a rapid growth of the informal sector, including callings such as street vending, and of unregulated work in factories, particularly in the export processing zones. In most cases, "the workers have become more vulnerable and are subjected to abusive working conditions. Their marginalised and unregulated areas of work are not visible and thus, not subject to labour laws and regulation".[13]

However, it can be argued that, the UN Trafficking Protocol i.e. "the United Nations Protocol to Prevent, Suppress and Punish Trafficking in Persons, Especially Women and Children, provides, a roadmap for "cross-national collaboration as well as recommendations for enacting effective domestic human trafficking laws".[14] Despite of its ratification of the UN Protocol, India continued to lack a unified comprehensive policy for human trafficking. In fact, India's anti-trafficking policies have broadly operated under a fragmented and piecemeal set of laws addressing various components of "human trafficking such as slavery, child labour, and child marriage".[15] In addition to that, Indian law did not contain a comprehensive definition of human trafficking. Since, the Constitution of India prohibits trafficking of human beings and forced labour, but it does not define either term.[16]

Although, "India penalizes many forms of forced labour under, "The Bonded Labour System (Abolition) Act",[17] "The Child Labour (Prohibition and Regulation) Act"[18] and "The Juvenile Justice (Care and Protection of Children) Act"[19] In addition to the above Act, India have also enacted the "Immoral Traffic (Prevention) Act i.e. referred as the IT (P) Act which criminalizes most forms of sex trafficking including some transactional aspects of voluntary sex work (e.g., solicitation). It thus ends up punishing both sex workers who solicit sex work voluntarily and sex trafficking victims who are coerced into doing so".[20] Furthermore, in order to fight with trafficking, "India enacted groundbreaking legislation in March 2013 i.e. the Criminal Law (Amendment) Act of 2013 which amended various Sections of the Indian Panel Code including provisions on human trafficking".[21] In other words, it can be point out that, this Act redefines the offence of human trafficking under Section 370 of the Indian Penal Code to closely parallel the definition in the UN Trafficking Protocol. Although, "these reforms have brought India into closer alignment with international standards, gaps still remain between India's current laws and the UN Trafficking Protocol".[22]

Moreover, it may point out that, it has been paradigm shift in India's trafficking laws; still traffickers have been operating either in an organised or unorganised sector. But in most cases, they operate as part of a nexus and some are one-time traffickers. As far as "Commercial Sexual Exploitation" (CSE) is concerned, in India, the initial traffickers are often known persons from the village, sex workers or madams, men who marry to sell their wives, a family, or in some cases, strangers who lure the victim with the promise of a better job. Trafficking requires the support of numerous factors, such as the initial procurers, the transporters, the middlemen or agents who facilitate the selling and buying of the trafficked, those who arrange for forged identities and travel documents, and the final buyers. The agents, brokers and employers involved often have links with organised crime. Members of the law enforcement machinery, more specifically, the border forces and armed forces, are also involved in the trafficking. They usually take commissions from the traffickers at the borders, or from brothel owners in the red-light areas.

Trafficked people are employed in various forms of exploitative work, including CSE, domestic servitude, camel jockeying, circuses, and other hazardous and slavery-like practices. Trafficking may involve some or all of the following components - force, coercion, fraud, deceit (including voodoo practices), trickery, complicity, ignorance (including the administration of drugs), cultural practices, gentle persuasion, luring the victims with the temptation of marriage or better economic prospects, and misinformation. It entails the transportation and movement of a person, through these methods, from one place to another for exploitative work. Finally, the victims are ignorant about what really awaits them at their destination.

The testimonies of the victims show that there is a commonality in the methods of persuasion used by traffickers, and research and literature reveal set patterns of abduction, as well as similarities in the circumstances of those who are trafficked. With regard to definitions, D' Cunha remarks that several authors, such as David, Polasky and Gagnon, relate prostitution to promiscuity and 'indiscriminate sexual intercourse', while a few others, like Barry, give recognition to the factor of coercion involved. D' Cunha, however, points out that these definitions do not take into account two points. First, that although slave labour (coercion) exists in prostitution, "it is not the only form of prostitution". Second, "not all women who are subject to sexual exploitation can be considered slaves, even when they cannot get out of the situation", i.e., other compulsions may keep them in the trade even when they are not explicitly coerced".[23] D'Cunha, therefore, feels that there is a need to adopt a more holistic view of prostitution. In this context, she points to Truong's study[24] which notes, among other things, that the act of prostitution must not be seen only at the level of individual motives. Instead, it must be analyzed in relation to the prevalent structure of relationships between men and women in a given society, as well as the existing class structure, as these "structures generally condition the act of prostitution itself".[25]

1.1 Classification of Commercial Sex Labour

Commercial sex labour, which can be carried out with or without the consent of the person concerned may be classified on the basis of the place where it is carried out and the form it takes. Moreover, different types or forms of sex work include brothel prostitution, hidden prostitution or prostitution carried out in hotels and bars, prostitution within small flats/apartments, street and slum prostitution, and prostitution with socio-religious sanction. Under the IT (P) Act, the term 'prostitution' covers commercial sexual exploitation, though it is interpreted by the enforcement agencies to also include commercial sex work. The classification of prostitution according to the workplace is of vital importance, as it accounts for the nuances of working in different settings. It gives us an idea of the sex workers' lifestyle, the extent of their freedom, their rights, their working conditions, their income and their vulnerability. The different forms of prostitution as per the workplace are described below.

1.2. Brothel prostitution

Brothel prostitution is prostitution carried out in specific areas, which are recognised as red light areas by the people and the police. "Red light areas in Delhi, Mumbai and Kolkata are home to a large number of persons in the commercial sex trade".[26] It has been observed that, the Sonapur red light area, located a few kilometers from the Bhandup Railway Station, in Mumbai was reported to be the most notorious area for prostitution of minors".[27] The other red light areas in Mumbai include places adjoining DB Marg, VP Road and the Nagpada police station, areas near the Grant Road station and areas in Worli. Besides, the red-light area where most of Delhi's brothels are located is GB Road and even though, private flats also operate as brothels. Another red-light area of Kolkata, found that some of these areas cater to customers from a low-income group, who rarely pay more than Rs 25 per visit. These include Loker Math, which has 21 houses with approximately 55 to 60 sex workers. Sonagachi is the only red-light area, which caters to high-income clients. According to some reports, it had been that 45.5% of the clients had a monthly income of less than Rs1000 and 13.6 % had a monthly income of over Rs 2500. Most of the clients were in service or business whereas the students who formed 8% of the clients. It has been seen hat 87% of the clients were literate and 25% had gone up to the level of higher education. These clients were called as "babus" or the clients with whom the women had a special arrangement were found to be slightly less educated, 74.3% were literate and only 9.1% had reached the level of higher education".[28] She has pointed out that, clients who buy the services provided by persons in the commercial sex trade can be classified into different categories; according to their economic status and their commitment to the persons they visit. These are temporary clients, fixed clients, local clients who include rich local people and tourists. The younger women prefer half hour clients (temporary clients), whom they can charge and avoid getting emotionally involved with. On the other hand, older women who are financially insecure prefer fixed clients, as the latter can give them a regular monthly sum and might also be able to offer a satisfying relationship.[29]

1.3. Types of Clients

(a) **Temporary clients**: These include persons who come out of curiosity. They could be one timer, such as young men and adolescents. Truck drivers, who are regularly on the move and visit sex workers on highways in different places, are also temporary clients as far as the sex worker is concerned. They might visit sex workers regularly, but for the sex worker they are temporary clients.[30]

(b) **Fixed clients**: These clients regularly visit the same woman for a period of a few months or years. Some of them pay the woman a fixed monthly sum and live with her. Fixed clients pay less per visit than temporary ones, as they provide the woman with greater financial security than the latter. The behaviour of fixed clients differs. Some stop visiting the woman if she gets pregnant, while others might get more involved with her life and even send money to raise the child.[31]

(c) **Local hoodlums**: Some of the local hoodlums who are clients are also landlords. They are inclined to be violent and keep the woman without her consent. Women who are part of the *chukri* system almost live in bondage to the pimps and do not have any control over the selection of their clients.[32]

(d) **Hotel clients**: These consist of wealthy local people and tourists. They pay around Rs 200 – 300 for an evening with a woman and if she stays overnight, she may be paid anything up to Rs 1500.[33]

1.4. Street Prostitution

This refers to prostitution which is not carried out in organised brothels in red light areas, but off the streets, as is most frequently the case in Kerala. Both men and women engage in this type of prostitution and in fact, a large number of males are found in street prostitution. According to a study conducted by the International Organisation of Migration· 75% to 80% of trafficked women belong to this category.[34]

1.5. Hotel, bars/ hidden prostitution

Prostitution is carried out on a large scale in massage parlours, hotels, beer bars and dance bars. Beauty/massage parlors in Mumbai serve as a façade for sophisticated prostitution rackets, and are popular with Arab and American tourists.[35] Over the past few years, the social service branch of the Mumbai police has conducted several raids on bars and beauty parlors where prostitution is practiced by girls and women. Some other forms of prostitution, which may not specifically fall under the categorisation of the workplace, are:

(a) **Call Girls:** Call girls practice prostitution with a certain amount of autonomy and hence, a relatively smaller number of trafficked persons are found engaged in this form of sex work. Call girls have much more control and influence over their working conditions than do other prostitutes. Their relation with their male clients is also less exploitative they often operate with the help of managers, who negotiate clients for them.[36] However, it has been found that, in some cases, call girls have regular and fixed clients.

1.6. Prostitution with Socio-religious Sanction

"This type of prostitution includes the Bedia, Jogin, Devadasi and Basavi systems". It was practiced in certain parts of India, including Uttar Pradesh, Andhra Pradesh, Orissa, Maharashtra, Goa, Karnataka, Tamil Nadu and Kerala. "Under these systems, young girls, usually belonging to the Scheduled Castes" and ironically, they have been dedicated to local deities and then sexually exploited by men belonging to the higher castes. For example, Bedias, irrespective to age and sex refer to prostitution as khandani pesha or hereditary occupation. They see nothing wrong with prostitution. Even though their acceptance of this way of life, is so ingrained that many of them tend to view it as the essential occupation for the sustenance of the family. In addition to that questions of morality, values, legality, exploitation, etc. do not seem to bother them. However, it can be argue that, "the growing incidence of trafficking of women and children for prostitution across India is a matter of serious concern and has been highlighted time and again in Parliament, by the courts, media and in national and international forums. The last decade has witnessed a significant shift in the perception of the flesh trade in differentiating prostitution from trafficking by seeing it not merely as a moral or law enforcement problem, but as a human right including legal and democratic rights violation, linked to gender discrimination and disparity in development".[37]

Trafficking and sexual exploitation including "commercial sexual exploitation of women and children have emerged as one of the" major problems for India. Fragile socio-economic condition leads many women and children to become victims of trafficking, prostitution and other forms of violence. Little or no legal support further aggravates the situation. Although there exist tough and appropriate laws against these sorts of crime but laps, gaps, anomalies, loopholes in the laws and lack of implementation due to various reasons make the laws unable to protect women and children from being victimized. As a result, "trafficking in women and children within the territory and across the" border and sexual or commercial sexual exploitation is gradually increasing. Under the present situation the laws of the land "relating to trafficking and sexual/ commercial sexual exploitation and the process of" its implementation should be reviewed to explore ways and means to improve the situation.

Now the question arises: Whether the "role and function of the law enforcement and adjudication machinery in deals with the problem of trafficking for Commercial Sexual Exploitation?" Whether the functionary's concerned working effectively towards achieving the desired objectives emphasised in various laws? What are the lacunae specific to each component, namely, the "police, the prosecution, the judiciary" and the correctional institutions, those are responsible for the ineffective "functioning of the criminal justice system (CJS)?" Whether the victims of the offence accorded justice and the perpetrators punished according to the established law of the country? Whether changes can be made to improve the functioning of various components of the Criminal Justice System in dealing with the issue? Whether the existing regime adequate to deal effectively "with the problem of trafficking for Commercial Sexual Exploitation".

To understand, analyze and evaluate the effectiveness of legislation concerning "trafficking in women and children for Commercial Sexual Exploitation" in India in the following manner: to study the socio-cultural-economic status of Bedia community. To analyse the occurrence of human rights violation of women in prostitution and understand the reintegration of women in prostitution, all within a context that protect individual's rights. To understand and critically analyse, role and functioning of the "law enforcement" and "adjudication machinery" in dealing with the issue of "trafficking for Commercial Sexual Exploitation. To evaluate the effectiveness of various components of the Criminal Justice System in preventing trafficking for Commercial Sexual Exploitation, and to understand the strengths and problem areas in its functioning. More importantly to investigate the processes, such as reporting, investigation, prosecution, etc., involved in the adjudication of cases of trafficking, and to analyse the impact of these processes on the victims as well as the perpetrators of the offence. Finally, to bring out a scientific solution that are pragmatic in nature for the maintenance of human rights standards in law enforcement.

It has been found that, thesis Bedia Community of central India mainly engaged in prostitution as a source of survival. Prostitution being their inherited profession ever since their birth because they send their daughter for dancing at early age instead for schooling and gradually prepare them to enter in the profession of prostitution. The major sustenance of Bedia Community is on the income of their females, which they earn through prostitution, as their male members by and large do not work. They enjoy both power and control over be brothels in the city red-light areas. After reviewing available literature and the objective laid down for the study, the following hypothesis are developed in socio-legal context of the present study: firstly, trafficking for prostitution among Bedia community has been a traditional cultural practices supported by family and community which gives tacit support to this tradition; secondly, Bedia women face gender discrimination and family members prefer male child and they deny property rights to women; thirdly, legislation concerning "trafficking in women and children for Commercial Sexual Exploitation" are not effective enough due to lack of implementation by enforcing agencies.

Of immoral trafficking of women for commercial sexual exploitation. The chapter further discuss about the difference between migrations, smuggling and trafficking etc.

The first chapter begins with the conceptual understanding of immoral trafficking of women for commercial sexual exploitation. It discusses about human trafficking which has been identified as the third largest source of profit for organised crime, followed by arms and drug at the global level. Further, it also analyses how India becomes a source, destination and transit for both in country and cross border trafficking. The chapter further discuss about the difference between migrations, smuggling and trafficking etc. This chapter also briefly focuses on the following aspect:

1.1. Classification of Commercial Sex Labour

1.2. Brothel prostitution

1.3. Types of Clients

14. Street Prostitution

1.5. Hotel, bars/ hidden prostitution

1.6. Prostitution with Socio-religious Sanction.

Second chapter focuses on historical and cultural aspects of trafficking that violates basic human rights in general and exploits women and their relationship with trafficking in particular. It tries to analyses the phenomenon of 'trafficking in persons' which has been linked to prostitution in ancient, medieval, modern and Bedia community in India. It tries to seek the connection between trafficking and prostitution because both are usually used as synonyms but they are not the same. In fact, trafficking is a broader concept and prostitution is one aspect of trafficking and furthermore, trafficking is the genus and prostitution is its species. This chapter divided into four sub-parts.

2.1. Status of Prostitution in Ancient India
2.2. Status of Prostitution in Medieval India
2.3. Status of Prostitution in Modern India
2.4. Origin of prostitution as a Hereditary Occupation Among Bedia Community

Third chapter discusses about various dimensions of inter-state trafficking in India which has been the focus of debate across national, regional and international levels. It also deals broadly with different pattern, trend and causes of inter-state, intra state and transnational trafficking. Further this chapter divided into three sub-parts.

3.1. Pattern of Inter State Trafficking in India
3.2. Pattern of Transnational Trafficking
3.3. Pattern of Cases under Immoral Trafficking Act

Fourth chapter focuses on legislation and law enforcement to identify, prosecute and prevent 'trafficking of women for commercial sexual exploitation'. Also discuss various international and regional conventions related to trafficking of women as well as brief over view of legislation procedures and rules concerning trafficking women for commercial sexual exploitation in India. Further this chapter is divided into three subparts.

4.1. International Conventions to Combat Trafficking for Commercial Sexual Exploitation
4.2. National Legislations to Combat Trafficking for Commercial Sexual Exploitation
4.3. Law Enforcement
4.4. Debate Concerning Legalisation of Prostitution in India

Fifth chapter based on empirical research which include the preparation of a case study by way of analyzing the data which was collected from courts, police stations, state home and 'victims of commercial sexual exploitation' as well as women of Badia community. Furthermore, I have tried to analyse the facts and figures collected from the courts and police stations in Agra district and examine the facts related to women of Bedia community who indulges in prostitution. This chapter divided into three subparts.

5.1. Law Enforcement in Agra District

5.2. Interactions at State Homes

5.3. Findings of Study Regarding Women (CSWs) in the Bedia Dominated and Red-Light Area of Agra District

In the six and the last chapter, I have sum up the main findings of my field survey related to immoral trafficking for commercial sexual exploitation among women of Bedia community of Agra district which may prove prudent in shaping the future policy for trafficking and it may contribute to large extent for the well-being of trafficked victims in general and Bedia women in particular.

NOTES

1. Government of India, India Country Report to Prevent and Combat Trafficking and Commercial Sexual Exploitation of Children and Women (Ministry of Women and Child Development, 2008).
2. United Nations, The Protocol to Prevent, Suppress and Punish Trafficking in Persons, Especially Women and Children (December, 2000).
3. *Supra* note 1.
4. Elaine Pearson, *Human Rights and Trafficking in Persons: A Handbook* 38 (Global Alliance, Bangkok, 2000).
5. Alexis A Aronowitz, *Human Trafficking, Human Miseries: The Global Trade in Human Beings* 4-5 (Praeger Publishers, USA, 2009.
6. John Salt & Jeremy Stein, "Migration as a Business: The Case of Trafficking" 35 *International Migration* 467-494 (1997).
7. *Supra* note 6.
8. *Supra* note 5 at 477.
9. *Supra* note 5 at 479-480
10. *Supra* note 5.
11. *Supra* note 5.

12. Sen S, Nair PM. *A Report on trafficking on women and children in India 2002-2003* 440 (Institute of Social Sciences, NHRC & UNIFEM, India; 2004).
13. European Union, Report on Trafficking in Migrants (International Organisation for Migration (IOM), 2018).
14. *Supra* note 2.
15. *Supra* note 2.
16. J.N. Pandey, *The Constitutional Law of India* 300 (Central Law Agency, Allahabad, 45th edn., 2008).
17. National Portal of India, *available at:* https://www.india.gov.*in/. (Last visited on June 30, 2019).*
18. *Supra* note 17.
19. *Supra* note 17.
20. The Immoral Traffic (Prevention) Act, 1956 (Act 104 of 1956).
21. The Criminal Law (Amendment) Act, 2013 (Act 13 of 2013).
22. *Supra* note 21.
23. Jean D' Cunha, "Prostitution Laws: Ideological Dimensions and Enforcement Practices" 27 *Economic and Political Weekly* 34-44 (1992).
24. *Supra* note 23.
25. *Supra* note 23.
26. Anita Katyal, "Murmurs at SAARC over Pact Against Trafficking", Times of India, 27 January 2013.
27. *Supra* note 26.
28. Carolyn Sleightholme & Indrani Sinha, *Guilty Without Trial: Women in Sex Trade in Calcutta* 114 (Rutgers University Press, UK, 1996).
29. *Supra* note 28 at 113.
30. *Supra* note 28 at 114.
31. *Supra* note 28 at 115-116.
32. *Supra* note 28 at 119.
33. *Supra* note 28 at 122.
34. Migration Information Programme (IOM), Trafficking in women for Sexual Exploitation (Brussels, 1996).
35. Gracy Farnandes, "Raids, Rescue, Rehabilitation: The Story of Mumbai Brothel Raids of 1996-2000 12 (Concept Publication, Delhi, 2001).
36. *Supra* note. 34.
37. *Supra* note 1.

Chapter - 2

Historical and Cultural Aspect of Trafficking in India

This chapter focuses on historical and cultural aspects of prostitution that violates basic human rights in general and exploits women and their relationship with trafficking in particular. In order to know about the phenomenon of 'trafficking in persons', the chapter deals about the historical and cultural aspect for trafficking which has been linked to prostitution in Ancient India. Moreover, it traces the genesis of these aspects and their prevalence in India, while linking these practices of trafficking. Trafficking of women for prostitution is an old phenomenon which was practiced in India since ancient time. However, there has been no specific definition of the concept of trafficking in women. It often stated that, trafficking in women refers to the—recruitment and transportation of women for work and other services by means of some form of coercion".[1] Before going into the historical and cultural aspect of trafficking, it is very important to understand the relation between 'trafficking and prostitution'. The term, 'trafficking' and 'prostitution' is usually used as synonyms but they are not the same. In fact, trafficking is a broader concept and prostitution is one aspect of trafficking. Furthermore, trafficking is the genus and prostitution is its species.

Prostitution is formerly defined as "the practice of offering sexual intercourse in return for pay".[2] It considered as the world's oldest profession and it was the most respected one as well. A profession of choice, prostitution is often confused with 'human trafficking and the euphemistic terminology of prostitution' must be blown away; as "prostitution is what an independent woman chooses to do and human trafficking is what one is forced or manipulated into. Other reasons for entering into the profession may include economic distress, social abandonment or psychological factors".[3] One of the "earliest traces of women practicing prostitution as a sacred ritual found among the Sumerians, followed by the Babylonians who considered it as a tradition needed to be followed by each woman, at least once in her life".[4] This was followed in many of the ancient civilisations like Greece, Rome etc. It must not come as a surprise that even in India, 18th and 19th century had a custom of "prostitute women or tawaifs, one that was considered to be symbol of nobility".[5] Prior to that, in the times of Chandragupta Maurya and his chief advisor- Chanakya- prostitution was a profession well know. Sex workers (Ganikas) were specifically mentioned in the Arthshastra and their maintenance process was elucidated in the same-pointing out to the fact that "prostitution was earlier legalised and regularised as well".[6] 'Rambha and Urwashi' are well known names of apsara or rather the "divine prostitutes".[7] In addition to that, Devdasi system followed in ancient, medieval and even the modern is another example of "prostitution".[8]

Trafficking in India is a complex process, and often starts with family members handing over responsibility for the safety and well-being of the trafficked person to others known to them, but then ending up trafficked by a third set of persons and into the profession as a "commercial sex worker commonly known as a prostitute".[9] According to Oxford dictionary, trafficking implies deal in something illegally. It also offers new terms like "drugs trafficking, arms trafficking and human trafficking". The conceptual meaning of "human trafficking refers to the criminal practice of exploitation of human beings where they are treated as commodities for profit and after being trafficked, are subject to long term exploitation".[10] It can be said that trafficking in persons is a serious crime and a grave violation of human rights. As Alex has rightly pointed out in his book *Human Trafficking, Human Miseries*, "Every year, thousands of men, women and children fall into the hands of traffickers, in their own countries and abroad. Almost every country in the world is affected by trafficking, whether as a country of origin, transit or destination for victims".[11] As per Article 3 of the Protocol to Prevent, Suppress and Punish Trafficking in Persons, "trafficking in persons as the recruitment, transportation, transfer, harbouring or receipt of persons by means of threat or use of force or other forms of coercion, of abduction, of fraud, of deception or of the giving or receiving of payments or benefits to achieve the consent of a person having control over another person for the purpose of exploitation".[12] It is one of the most despicable forms of human rights violation which involve the "transportation", "harbouring or receipt of persons by means of threat or coercion, abduction or fraud for the purpose of exploitation". In other way, trafficking becomes a social problem which is the most "serious threat to human dignity" and their rights which leads to gross commercialisation and commodification of human lives.

Despite that "Indian Constitution specifically bans the traffic in persons according to Article 23 of the fundamental rights that prohibits traffic in human beings and other similar forms of forced labor".[13] Still traffickers exploit the trafficked person and forced them to live like an animal. As we know that "women and children are the weaker and vulnerable section of the society" and they are the main subject of trafficking which cause grave violation of their dignity and human rights and for that society is also equally responsible for this menace. In this way, "human trafficking is regarded as one of the three most lucrative types of organised crimes, after drugs and arms".[14] Moreover, it is to be noted that this "organised crime has reached a scary magnitude because the extent of violations of human right which is unbelievable and unimaginable".[15] That's why it is considered as modern-day slavery. It is found that, there is very "little awareness of this crime among the masses and it is also because of its highly secret and clandestine nature".[16]

For the sake of clarity and precision, I shall divide the present chapter into four parts. In Part I, I will discuss historical and cultural aspect of prostitution during Ancient period. It is to be noted that prostitution had been a prevalent phenomena since the beginning of civilisation in one form or another. As there was no institution of marriage during prehistoric time and both men and women living together just like an animals. As per the finding of archaeological survey it was believed that the 'Indus Valley Civilisation' was a urban settlement but there was no definite evidence of institution of prostitution at that time. For instance, the "bronze figure of dancing girl of Mohenjo-Daro indicates about sacred prostitute who performs her duties within the premises of mother goddess" but there was no evidence of any reserved area in town planning for prostitutes as it was evident later on. Unlike Indus Valley Culture, in Vedic society, the offering of slave girls to Rishis by the King clearly indicates the existence of institution of prostitution. Furthermore, this practice was rampant during the time of Chandra Gupta Maurya and Patliputra was known as centre for prostitution. Since the state for the first time gave its attention and tried to control this profession for the benefit of state and for this state has constructed colonies for them. Even though "Arthashastra of Kautilya" has clearly mentioned "rules for prostitutes and their activities as well as gives an account of how they should behave". He also mentioned that the "prostitutes were state property and any injury to them meant a loss to the State and prescribed a deterrent fine for killing prostitutes".

In Part II, I' ll discuss about the status of prostitution in medieval India. However, at this time prostitution was regulated and restricted; for example, some rules was made by Akbar to regulate and restrict services of prostitutes and confined them to outskirt of the cities only. At the same time the Rajput rulers availed the service of singing and dancing in their courts from these public girls and enjoyed a privileged position. Even though in Mughal times, women used to accompany with army for the purpose of their entertainment. However, prostitution was rampant when Europeans came to India for trade. At this time, British for the first time consider to control and regulate prostitution by several legislation related to "immoral traffic" was enacted by them i.e. the "Contagious Disease Act, 1868". This act started a new beginning in the chapter of prostitution in India. Since it provides for the establishment of brothels and permitted to run prostitution in prescribed manner. Besides this act, the Suppression of Immoral Traffic Act, 1923 was enacted for Bombay, Calcutta and Madras presidencies to regulating and controlling prostitution which may consider as the beginning of legislative control of prostitution.

In Part III, I will discuss the modern aspect of prostitution as a human rights violation which assault on the dignity of human being. In other words, prostitutes were in such conditions where their dignity, respect and freedom were compromised. At the same time they are reduced to a mere object of sexual exploitation coupled with abuse and violence regularly. Although from the end on 19th and the beginning of 20th century British rulers have taken several steps to encourage, facilitate and regulate prostitution to transformed prostitution in India with British culture and ethos. However, the British supremacy is also one of the reasons for regularisation of prostitution.

In part IV, I will discuss about origin of prostitution as a hereditary occupation among Bedia Community of central India which was earlier known as a "denotified nomadic tribe". They mainly engaged in singing and dancing traditional folk dance as a source of survival for their community. Prostitution being their inherited profession ever since their birth because they send their daughter for dancing at early age instead for schooling and gradually prepare them to enter in the profession of prostitution. The major sustenance of Bedia Community is on the income of their females, which they earn through prostitution, as their male members by and large do not work. Bedia involvement in the business of prostitution does not end with the induction of their own girls into it. Bedias indulge in the sale and purchase of girls from other castes and communities. Those girls forced into prostitution by the Bedias are called 'Lonchi'. They enjoy both power and control over be brothels in the city red-light areas. Women in the trade are treated at par with the male siblings and have an equal share in the family property along with their brother.

Coming to the basic issues which I am discussing in the above four parts, I would like to point out that, prostitution is practiced since the origin of organised society in almost every country and society in one form or another. "Prostitution and the accompanying evil of the traffic in persons for the purpose of prostitution are incompatible with the dignity and worth of human person and endanger the welfare of the individuals, the family and community".[17] That's why it called as a "public molestation and humiliation to civilisation. Since many observers contend the absence of the love element is the one essential factor that stamps the woman as a prostitute".[18] It has been pointed out that an important ingredient missing from "prostitution is that, woman received no pleasure from her sexual services" and the sole purpose is to earn money for her services. Hence, prostitution referred as illegitimate sexual services for money. Prostitution is the practice of habitual intermittent sexual union, more or less promiscuous, for mercenary inducement. It is thus characterised by three elements: "payment, usually involving the passing of money, although 'gifts or pleasure may constitute equivalent consideration; promiscuity, with the possible exercise of choice; and emotional indifference, which may be inferred from payment and promiscuity".[19] The concept of prostitution has been defined by International Encyclopaedia of the Social Sciences, "Prostitution is the granting of sexual access on a relatively indiscriminate basis for payment either in money or in goods, depending on the complexity of the local economic system".[20]

In other words, it is also defined by the Suppression of Immoral Traffic in Women and Girls Act 1956, "prostitution means the act of a female offering her body for promiscuous sexual intercourse for hire, whether in money or in kind".[21] However, trafficking for prostitution is grave human rights violation and it has been one of the most debatable questions in the fallowing way:

1. One section believes that prostitution is existing because of patriarchal nature of society therefore they suggest total eradication of prostitution irrespective of voluntary concern of women.
2. Other section emphasis to provide them legal status and empower them to claim their rights and self-respect in society. One of the motivations behind this stand is that an approach which would ban prostitutions would not be realistic bearing in mind the "economic interest involves in the prostitution industry of today".[22]
3. Another section argues against the distinction between forced and voluntary prostitution because they belief that

this distinction only confines the problem to human rights violations and neglect the other basic reasons which leads women to adopt prostitution. Moreover it goes without saying that, "choice between criminalising, regulating or decriminalising prostitutions depends largely on the basic view adopted".[23]

It is evident that "women are one of the major groups considered most vulnerable to human trafficking"[24] particularly prostitution. "For purposes of sexual or commercial exploitation, women and girls are kidnapped, sold, and coerced by slavers in nearly every country in the world".[25] Further it can be argue that, "Though many human rights and governmental organisations agree that trafficking in women is a serious violation of human rights that needs to be fought, the complex and widespread operations of human trafficking make prosecution and punishment of traffickers nearly impossible in many cases".[26]

It has been found that trafficking in women is an "ancient enterprise that dates back nearly to the beginnings of civilisations where female slaves were often highly valued for use as prostitutes, concubines, or to breed more slaves"[27]. In other words, the most attraction for women trafficking in recent time is to widen aggressively prostitution business. Since the "traffickers often recruit or buy women from destitute areas, promising to smuggle them to a new country and find them work as domestic servants".[28] Furthermore, "women are often raped and abused by their recruiters, and then sent to brothels where they are sometimes literally held under lock and key".[29] It has also been found that, "Prostitutes will have to work in the sex industry until the debt for their transport has been paid off, which may effectively be for the rest of their lives".[30] Many health issues have been the major concern because officials insist that "trafficking in women causes significant health risks to the general public, especially in terms of sexually transmitted diseases".[31] For instance, "Women sold into prostitution are often discouraged or forbidden from using contraceptives such as condoms, and thus become high-risk candidates for the spread of diseases. Since these women are usually tightly controlled, they also have limited access to any type of health care, and are thus far more likely to suffer from illnesses of all kinds".[32]

"In order to understand the place of prostitution and its evil practices during ancient times, we should study the historical aspect so that we may look back to its inglorious past and present while analyzing all the facts concerning prostitution". Moreover, to address this problem, we need to revisit and "study the cultural, social, religious and economic states of prostitutes" in ancient, medieval and modern India and the role of state towards prostitution". With this brief remark regarding prostitution which is incompatible with human dignity; I shall come to the Part I of the chapter.

2.1. Status of Prostitution in Ancient India

Prostitution is an "age–old institution in India".[33] In other words, prostitution was controlled by state institutions since ancient times and status of prostitutes particularly, 'Ganikas' enjoyed great status in ancient India.[34] As Nag Moni has rightly pointed out, from early days of human history, the state has supported the idea of providing "sexual entertainment to the public using trained Ganikas".[35] It has existed in India since ancient civilisation and can only be well understood in its social and historical context. For instance, the "ancient roots of prostitution may be found in many historical accounts of Buddhist literature, Kautilya's Arthashastra, Vedas, Puranas, Mahabharta etc. The Purana states that the very sight of prostitutes brings good luck".[36] Moreover it literary socurces states that, The women prostitutes in those times were classified into three categories and these are "Kumbhadasis, Rupajivikas and Ganikas". Their act had religious and cultural sanction and these women enjoyed considerable respect within social hierarchy as the "courtesans of king".[37]

As Shailendra Nath writes in his book *Ancient Indian History and Civilisation*, "Courtesans or prostitutes (in Mauryan period) enjoyed a social status not accorded to them anywhere in the world".[38] However, "prostitution in Ancient India was largely regulated by the state institution and not considered as an act having loss of dignity but a profession that was adjusted with the social institutions in an otherwise male dominated society".[39] Often prostitution implies, "selling sexual services for material, commercial and economic benefit".[40] In other words, a prostitute hires her body to sexual services and during this process, love and other emotion does not play. That's why Vātsyāyana who lived during the second or third century CE has written a famous ancient book on sexuality i.e. "Kama Sutra"[41] where he has classified Vrasta from the Vaishyas. The former is a "concubine and adulterous wife who have a lover are not prostitutes while the latter implies that women carries on liaison with men for the satisfaction of lust".[42] Historically, it has been found that, "Before the dawn of civilisation there was no system of marriage. In the prehistoric age men and women cohabited in the manner of birds and animals".[43] Moreover, "sexual promiscuity obtained within the limits of each tribal group. Men and tribes always quarrel for women and changed his mate frequently".[44] Besides it has been mentioned that the "primitive woman enjoyed herself at her own sweet will".[45]

However, prostitution as a profession appears in the "literature of a few centuries after the Vedas"[46], even though it must have been common practices in society much earlier. In order to trace the history of prostitution from the beginning, "archaeological findings have thrown a light on the urbanised culture of Indus valley which has been known for its economic prosperity. Still we cannot definitely confirm or refute the existence of sacred prostitution in the absence of any concrete evidence".[47] As Chandra Moti has rightly argues in her book – "The World of Courtesans", "Indus valley culture is known for its economical progress. Its wealthy merchants could afford to spend lavishly on wine and women".[48] Furthermore, As Joseph Gathi argues, "The bronze figure of dancing girl from Mohenjo-Daro shows a sacred prostitute carrying out her duties within the precincts' of the temple of mother goddess".[49] It shows that there is the possibility that the "bronze figure of the dancing girl from Mohenjo-Daro represents a sacred prostitute within the boundaries of the temple of the Mother Goddess, a cult which was very popular in the Indus Valley culture".[50] But, in the "absence of any concrete evidence to support this view, we cannot be sure that the existence of prostitution during pre-Vedic age"[51]. It can be argue that during the period of "Indus valley civilisation women enjoyed very high status and were highly respected. Since the figures of mother goddesses affirm the fact that women were not only a source of entertainment and house-keepers but also worshipped in the society in the form of mother goddess".[52] Moreover, it is not known whether "any special place was reserved in town planning of cities for prostitutes as was case in later times".[53] Still, there is "no way to find out the exact time when prostitution in India arose as a recognizable profession, or how much payment the prostitute received for her services".[54]

It shows that the process of the "emergence of prostitution must have been slow, varying from region to region and from age to age. By the later Vedic age, i.e. around the eighth or seventh century B.C.; we have references to a more regularised form of prostitution recognised as a social institution".[55] It can be argue that "prostitution is a by product of marriage institution"; however, it is not confused with "illicit sex union of lovers". Furthermore, "prostitution has certainly existed through institution of marriage and the earliest existence of prostitution occurs in the *Rig Veda* - the most ancient literary work of India. At firs however, we hear of the illicit lover, '*Jara*' and '*Jatini*'- male and female lover of a married spouse".[56] Now it is very important to distinguish between prostitution and illicit lover; however, "what distinguished such an illicit lover from the professional prostitute or her client is the regular payment for favours received".[57] It can be argue that "when we hear of an illicit lover, there may or may not have been an exchange of gift; in a case of mutual consent, gifts must have been optional".[58] According to Sukumari who argues in "Prostitution in Ancient India", "In the remote days of barter economy when money or currency was yet unknown, such gifts were equivalent to payment in cash. Hence love outside marriage was a familiar phenomenon even in the earliest Vedic age"[59]. Furthermore, she pointed out that the "extramarital love may have been voluntary and unpaid but it might have been regarded by the male partner as a form of service for which he was obliged to pay in some form. But till it was confined to a particular person, it was a temporary contract and not regarded as a profession".[60] In other words, "we have oblique references to women being given gifts for their favours, but the contexts leave us guessing whether the woman was a willing partner or whether she agreed to oblige in return for the gifts she received. But clearly, even in the earliest Vedic age, love outside wedlock was a familiar phenomenon and unions promoted by mere lust are mentioned in quite an uninhibited manner".[61]

Prostitution is a global phenomenon which was evident since the beginning of the organised society and India is not an exception because the "primitive non-Aryans Dravidian) were originally animists, phallic worshippers. They worshipped phallus and Yoni as the supreme manifestation of the creative force in nature".[62] Besides Dravidians, the "Aryans were probable nomadic pastoral tribes flowing across the central Asian land mass".[63] It has been found that the "Aryan merchants established trade relations with Dravidians". "While their commercial transactions with the Dravidians they presented women accomplished, beautiful and maiden in token of friendship to kings".[64] In this way the "Aryan merchants" came in contact with "guest prostitution".[65] Moreover it has been found that, "Aryans settled down as agriculturists and they had to look forward to the onset of regular rains and to protect their corns. But it was beyond the control of themselves; they thought about Supreme Being – the Devas, the chief among them was Indra. For his invocation some sort of sacrifice was introduced".[66] Moreover the "sacrificial rites were accompanied with a mild intoxicating drink, the juice of Soma plants. And the end of which there was probably a manifestation of natural promiscuity".[67] However, it has been often argue that "if there be no marriage institution existent in the society, promiscuity can't be called prostitution".[68] Westemarg has rightly pointed out in "*History of Human Marriage*", "A state of sexual prevails in the beginning of all human development, but it lasted a short time only to be followed by a kind of semi-promiscuity. It gave rise to group marriage and polyandry. This led to establishment of matriarchal society. After this promiscuity was only resorted to in religious or political celebrations".[69] "In the times of the later Rig and Yajurveda, marriage institution established, however it took hundreds of years". "Although the later Vedic literature tacitly assumes and sometimes even overtly mentions prostitutes and in order to demonstrate the prostitution that is the by-product of marriage institution".[70] "Sexual union of two persons or more (as in polygamy), temporary or permanent, having one of its chief objects the procreation and care of the offspring – and union that's sanctioned by the society through the performance of a definite ceremony, is called marriage".[71] However, it has been found that the "social potentates of the early Aryans, tried to stem the tide of sexual relationship to a monogamous channel"[72]. Even though in Vedic age, "there was laxity of marriage laws, so prostitution outside marriage was hardly felt necessary. The concubinage relationship was probably not in demand after marriage–institutions were established but there are references about dancing girl in Rig Veda".[73]

In other words, the "emergence and the recognition of prostitution as a profession was concomitant with the institution of strict marriage rules, especially the wife being regarded as the private property of her husband"[74]. Take for instance, "when an Indian woman does not belong to one man but obliges many; since she is not seen to be the responsibility of one man".[75] More importantly, "the terms *Varangana, Varastri* and *Varamukhya"* signify a woman who is not the responsibility of one man but many and she looks after herself. She does by accepting payment from each of the men she obliges; she then becomes *panyastri,* one whose favours can be bought with money.[76] In other words, the terms "*sadharani or samanya* (common), synonyms for prostitute, distinguish her as a woman possessed by not one man; this is the desideratum".[77]

In Rig Veda, "there is one instance which clearly pointing towards the existence of prostitution by offering the present of slave girls to Rishis by kings"[78] which pointing towards the "existence of institution of prostitution in Vedic time".[79] It may point out that, the sexual life of Vedic people, certain institutions seem to have played an important part and these are samana and the Vedic Sabha.[80] The first and foremost institute of prostitutes was Samana which considered as one of the important institution of prostitutes where "free love seems to have been encouraged".[81] Moreover, "Samana which was held during tournaments, women were present and they seemed especially attracted chariot – racing. They spent whole night wooing their lover and dispersed at down"[82]. "Samana was a general popular festivity to which women went enjoy themselves – young women and elderly women sought thereof find a husband and prostitutes make profit of the occasion".[83] Besides Samana, the second institutes of prostitutes were the "Vedic Sabha which usually connotes an assembly as well as the hall where it met and though there seem to have been several types of Sabha, it is possible that the same sabha served multiple functions".[84]

According to Chandra, "Rig Veda refers Sabha as a sort of drawing room of a private house. One night read in Sabhavat Yosha of the Rig Veda, a reference in this particular context to women visiting a Sabha hall. If this interpretation is correct, Sabhavat Yosha may have meant a prostitute. Bearing in mind the pejorative sense of the word Sabha as a place where gamblers gathered, the presence of prostitutes there is probable, for in later times gambling, drinking and prostitution went hand to hand".[85] Still the emergence of prostitutes changing from "early Vedic age to the later Vedic age since we have references to a more regularised form of prostitution recognised as a social institution during the Brahamana period".[86] Moreover, at this time, "prostitution was accepted as a profession by society and the prostitutes were called as Vishya. This class had been creed to aid to the Vish or Vaishy caste (i.e. Merchants who led a town – life cut off from their home.) Vishya gradually changed into Beshya which lost its original derivative root and was framed from the root (to enter) and which meant one who is approachable to and by all or one who nicely bedecks herself".[87]

During this period, "prostitutes were variously known as Ganika, Bandhki, Rupjiva, Varangana, Kultani, Sambhali, Pumscali etc and concubinage relationship showed its head. Concubinage was an interpersonal relationship in which a woman engages in an ongoing sexual relationship with another person whom they could not be married".[88] In other words, "the kings sometimes retained hundreds of slave girls in their palaces. These slave girls could dance and sing perfectly and acted as concubines".[89] It has been found that, in this period "Marriage with the prostitute was not looked upon. The great sage Vashistha, was the son of women engaged in prostitution".[90] According to Salla Sariola argues that, "There is no account about elucidation the life of the prostitutes, their habits, modes and manners and the laws relating to and regulating them in Brahamana literatures".[91] Besides, there are several epics regarding the origin of prostitutes. In other words, it can be argue that the status of prostitution has been the paradigm shift in "Epic period" because the "institution of courtesans had a legal status".[92]

At this time, "prostitutes, particularly Ganikas were highly esteemed persons as many women, if only their social status allowed them to do so, had chosen to become prostitutes in ancient India. They enjoyed great status".[93] It can be substantiated by several instances, "king Virata, after victory, sent messengers to the city and asked young girls and ganikas to meet him, when he returned from victory expedition".[94] Similarly, in the "Ramayana",[95] "when Rama was to be consecrated, Vasistha ordered that the prostitutes should attend the ceremony and when he returned from the exile, ganikas had to be there to honour him".[96] Also when king Kusika returned to his home, he was received by courtesans".[97] Similarly, "when Krisna came to the court of the Kauravas, he was greeted by courtesans".[98] It has been found that, "when the king entered his home after returning from a distant journey, he had first to see prostitutes and then other insignia of royalty.

In other words, when "Gandhari a wife Dhrtarastra was pregnant a prostitute (Vesya) waited upon Dhrtarastra".[99] There are other references about the importance "Bharata ordered courtesans to join the welcome festival or occasion of the return of the triumphant Rama".[100] It makes clear that "veshyas were common during the reign to Pandavas and Kauravas and plays an important role in the courtesans. Moreover, they had to put on red cloths, red garlands and use ornaments of red gold in the participation of social functions. The red colour is regarded as colour as the symbol of Yama. This rule was framed to distinguish easily the prostitutes and for warring the people about the dangerous effect of sexual union with a prostitute"[101]. Further, in the "Jatakas, the prostitutes were called ornaments of the town (nagaras obhimi). We also learn that prostitutes used to follow the army of the king and in the army of Duryodhana, there were interalia. Ganikas in huge number and the army of Pandavas was also accompanied by courtesans. Dashratha had also ordered that the army of Rama be accompanied by prostitutes".[102] "In Mahabharata courtesans of Indra Puri have been variously depicted. Mahabharata has recorded the name of forty-two apsaras in all and the stars amongst were Urvashi, Menaca, Tilottama, Rambha and Ghritachee".[103] Hence, it can be seen and presumed by the above examples that prostitutes had enjoyed a very dignified and honourable status in ancient Indian society. It can be argue that "prostitution since the time of the epics had been gathering forces and making inroads into every available nook and corner of society" but "the position of prostitutes were depraved in the Smriti period". In other words, it can be said that, the influence of "later Vedic literatures like Smriti, Sutra, Purana and their religious injunctions have adversely affected the status of women".

During the "Smriti period, some new notions got established in the society, eventually affecting the position of women". At this time, it was also noticed that there was deterioration in the status of women by Manu who believes that, "Day and Night women must be kept in dependent by the Males (of) their families, her father protects (her) in childhood, her husband protects (her) in youth and her sons protect (her) in old age, a woman is never fit for independence".[104] It has been found that, "women were exploited in all walks of their lives and termed as Dark Age for women's progress. Moreover, the "Dharmashastras- law books of Manu" shown "new conventional usages and the developed political exigencies further enhanced the criminal victimisation of women" and projected the thoughts which they regarded as ideal for their Brahminical class without portraying the actual state of things in society. In other words, the references of "prostitutes in Jatakas and all shasrakaras such as Manu, Gautama etc. recommended for suppression of prostitution". In the prevailing unfavourable atmosphere of this era, many crimes like Sati, Devadasum Child Marriage, Dowry and Female Infanticide evolved and women were victimized in all aspects of the society. During this period, the noble religious Devadasi system in rolling of times changed as a corrupted system and Devadasis turned as temple prostitutes. Thus, Devadasi, being the women torturing institution, is kept alive in temples of worship.

While analyzing the historical records of our country, it "throws light on the position of women" in different ages which prove that deterioration in the status of women and their criminal victimisation are the outcome of the "influence of later Vedic literatures like Smriti, Sutras, Puranas and their religious injunctions. Moreover, in the later

Smriti age the new conventional usages arose from the exigencies of political and other situations resulting in increasing victimisation of women". "The ganikas were the castaways of society and hence food from them was unacceptable to a well-bred Aryan. But the state protected them and gave all human facilities to play their profession".[105] It is to be noted that there are some literary sources which clearly shows that despite of various social prohibition, Ganikas tried to uplift themselves and her status in various manner.

Since Nagendra Kumar has rightly pointed out in his book – "*Divine Prostitution*", "The Ganikas sometime gave themselves in marriage with Brahmins and Kshatriyas in accordance with the Gandharva system, by virtue of which they could occupy an exalted position in society. The accomplished ganikas always had the chance of being up-lifted to the ranks of a concubine and of being comfortably ensconced in an aristocrat's harem".[106] "The severe law givers of the Epic Age tried to keep this vile commerce in check and clearly define the diverse rights and privileges of chaste of unchaste women. Purana makers one and all have freely fabricated many outstanding tales of heavenly nymphs – their relations with the mortal's and their coming on earth either to break the chastity of sages or despoil the integrity of mighty kings. The love affair of Pururava and Urvasi was very widely described in various Puranas".[107] But during Buddhist age, women were not honoured as much as they were during the Vedic period. For instance, Buddha himself did not allow women to be included into the "Buddhist Sangha in the beginning and later on when admitted as Nuns, were placed in an inferior position to male Monks".[108] Moreover this period begins from 600 B.C. and end to 600 A. D. which "produces the great founders of world religions and vast empires like the Lord Buddha, Mahaveera, Chandragupta Maurya, Emperor Asoka" etc. For instance, "Buddhist and Jain's literary sources" tells us about the "history of Maghadha, Anga, Kosala, Kashi and Vaishali and the other parts of India" where famous courtesans practiced at the towns by these kingdoms.

"And the apathetic attitude or carelessness on the part of the administration in dealing with the courtesans would put the State as well as the society into many inconveniences and loss".[109]

During "Mauryan government" under the foster care of "Chanakya", "prostitution recognised as a part and parcel of the society". The literary sources shows that "Pataliputra was at the time of Chandra Gupta Maurya a flourishing centre of prostitution and it was the first time the attention of the State was drawn to the colony of prostitutes for its effective control and to bring it under the obligation of a stabilised taxation system".[110] Moreover, "brothel keeping was looked upon as a source of government revenue".[111] "Kautilya has used the words such as Ganika, Praganika, Dasi, Devadasi, Rupijiva etc. for the prostitutes and courtesans".[112] According to P.C. Sahoo, "A study the on Arthašāstra, the masterpiece on State craft reveals various aspects of royal administration in ancient India"[113]. It has been widely accepted that its author "Kautilya was a matured social and political thinker who could produce such a treatise in Sanskrit during the early Mauryan era for providing a complete guide line for the then rulers with an intention to establish an ideal and welfare State in which all minute details of State policies on administration are dealt with".[114]. Even though, "Kautilya never hesitated to deal with an ignoble social affair called prostitution and laid down administrative provisions in this regard for yielding maximum benefit to the State and simultaneously keeping his view on the overall welfare of the practitioners. Intelligently enough he could realise the fact that sex business, an age-old practice, is impossible to be abolished altogether from the human society and it needs, therefore, to be organised and regulated properly through State's administration".[115]

Furthermore, it can be argue that, "entire chapter (27th) of the second book of the Arthašāstra (2.27) has been devoted to this subject under the topic on the duties of the Ganikădhyaksa Superintendent of prostitutes. This officer of the State heads an independent department dealing with all the sex workers working inside the State".[116] Furthermore, it appears from the text that, "there were two types of such workers, one working under State's service being fully controlled and protected by the administration and the other type of practitioners running their business privately by paying timely taxes to the State"[117]. "The term Gaņīkā in the text mostly stands for the former practitioners and the latter sex workers are known by the terms like rūpāfivā, pumšcalī, vesyã, dāsī etc. Both the types of workers do their business under the strict vigilance of the concerning officer".[118] In this way "Kautilya mentioned rules for prostitutes and their activities gives an account of how prostitutes should behave and how their lives be ordered. The function of prostitutes was not only entertainment, but their services were also used for political purposes, especially in espionage work. Courtesans were exclusively in the service of the king".[119] Further, Chanakya has tried to focus attention on the purpose and benefits of the office of prostitution. Chanakya divided it into three categories namely; firstly, royal prostitutes, secondly, city-level prostitutes and thirdly, private prostitute or a group of prostitutes under the control of a private person and all these classes of harlots were under the control of the state. The institution as a whole yielded an enormous amount income to the state exchequer and it is quite likely that unemployment on the part of woman would have been solved. In other words, the stamped harlots of the Mauryan Empire were connotated as a "ganika which denotes a prostitute and also government servant".[120] Furthermore, the "terms used by Chanakya are pratiganika, rupajiva, Vesya, dasi, devadasi, pwnschali, silpakarika, kausikastri and rupadasi which meant special kinds of prostitutes. The individual prostitute i.e. rupajiva".[121] According to Curtius, "when Indian rulers went on a hunt, the courtesans bowed to them and to the accompaniment of their songs the kings hunted. Their food was prepared by courtesans, when they fall into a drunken sleep; their courtesans carry them away to their bedchamber".[122] In this way "Arthashastra shows the different roles played by courtesans to help the State revenue. Moreover, prostitute's rights and privileges were recognised and their profession was an important source of revenue to the State". "For Kautilya", "the prostitutes were State property and any injury to them meant a loss to the State; therefore, he prescribed a deterrent fine for killing prostitutes".

Besides Maurya period, during Gupta, "the institution of the courtesan became fully evolved and played a very important role in the social and cultural life of the people". "The Kamasutra of Vatsayana and the Natyashastra of Bharata have mentioned about courtesans and their customers. According to Chandra Moti, "courtesans and the prostitutes had separate quarters assigned to them. The cultured and the boorish, the rogues, the rakes and even pundits and philosophers could meet them".[123] According to Sinha & Bose, "Vatsayana has mentioned about the foreign soldiers were the most liberal patronizes of the local prostitutes and no wander that these women ever eager to serve the pleasures of their customers".[124] On the other hand, "Bharata supposed to have flourished at this period has given a nice portrait of an ideal Ganika in his Natyashastra" and he says "A woman who knows the practical application of various arts, who has a thorough knowledge of the science and literature, who is well-versed in the sixty – four recognised Koalas and particularly in dancing to the accompaniment of music".[125]

More importantly, "courtesans women's conduct is marked by a respect to the superiors (in age, social status, riches, learning etc.) by graceful and engaging deportment, by lively gestures and luscious blandishments, who possesses strength of mind and tenacity of purpose, punctuated with a sense of delicacy and sweetness of temper, who is free from the characteristic drawbacks of the average woman, who speaks sparklingly with a clarity of expression, who can work intelligently without getting easily fatigued – is then to be designated a Ganikas".[126] Besides it, "courtesans from their childhood have attended public schools which known as Gandharvashalas" so that they can "learn the sixty-four arts supplementary to the highest technical knowledge of erotics". Take for instance; "Ujjain in that period was great centre of learning Gandharva Kala. This art was also included all kinds of information on courtesans appears to be current because in this period the quarters where the courtesans lived had their own importance. The intimate contact between the dancing girls and temples and the courts gave rise to difference sorts of rules and regulations which governed and regulated their relationship with these institutions".[127] It makes clear that, prostitution as a profession at the time of ancient India enjoyed social acceptance while practicing bodily services. Moreover, "courtesans have played an important role in almost all King's court functions"; festivals and even they used to accompany an "army on the march throughout Indian history".

Besides, "they contributed an important role in "political, social and religious life and therefore they were treated with respect of course".

2.2. Status of Prostitution in Medieval India

Medieval Indian history begins from the eight centuries to the eighteenth century under the indigenous rulers that included the "Chalukyas, the Pallavas, the Pandyas, the Rashtrakutas", the Muslims and at last the Mughal rulers and their empire. Shadab Bano has rightly pointed out in her article, "Women Performers and Prostitutes in Medieval India", "Music and dance, the esoteric performing arts, being markers of culture in medieval India; a number of these differing forms and varieties developed into well-recognised and reputed arts overtime. The progress of these art-forms and in relation to each other varied, as preference and patronage to these did not remain same throughout. These practitioners accordingly were regarded as agents of refinement and culture. At the same time, music and dance had also been among the most popular forms of entertainment".[128] In other words, "each of them gave patronage to arts and letters including temples".[129] Moreover, this period brought an important change in north and south India which had "profound effects on the social, economic and religious living patterns of the prostitutes".[130] "There being a traditional linkage of these art-forms with entertainment/and physical pleasure as well tied to such forms of entertainment. These remained crucial in classifying musicians, singers and dancers as entertainers alongside the prostitutes".[131]

"During this period courtesans has to learn arts like music, dancing, casting side glances, a deep knowledge of sex, of the wiles that can ensnare a lover, the knack of double crossing a friend, drinking, love – making, embracing, kissing, shamelessness, flurry, confusion, jealousy, weeping, scratching, stealing, talking of one's own deficiencies, anointing the body, horticulture hair dyeing, devotion to monks and hermits etc".[132] It becomes clear that the "origin of the custom traceable to the practice of ritual dancing which becomes an integral part of the ritual service of gods and goddesses to please the deity".[133] Moreover, the "deity of an early medieval temple can be compared to a feudal lord who was provided with all the amenities and pleasures of life were needed by a feudal lord. The divine prostitutes had therefore to be employed to give company to the god as wives and concubines"[134]. According to "Huen -Tsang there were several dancing girls in the Sun temple of Multan".[135] In other words, the "association of dancing girls with the temples was beneficial for the development of temple and temple economy during the early medieval and later medieval periods".[136] In medieval period, "temple emerged as the owner of vast land property and the employer of a large number of religious and nonreligious functionaries".[137]

"The religious functionaries included the priests, dancing girls, dancing masters, singers and others. The temple Pidariyar in Kolar had twenty-four dancing girls".[138] "These singing girls were usually prostitutes and even they have recommended purchasing of beautiful girls for their dedication to temples"[139]. However, it can be argue that these dancing girls came from "low caste, non-Brahmin" and "other higher caste women were very rare". Moreover, it has been found that "parents from lower casts offered their girls to the service of temple out of their religious beliefs and devotion to god and goddess". For instance, there has been a practiced of "temple women" were called as Devdasis which literally means "God's (Dev) and female servant (Dasi). According to this ancient Indian practice, young pre- pubertal girls are married off, given away in matrimony to god or local religious deity of the temple" and "dedicated their lives to the service of God". During medieval period, "Sanskrit was regarded as the language of high culture and large number of scholars" who wrote in Sanskrit which provides information about the status of prostitution and role of states towards prostitute. For example, "Sanskrit literary sources of Kuvalayamala (779 A.D) written by Uelyotanasuri at Jalod in Rajasthan, Sringaramanjari Katha of Bhojadeva the famous ruler of Malwa, the Nammayasundari Katha of Mahendra Suri and Manasollas of Someshwara written in 1131 A.D are the literary sources which described the picture of the courtesans of this period and the environment in which prostitutes worked and lived".[140]

More importantly, "There have been within the class of women who prostituted, the courtesans trained in skills of music and dancing, educated and cultivated in fine arts, who were treated more as embodiments of culture. The elite status of courtesans made the class stand apart from the ordinary prostitutes".[141] Furthermore, a prostitute who lives in the quarters known as "Vesyasraya, Pura, Vesa" and drinking was "essential habit of them and therefore, "medieval Sanskrit dictionaries contain the names of wines, the methods of fermentation, the ingredients", etc. Besides, "Abhidhanachintamani" written by "Hemchandra where he has mentioned the following names for a prostitute and they were:

1. Sadharanastri (a strumpet),
2. Ganika (a courtesan), Panapanyangana (a woman who could be enjoyed for a pana),
3. Bhujishya (a mistress),
4. Lanjika rupajiva (one who lived on her beauty, a demimonde)[142]
5. Varavadhu, Varamukhya (a chief courtesan)
6. Kuttani (a bawd) and Sambhali (a prostitute).[143]

As Kambale Uttam says in his book, *Devadasi ani Nagnapuja,* the process of sanskritisation continued, the non-sanskritic shrines, which were mostly dedicated to Mother Goddesses, got sanskritized. The Brahmained priests added a mail deity to the shrine and also created myths saying that the new mail deity is the husband or master of the Goddess, when this was accepted, the priests also demanded sexual union with the priestesses of the local tradition. [144] Moreover, it has been that the emergence of religious prostitution is the part of Sanskrit religious tradition that offering something to the deity was rewarded bountifully. When the devotees came to the shrines with the problems such as bad health, poverty, barrenness etc. the priests interpreted these as the worth of the deity and suggested that a vow should be taken by the devotees, such included the offering of one of their daughters to the service of the deity".[145] It essentially encourages young girls to "engage in the sexual exploitation of their bodies". As James Frazer has rightly pointed out in "*The Golden Bough: A Study in Magic and Religion*", "the origin of sacred prostitution to the ancient custom of worshipping earth or Mother Goddess".[146]

Generally, it is believed that from the "sixth century onwards; the practice of dedicating girls to Hindu gods became prevalent practice that eventually developed into prostitution under the name of religion". In other words, "Devadasis performed a number of ritual and religious roles in the temples. They were celibate dancing girls belonging to ritually and economically lower castes, served as a link with the higher castes, by serving as the sex objects".[147] More importantly, "Devadasis were also present at marriages and other family gatherings".[148] In ancient India "Devadasi has an important position in society. Her presence as Sumangali was supposed to be auspicious".[149]According to Chakraborthy, "Their official duty consisted in dancing and singing within the temples twice a day, morning and evening and also at public ceremonies".[150]

"Many of them were proficient in the field of fine arts, especially music and dance. Originally, they were employed in the temples for cleaning the premises, washing the vessels, preparing the flower garlands and doing other jobs. But in the due course of time they took to dancing and music also. Gradually, due to the laxity of morals among the priests, the system was missed by them for immoral purposes".[151] It has been evident that those "girls who are form poor family and to low caste were sold at private auctions and later dedicated to the temples and then initiated into prostitution". "The account of the Arab traveler Abu Zaid al Hasan, who came to India in 867, states divine prostitutes earning from prostitution went in to the hands of the priests and was used for defraying the expenses of the temple".[152] Another foreign traveller, "Al Baruni (in the eleventh century) have recorded that the income from prostitution in temples used to be taken by the kings for meeting the expenditure of the army".[153] These examples have shown that, "under the grab of religious dedication of girls to temples, clandestine prostitution emerged. Besides, the institution of divine prostitution's property and earnings helped to enrich the 'wealth of the temples and went to the state treasury'. However, Trivadi argues in *Scheduled Caste Women: Studies in Exploitation,* in Hindu society Devadasi had a divine status and role as amorous form of mother Goddess. In Muslim period, they were pulled out of their ritual sphere and further lowered to the status of entertainers in royal courts. In British rule they were reduced to still lower status as commercial prostitutes in red light districts, to entertain their personnel.[154]

Furthermore, during Delhi Sultanate, music and dance received great patronage by the sultans and formed distinct art-form. It started from 1206 to 1526 and 'Qutb-ud-din Aibak, a former slave of Muhammad Ghori was the first Sultan of Delhi. It has been found that, "The prostitute-houses in the Sultanate come up as distinct establishments with state having a direct interest to regulate the profession in order to earn revenues out of it. "Alauddin Khilji's order came out with scheduled rates for sexual service and prostitutes classified as first, second and third to regulate the profession of this class of public women."[155] Moreover the 'legal position of the prostitute was also specified'.

A woman had to be registered as a prostitute and the state recognised a professional prostitute as a full person. While there was a recognition that a woman out of her will might also turn into a prostitute and for that her relations sever off all ties with her and turn out from the house. Her status was made low to the professional prostitute who could appear as witness in the court. We also hear words of praises about the professional ethics of prostitutes.[156] Perhaps, in making such distinction in status between a professional and a non-prostitute turning into a prostitute, while the state made available adulteress women for use in prostitution, there also appears a tacit recognition of other factors in the making of prostitutes.[157]

At this period, "dance and music by public women were integral to social pleasures and entertainment". According to Shadab Bano, "Interestingly, there appear no religious or ethical issues raised against prostitution and no attempt by the state to prohibit it".[158] Moreover, the Sultan and his chief nobles enjoyed dance and music, for instance, "Firuz Tughlaq came out with a treatise on music and dance, (however referred as Paturbazi)".[159] "The special interest in music of Sultan Sikander Lodi is also noted and he employed the best musicians of his kingdom and had them perform in late hours of night and early morning within his bedchambers on particular ragas and instruments he preferred".[160] Dance and music "in the early Sultanate chronicles was seen a performances mainly by the captive-girls". "Ibn Batuta's *Rihala* has given an account of festivities at the Delhi court. Male musicians and singers were there, a number of them being slaves, but male dancers were not mentioned among the performers at the court. Dance at the court particularly at that stage was performed by only women dancers. These singing and dancing girls were prised ones to be given as presents to distinguished guests on occasions".[161] However, the "dancing girls serving the court and aristocratic circles were a class apart compared to the ones who performed in the streets and bazaars. Dancing girls were also maintained by the merchants who organised their shows from place to place".[162]

"The professional 'dancers' of the market with their skills at singing and dancing, were not the same as ordinary prostitutes, who were mainly to provide sexual service as Ferishta writes cause ruin of soldiers so many youth. Still the prostitutes might have lured the clients with singing and dancing to heighten pleasure, in the same way as professional dancers and singers might bestow sexual favours along with providing a cultural entertainment".[163] Balban raised a "serious concern about men's sexual nature, as men will pounce on other men's wives" and as adultery could not be tolerated, "prostitution was regarded as safeguard against the passions of unruly men".[164] At this time, "brothels thereby came up in every city, in army stations to which all soldiers used to flock. When in Alauddin Khilji reign prostitutes were conferred in marriage, it was to relieve the profession of too much congestion, rather than on moral grounds".[165]

There have been "different classes of dancing girls appear in the 16th Century account" such as "Domnis, Patars, Kumachnis, Pari- Shans and Lulis. Each of these was in bands of thousands in the court of Sultan Bahadur of Gujarat. The Paturs was a celebrated caste of performers belonging to the Hindu branch, while the Lulis were the Muslim ones".[166] "The ruler could keep them and then pass on to friendly ruler or nobles as gifts and favours. When Sher Shah ordered the paturs kept by the amirs to be taken by force, there was no ethical question involved here, but the ruler simply tried to deal with his nobility and snatch from them these markers of status".[167] Besides "women performers had become cultural embodiments prised for their dancing, singing skills, beauty and charm". Still it has been found that "secret prostitution became general among the women living in the vicious atmosphere of the harems".[168] At this time, "women were generally corrupt and carried on love intrigues and their motive was mainly satisfaction of lust".

During the Vijaynagar Empire, prostitution was much in vogue and "organised prostitution for the benefit of the state". It has been found that "Vijaynagara emerged as the most powerful and wealthy state in the south during the first half of the fifteenth century".

According to H. M. Elliot, "Behind the mint is a sort of Bazar, there are several brothels within these seven fortresses and revenues from them amount to 12000 fanams, go to pay the wages of the policemen".[169] Abdur Razzak have visited Vijaynagar in 1442 A.D. and stated in the following manner:

1. "Opposite the darab – khaneh (the mint) is the house of the Governor, where are stationed twelve thousand soldiers as a guard, who receive every day a payment of twelve thousand fanom, living on the receipts of the houses of prostitution.
2. The magnificence of the palaces of this king, the beauty of the young girls collected therein, their allurements and their coquetry surpass all description. Behind the darab – khaneh is a sort of bazaar. On the two sides are ranged chambers and estrades.
3. Immediately after the midday prayer they place before the doors of the chambers, which are decorated with extreme magnificence, thrones and chairs on which the courtesans seat themselves, youth Good looks, good qualities and liberality are the chief and most natural means of making a person agreeable in the eyes of others but in the absences.
4. Each of these women is bedecked with pearls and is dressed in costly garments. Any man may enter their locality and select any girl that pleases him, and take his pleasure with her".
5. Anything that he carries with him is delivered into the keeping of those engaged in the service of the houses of prostitution, and if anything is lost these latter are responsible for it."[170]

Prostitution and their conditions under Vijaynagar Empire have been described by a number of foreign travellers. For instance, famous Italian traveller "Paes" who spent a number of years at "Krishna

Dev's Court" and highlighted emphasised that "dancing girls were also summoned during the feasts". "For these feasts are summoned all the dancing – women of the kingdom, in order that they should be present and also the captains and kings and great lords with all their retinues".[171] Moreover, "Al Beruni has also pointed out about the sacred prostitution in the institution of Devdasi has been prevalent in Vijaynagar".

During Mughals, "prostitution had a strong nexus with the performing arts". "Mughal Empire (1526 - 1707) was ruled by Akbar, Jahangir, Shahajahan and Aurangzeb". However, during this time, "rulers had to face many political and administrative problems", but in "economic and social spheres, particularly from the beginning of Akbar to the end of the seventeenth century, there were important social and economic developments". Basically "Mughal kings were great patrons of fine arts of music and dance, which flourished during their regime. Many a time the prostitutes were employed as dancers and singers in public social and religious functions".[172] Take for instance, a large number of "girls were attached to the Mughal courts for dancing and singing". According to foreign travellers such as Thomas Bowrey and J.B. Travernier, "Prostitutes had to pay some amount to the Governor of that of country and every Thursday's night pay visit to the house of governor and kotwal (Inspector) (Justice of peace) before whom they do and must dance and sing and make salams".[173] In other words, "some of them were highly accomplished ladies, adept in various arts and skills such as music, poetry, sorcery and spying. They lived there as the concubines and enjoyed a privileged position. A few of them were very loyal to the king, even going to the length of burning themselves to ashes after the death of their kings".[174] "Many of them maintained a large harem of women".[175]

For example, "Nur Bai was dancing girl of Delhi court and Nadir Shah was highly fascinated by her music that he used to pay her Rs. 4500 and wanted to take her Persia with him but she had categorically refused".[176] Besides, Nur Bai, "Anarkali was the most famous dancing girl of Akbar's court and it has been believed that Akbar's son Salim or Jahangir who fell in love with her and built her tomb at the outskirts of Lahore".[177] Besides, the "Mughal nobles maintained a large train of servants and attendants and a large stable of horses, elephants etc. Even women even accompanied the Mughal army and moved with them from place to place for the entertainment of the army personnel".

During Mughal reign, many European travellers as well as traders "came to India and some of them have mentioned about the social and economic conditions of the country". For example, the famous traveller- Blochmann has translated "*Ain E Akbari*" where "Abul Fazal" argues about the concubines and favourite slave girls and "Eunuchs or Hijras were entrusted with keeping guard over the women in a harem". He also pointed out, "Akbar maintained a seraglio in which there were 5000 women, and it had a separate staff of women officers who looked after its management".[178]

As "Durga Quli Khan, *Muraqqa-i-Dehli*", "These women referred to as rupajivas, literally meaning those earning a living by means of their beauty and were typified as samanya that is who is property of none and is concerned only in moneymaking".[179]

In order to restrict prostitution, "Akbar has made some regulations so that the services of prostitutes might not be available very easily to the public. He made an arrangement in such a way that the prostitutes were confined to a place outside the capital city".[180] In this way, Akbar took steps to check prostitution; even though, he appointed "A Darogha (superintendent) and a clerk were appointed for it who registered the name of visitors of prostitutes".[181] Despite of Akbar's restriction against prostitution, during Shah Jahan's reign, prostitutes "enjoyed much freedom and were in great numbers" but during Aurangzeb's reign, "most of rules were directed towards the prohibition of prostitution, but he failed". Darga Quli Khan has pointed out in his book "Muraqqa-i-Dehli", "Another description of these professionals comes from a rather retrospect account of Gujarat, which says that there was a great thrust to remove these women from bazaars of Anandabad City".[182] Since, prostitution received great encouragement from the rich section of the society such as Hindu rajas like "Baz Bahadur who was the ruler of Malwa and Raja Indrajit Singh the ruler of Orchha were great patrons of prostitution". It has been evident in "Manrique's account of the caravansera is (way-stations) for the passengers and merchants there are no speculations because he clearly mentions that these places were a site for this gainful profession and further that the women paid taxes to the state for allowing them to continue with their business".[183]

During the time of colonial period, the "rapid urbanisation and industrialisation increased the prostitution". At this time, status of prostitution becomes more vulnerable after the entry of Europeans such as the "Portuguese, Dutch, the English and later the French came to India for the purposes of trade". They have profoundly distorted the social, economic and political environment because they "used to visit houses of prostitutes which were like honeycombs in areas adjoining sea ports".[184] Firstly, during the end of fifteenth century, "Goa was a centre of Portuguese civilisation in India" and they were very corrupt. Dennis Kincaid has rightly pointed in "*British social life in India (1608 – 1937)*".

"The gambling houses and resort of dancing girls were run under the patronage of the Government. Some of these Portuguese captives brought to Surat and some were bundled into the harems of local officials and never heard again".[185] Secondly, during the seventeenth century, French came to India and many of them took concubines. It has been recorded that "General De Boigne who was European adventurer of the 18th century took one woman to Paris and embraced the Catholic religion".[186] Thirdly, "East India Company's servants were the British who kept native concubines. Many of these servants kept slave-girls as mistresses. Henry Crittleton, a Company's officer, kept a Brahmin mistress called Raje and in his will he refers to her wit obviously sincere gratitude and devotion leaving to her all his property".[187] According to Dennis, "General Pater was so fond of his mistress Arabella, that when on her death, the chaplain refused to bury her in consecrated ground, he has her body interred in a field and then built a Church over it, the Church of St. Mary's, so that in spite of Chaplain she should lie in consecrated ground".[188] In order to regulate prostitution, law dealing with immoral traffic was enacted and this was called the "Contagious Disease Act, 1868" which opened up a "new epoch in the history of prostitution in India". It enacted rules for controlling the increase of venereal diseases in the presidency capitals and regulating the "activities of prostitutes in the towns neighbouring to cantonments were behind this legislation".[189] It also "sanctioned the establishment of brothels and allowed prostitution in a regularised form and every brothel keeper and prostitute was provided with identity cards with details of registration. Every Prostitute was required to be periodically medically checked that she was not infected with venereal diseases".[190] However, protection of prostitute's health was not the main purpose of the medical check rather protecting the customer from contracting sexually transmitted disease. It can be argue that it worth mention here, unlike ancient India, in medieval period; some substantial steps had been taken by the rulers of that time to regulate the profession of prostitution and maintained the dignity of women. For instance, "the Contagious Disease Act, 1868", the "Suppression of Immoral Traffic Act (S1TA), 1923" was passed for "Calcutta, Madras and Bombay presidencies" and the "Nayak Girls Protection Act" and "Minor Girl Protection Act in Uttar Pradesh to regulate and control prostitution in legislative sense".

2.3. Status of Prostitution in Modern India

It has often been argued that, with the expansion of the globalisation, various social problems came into existence and prostitution is considered to be one of them. In other words, prostitution are closely related with urbanisation, trade development and places where people gather for tourism. Today prostitution is very common in India and big cities are worst affected. Moreover, an accurate and real situation of prostitution across India is not known because "sexual exploitation" and women's traffic are generally not reported. "The Coalition Against Trafficking in Women has highlighted about prostitution and according to its publication on trafficking, there are about 2.3 million prostitutes in India".[191] Although prostitution is technically illegal in India but usually it practiced across India. Even though, several laws have enacted from time to time to suppress prostitution. Take for instance, "The Suppression of Immoral Traffic in Women and Girls Act (SITA), 1956" and it renamed as "The Immoral Traffic (Prevention) Act (ITPA), 1956". But this act unable to achieved desire goals; therefore, Government must need to address this issue effectively at the earliest.

In order to mitigate prostitution, it is very important to focus on the causes of this menace. As M. Orhant has rightly pointed out in article entitled "Trafficking in Persons: Myths, Methods and Human Rights", "the root cause of prostitution is mainly due to poverty, unemployment and a lack of education".[192] Besides above causes, lacks of awareness, religious and cultural myth have been the major factor which leads women to enter into prostitution so that they can improve their living conditions. To reduce the number of people being trafficked for prostitution, globally, regionally, nationally and locally, various steps have been taken by governments and other institutions to undertake above causes that encourage this practice.

According to Samarasinghe & Burton, "The roots of sexual exploitation and trafficking are systemic and structural; prevention efforts should at the very least address some of the most fundamental issues that render women and girls vulnerable to trafficking. These issues clearly include the disadvantages for women in regards to poverty, education and wage employment".[193] Moreover, India is a developing country where 1/3rd of India's population lives in poverty. It shows that almost 33 percent people cannot meet their basic necessities. According to Robinson, "poverty plays a major role particularly in female prostitution".[194] In India, it has been noticed that, when the incidence of poverty comes on women's lives, it aggravates already "existing imbalances in power and therefore increases the vulnerability of women those who are at the receiving end of gender prejudice".[195] In other words, "in patriarchal set up, the section in families in societies that is affected is women and girl children. This poverty is often cited as the root of India's growing prostitution problem".[196] For instance, it has been observed that, traffickers usually victimize poor, uneducated, divorced, widowed and unmarried women etc. Besides, it has been found that, traffickers easily convince young girls from rural areas and offer them for job opportunities in cities to convince them easily to accompany them without suspecting their intention. Now it becomes clear that "trafficker forced young girls into prostitution which is modern day slavery" imposed on them by procurers. Moreover, such type of forced prostitution diminishes women's dignity to mere "sex objects and marketable commodities". In addition to poverty leads to prostitution, there other factors to be conducive to prostitution and these are namely:

1. Prostitution and Religion: "The inhuman system of prostitution with religious sanction exists in the states like Maharashtra and Karnataka of India. The most intense Devadasi practices still practiced in 21st century of progressive and democratic country where every year, thousands of young girls offer to God by their parents to escape from the poverty and later on these young girls serve as prostitute in their village".[197] Although religious prostitution like "Devdasi System" has been banned in India. Still it is widely practiced which "contributes to about 10 per cent of total prostitution in India".[198] In this way, several religious traditions and its practices in India aggravate the evil of women's trafficking in present society.
2. Prostitution and Culture: The evil of prostitution is embodied as a part of culture in Indian society since the Ancient time. For instance, tribes such as "Bedia, Banchara, Santhal" etc.; "practice prostitution as a tradition due to economic and social marginalization".[199] "Like most forms of religious prostitution, the tribal system automatically falls under the category of prostitution since they mandate that their girls be initiated by puberty at the latest".[200] In the present day society, evidence shows that, every year, around twenty thousand women have been trafficked within India in which fifty percent are from states where prostitution is the part of their culture.
3. Prostitution and Rape: It has been found that six percent of the rape victims forced to choose prostitution as their profession. It is regarded as a social stigma and when the victim don't find conducive environment and unable to find any prospect and finally they end up to brothels. As Robinson has highlighted that, "individuals who are victims of prostitution and or sex trafficking, who endure rape".[201] Moreover, around eight per cent of victims entered into prostitution after the occurrence of incest and in some certain circumstances; evidence shows that victims pushed to brothels by their own fathers and uncles after subjecting them to incest for monetary gains. "This is degrading to women because human bodies should

not be seen as commodities which can be sold and bought by peoples for sexual pleasure".[202] Besides above, "women's bodies should not be marketed for others to purchase. The buying and selling of women's bodies exemplifies women's second-class status in many countries including India".[203] Moreover such forms of "prostitution violates one's right to physical and moral integrity by the alienation of women's sexuality by the fact that it is debased and turned into a thing to be bought and sold".[204]

4. Prostitution and Abduction: It has been found that abduction has been the major reason under which girls are being abducted from rural areas and sexually exploited them and trafficked into prostitution against their will. Today, thirty five percent of prostitutes enter in this profession due to abduction. However, "the belief that prostitution is a victimless crime which is far from the reality because when women are abducted for prostitution against their will then the beliefs succeed to acknowledge the fact that there are victims of crime".[205] Moreover, when one examines the issue of choice and consent as an analytical tool, it is pointless to understand "prostitution as an institution rather to understand that prostitution pre-exists as a system that requires a supply of female bodies and therefore women and girls will be kidnapped, deceived, enticed, or persuaded to ensure that supply".[206]
5. Prostitution and Marriage: Some time unsuccessful marriage also leads to prostitution. It has been found that approximately fifteen percent prostitutes are in this profession from this category. According to Joffres, "forced prostitution through marriages whereby young women and underage girls are married to grooms willing to pay poverty-stricken parents a dowry".[207] He has also pointed out that, "Once these young girls are married, marriage makes this form of trafficking difficult to challenge under the law, these wives are forced into prostitution by their husbands and are sold to a broker who resells them to a brothel".[208] It has been noticed that, this practice has been prevalent in "Indian states such as Bihar, West Bengal, Chhattisgarh, Orissa, Uttaranchal and Hyderabad. Destinations for girls and women forced into

arranged marriages include the Indian states of Punjab, Haryana, Uttar Pradesh and the nation of United Arab Emirates".[209]

6. Prostitution and Social Factors: Due to patriarchal society, "women have been treated as commodities for the sake of pleasure are the manifestations of Hindustan culture in India".[210] Moreover, it has been found that, "The social stigma leads a woman to believe that her life is worthless after her husband's death and is also attached to a woman whose husband chooses a different woman as his wife".[211] Furthermore, a woman without a husband, generally she do not have means of life and at last she finds a useful place as a prostitute. It can be argue that once social norms combined with poverty leads them into prostitution. That's why it is said that prostitution is "the most systematic institutionalised reduction of women to sex".[212]

In modern India the account of women who have been indulging in prostitution, primarily in brothel but also in street, massage parlours, strip club, escort, and other forms of prostitution. Tulsing & Davis has rightly pointed out in their article entitled "Prostitution in Indian Society: Issues, Trends and Rehabilitation", "Generally prostitutes can be classified on the basis of their modus operandi" which is as follows:

1. Brothel Prostitutes: "Their operations are carried out in the brothels situated in red light areas which are generally owned by an ex-prostitute. The prostitutes work for a commission based on her sexual service".[213]
2. Call Girl Prostitutes: "They generally operate independently from her place. She may be available directly or solicit customers through middlemen".[214]
3. Street Prostitutes: "This type solicits customers on the streets and takes the customer to a place of assignation".[215]
4. "Clandestine forms of prostitution are also found in massage parlours, amusement centres, dance clubs etc."[216]

In recent times, India becomes a "receiving, sending, and transit country for prostitution". Due to its geographical border with country like "Nepal, Bangladesh, Pakistan", Sri Lanka, Afghanistan, Bhutan,

Myanmar and China are neighbouring country of India and the movement of people between India, Nepal and Bhutan more or less unrestricted since there is no requirement of passport. So, the regular unauthorised cross border movement of people is a matter of routine. Moreover, the increasing incidence of prostitution in cross-boundary is due to excess demand of women for prostitution and rampant unemployment. It has been observed that, "increase in tourism and gain of high profits from trafficking trade has encouraged the exploitation and seduction of women from poor to tribal communities and even other sections of the society who have never practiced this profession but became victims".[217]

In modern India, "information technologies bring out global revolution in communications" but at the same time it is also encouraging sexual exploitation of women and girls. It has been found that, "New technological innovations are the tools of the sexual exploitation of women and children because people easily can buy, sell and exchange millions of images and videos of sexual exploitation of women".[218] Moreover, "sexual exploitation of women is a global human rights crisis that is being escalated by the use of new technologies".[219] Today there has been various sophisticated technologies which easily facilitate prostitution, for instance, internet and various websites are become a tool to facilitate women's exploitation. It has been seen that these platforms are used by various sections for buying and selling of women for flesh trade. Besides, pimps also use these platforms to promote their brothels as well as escort services directly to the clients in flesh trade. In addition to website; chat rooms also provide a popular means of communication by which perpetrators engage women in sexual conversation on the internet".[220] For instance there has been several "cases online stalking of adults that began with conversations in chat rooms, which led to physical meetings that turned into sexual assaults".[221] In present time, mobile phones are using by pimps to avoid their tracing by the police personnel and in this way they easily contact their customers. Hence, communications by mobile phones makes jobs of pimps very easy and also avoid detection. Moreover, pimps used his phone for a very short period and switched to another phone for the avoidance of tracing. Therefore, it can be argue that, prostitution is one of the global problems and India is not exception of it. Even though, prostitution becomes a modern-day slavery which dehumanises and degraded the dignity of women. However, there has been several laws have enacted to address this menace at international, regional and local level. Recently a large section of society raising voice for legalise prostitution and take them to mainstream development and to protect women's dignity.

2.4. Origin of prostitution as a Hereditary Occupation Among Bedia Community

Generally speaking, prostitution is old issue in our society as it considered a part of religious and cultural practices among some communities like Bedia. Evidence shows that for many communities, prostitution is the only source of income particularly the women in the Bedia tribe who has been engaging in singing, dancing and in prostitution. According to Arun Kumar Acharya, "This tribe, who traditionally served the prince armies of their region, turned to criminal activity, when the advent of British rule dispersed; the tribal people started robbing for their livelihood. During this time very often, the British imprisoned the tribal men for long periods of time with or without any actual justification and to earn a livelihood the women folk turned to prostitution. The men only showed resistance initially but over time accepted it for the easy money and gradually, the only means of survival developed into the rigid tradition of social organisation".[222]

For Bedia community, prostitution becomes a convenient traditional business but it diminishes their social position. "The Bedia community of central India was earlier known as a denotified nomadic tribe. They chiefly engaged in singing and dancing to entertain the Kings and Zamindars (Land owners) of erstwhile India. They have been using traditional folk dance as a source of survival for their community. In the Mughal era, Bedia women entertained Mughal soldiers by their singing and dancing skills and also provided sexual pleasure to them. This tradition continued even under the patronage of the British armed forces".[223] Arun Kumar Acharya has rightly pointed out in his article entitled "Impact of Cultural and Religious Practices of Prostitution on the Trafficking of Women in India", "The Bedia women became the principal earners of the family whereas the males either solicit clients for their daughters, sisters, or mothers. In this system, the mother of any girl has to declare during her childhood in the presence of the village deity *Narsima* whether she will introduce her daughter into prostitution or give her in marriage. The initiation of daughter into prostitution is an occasion for celebration. It is a mandatory caste rule that at least one daughter in each family be reserved for prostitution".[224]

Further, he pointed out that, "A married woman is fully debarred from the profession of prostitution. The prostitute is debarred from having sexual relations with anyone of the community. All these caste rules believed to have divine sanction and their contravention invites penalties and social boycott".[225] It is worth to mention here as Gathia Joseph argues in his book—*Child Prostitution in India",* "Bedia as well as other communities like Bachada, Kanjar, Koltas, Nat and Sansi had played a significant role in the Sepoy Mutiny in 1857 against the British crown, which later provoked the British authorities into including these communities in the Notified Tribes and Criminal Tribes list. Their stay overnight at any village was supposed to be reported to the local administration and the police. Such repression deprived them of the essential sources of livelihood".[226] Besides he also mentioned that, "After the war in 1857, the British government prohibited Bedia community from the right of ownership of agriculture land, and this cruel repression left them almost deprived. Such a system continued throughout the entire British period".[227] "Bedia community was also notified as a criminal tribe by the colonial state at the end of nineteenth and beginning of the twentieth century. The National Commission for Denotified Nomadic and Semi-nomadic tribes and the Ministry of Social Justice& Empowerment of the Government of India have included Bedias in the Scheduled Caste category according to the Indian Constitution Scheduled Castes Order 1950".[228]

The origin of Bedia community's identity are derived from two sources, firstly, from books and documentation by anthropologists and historians, and secondly, from the oral accounts given by members of the Bedia community. There has been a different theory propounded about the origin of the Bedias and the practice of their women who indulges in prostitution. However, there has been the same opinion regarding Bedia community originally being a nomadic one.

According to Russell and Hiralal, "Bedia communities are the caste of gypsies and thieves. In 1891, they numbered 906 persons in the Central Provinces, distributed over the Northern districts. In 1901, they were not separately classified but were identified with the Nats. Apparently, some generations ago two brothers resided in the Bharatpur territory of whom one was named Sains Mul and the other Mullanur. The descendants of Sains Mul are the Sansias and those of Mullanur the Bedias or Kolhatis who are vagrants and robbers by hereditary profession. Among the Bedias, women are professional prostitute and do not marry. In central India and in Bundelkhand 'Berni' (a term used for Bedia Women) is a synonym for prostitute".[229]

Historically, Bedia community has been visible in the period of Muslim invaders like Mohammed Gazni and Mohammed Gauri. During that time, there was no central authority in the Indian sub-continent but it was divided into smaller kingdoms. Moreover, people were superstitious and the rulers were fond of luxury and comfort. "During British rule they came to be known as 'criminal tribes' along with other castes like Kanjars, Nats Sansis, etc. They were frequently hounded for criminal offences and their movements were restricted. At night they had to report to the local police station. Somewhere along the line they sought protection against such surveillance from the princely states. It is believed that in exchange of the protection and security received from the aristocracy they gave their women. Thus, began the traditional practice putting Bedia woman into prostitution".[230] In the "post-independence period Bedias came to be known as Vimuki Jati or de notified caste, and are presently included in the broader classification 'scheduled caste' among Hindus".[231] Besides, studies by "Non-Government organisations with Action Aid India indicates that Bedia and other communities could not get any benefit from the state in spite of being in the reserved category and they are suffering from poverty, insecurity, prostitution etc. As a result, Bedias take part in sex work and also many have chosen prostitution as a convenient occupation".[232] Secondly, it has been found that, Bedia community originated during the 19th century. There has been a narrative about the thankurs wife who was widowed and accounts of her widowhood she as faced with various problems and not accepted by her parental and marital families. As a result, she moved into the jungles somewhere in Rajasthan where she started living".[233] Consequently men who brought their cattle to graze in the jungles met her and after that she gave birth to some children whose status by birth made them social outcastes. She therefore, put her daughters into prostitution and according to this particular village source, is the origin of Bedias and the tradition of their women partaking in flesh trade. From the above, the tradition of Bedia women's association with prostitution seems to be rooted in the peculiarities of community history.

Moreover, Bedia community known by several names and their identity with the type of work they do in different areas. For example, their origin is from Rajasthan where they are listed as scheduled tribe and in U.P. they are listed under scheduled caste. It is evident that in other areas, Bedias are identified either with Nuts, Sansis, Kolhaties etc., however, they recognised internationally very close to gypsies of Europe. In earlier days, they have no separate identity lf their own but identified with other allied, castes. Only in 1901, two brother who were resided in Bharatpur territory, one named Sains Mul and ancestors of Sainsmual become sansia and those of the Mullanur become Beria or Kolhaties in different place who are vagrant and robber living either in tents or huts. There are '12 sub castes' and those involved in such activities namely; Bedia, Bhantu, Kanjare, Chdiya, Kabootrey, Karval, Saperey, Banjare, Bhaat, Kolhaties, Sansi and Nuts. It has been found that Sansi, Berias, Kolhaties and Nuts are similar to each other. Moreover, "Bedia men are offensive and indulge in crimes like kidnapping children, making thefts and all other criminal activities while Bedia women are engaging in prostitution".[234] Since the inception of this tribe, they are involved in the profession of prostitute, criminal activates, thefts and kidnapping. Profession of prostitute is the bigger source of their earning which is still ongoing in all corners of the world".[235] No matter how they have been identified in different parts of country and world as reported by some community member it is quite astonished to hear that the entire community is yet involved in the profession of prostitution except 2 to 3 percent of Bedia population. It has also been reported by them that there are three types of Bedia

1. Pure breed of Bedia.
2. Mixed breed of Bedia which implies a woman (CSW) who is a Bedia but the caste of the client is unknown then the child born out of this meeting will be of mixed breed of Bedia.
3. Kidnapping of female children to whom they treat as their daughter and later on these girls are sent for the prostitution in metropolitan cities. This type of professional structure expands not only their profession in all dimensions but also increased the population of Bedia Community.

In addition to that, prostitution being their inherited profession ever since their origin, they send their daughter at early age for dancing instead of schooling and gradually prepare them to enter in the profession of prostitutes. It is a proud privilege for parents to send their daughter in this profession and for the daughters too. "Recent studies have revealed that Bedia women and girls are being made available to international customers for sex services through international agents and local pimps".[236] Since their daughter are sent to big cities and different countries where they can earn lucratively while kidnapped girls as their age advanced are sent to smaller cities where they can hardly earn their livelihood. "Women of Bedia community, who are among the most prominent of the groups to traffic their women into prostitution, are believed to travel up to Gulf countries as sex workers often in the guise of dancers. Not surprisingly, the families of these women are the main beneficiaries of these women's economic gains from such tours".[237] "Times of India have also reported on July 28, 2017 that Bedias were providing sex services to the customers of G. B. Road, Delhi."[238] According to "Trafficking in Persons Report: India", "Bedia girls and women were rescued from metro cities like Delhi and Mumbai, and also from some parts of West Bengal".[239]

In order to know about the involvement of Bedia community in prostitution, about 50 family members 24 children of these families and 80 C.S.W. have been interviewed. It has been brought to our notice that their own daughter lived in Bombay, Calcutta, Delhi and so on but they say our daughter are married and they are not involved in this profession while the fact is that they are engaged in CSW's. It has been noted that they don't know about the husband of their daughters.

"The Bedia families have no reliable sources of income and hence, unmarried women of the family are compelled to offer sex services within the village as well as outside the district".[240] As Anuja Agarwal writes in her book – "*Chaste wives and prostitute sisters: Patriarchy and prostitution among the Bedias of India",* "The major sustenance of Bedia community is based on the income of their females, which they earn through prostitution, as their male members by and large do not work. They are mainly involved in Kidnapping, making thefts and other criminal and unlawful activities and act as organizer, mediator to promote the business of prostitution. In earlier day this was the only job but gradual change has been observed. Few of them started sending their children to school. As a result, some of them had left their old profession and engaged themselves in the new profession for their livelihood. Except 2 to 3% of population, their males and females are primarily involved in the inherited profession, with all these kinds of activities they can earn a lot and have become very rich".[241] It has been found that, Bedia community is proud of this profession and earns huge money to live their luxury lift but it has certain disadvantages. Consequently, educated person who have engaged in other profession change their caste and almost boycott with their own community. As observe some of them adopted caste of Baniya, Sikhi, Muslims, Hindu any other caste and start living in good colonies and marry their children with other caste.

The prevalence of certain communities in the business of flesh trade has been in various studies and reports on the subject. Their involvement is not incident, because prostitution is the traditional occupation of the women in these communities. Usually when we speak of or refer to hereditary prostitutes when have in mind devadasis and their kind. "The association of prostitution with religion has been an age-old phenomenon, so in many parts of the country we can find the female dancers and singers attached to temples are generally referred to by the term Devadasi which literally means female slaves of the deity. Their dedication to temple services is considered as constituting a marriage with the deity. The cult of dedicating girls to the temple is prevailing all over India in different forms and names, such as Devadasi in Karnataka state, Maharis in Kerala state, Natis in Assam state, Murlis in Maharashtra state, Jogins and Basavis in Andhra Pradesh state, Thevardiyar in Tamil Nadu state and Bhavins in Goa state. As centuries passed, their services shifted from gods to earthly gods and lords. The women dedicated to the deity as Devadasi, usually lead a life of prostitute with religious sanction".[242] Besides religious form of prostitution like Devdasis, Basavi, and Jogin, Bhavins system, Prostitution in tribal societies of India has been prevalent since time immemorial. "In India, there are some tribes such as Banchara, Bedia tribe of Madhya Pradesh state, Domare tribe of Andhra Pradesh state, Santhal tribe of Orissa state and Bihar state, Rajnat tribe of Rajasthan state practices traditional form of prostitution because of economic and social marginalisation. Like most forms of religious prostitution, the tribal system automatically falls under the category of prostitution, since they mandate that their girls be initiated by puberty at the latest".[243] But, the devadasis, for whom prostitution is the inevitable way of life, differ from the hereditary communities like the Bedias. Gils from the Bedia are put into prostitution with family and social consent, while devadasis belong to diverse caste backgrounds (generally the weaker sections), who "dedicated themselves in the service of Goddess *Yellamma* on full moon day of *Chitra* month (March-April) or *Magha* month (December-January), where every year 1,000 to 5,000 young girls are brought to the Devadasi profession. The sites of most intense Devadasi activity are located in a belt on either side of the Karnataka or Maharashtra border districts like Belgaum, Bijapur, kolhapur, Solapur".[244]

"Most of the girls belonging to this group are from lower caste. Their families trapped by poverty often depend upon the income supplied by their daughters and money being funnelled down to them from higher caste, wealthier men who can pay for the services of a prostitute".[245] This act of dedication denies then the right to marry, leaving them with the options of begging and prostitution as means of self- sustenance. As Chakraborthy writes in *Women as Devadasis: origin and growth of the Devadasi profession*, "A Devadasi family receives regular gifts of presents and cash on those specific days dedicated to the goddess Yellamma from Hindus who worship this goddess".[246] Further she also pointed, most of the times the dedication ceremony is financed by a wealthy man, and after attainment of puberty this man has the right to the girl's virginity. At the time of 'deflowering' the man pays a large sum of money to the girl's family, hence the financial returns to the family of a girl are immediate, and they profit from her earning as long as she continues to work".[247] Perhaps a majority of them entered into prostitution and thereby, devadasis may give rise to a lineage of hereditary prostitutes. However, the origin of such a lineage is not essentially hereditary, but more the product is ignorance and religious folly. Their historical background, the social and cultural factors promoting the practice of dedicating girls, their involvement in flesh trade, etc. have been subject of research and have been studied in some detail. As a result, their position and problems are now known. Not only this information enabled the concerned sections to draw up rehabilitation, economic, and general developmental programmes for them, but it has also been possible to organize the women themselves against this humanly degrading practice of dedicating girls. Bedias irrespective their age and gender or sex, refer to prostitution as "khandani pesha or hereditary occupation". "During a discussion with a senior male member of Bedia community of village Chamarpura, Fatehabad area of Agra district regarding their tradition and culture, they responded that (Hum log kalakar hai, isliye hum mata Saraswati ke putra hai) they are artists and therefore they are the sons of Goddess Saraswati".[248] They have also emphasized that colonial government treated them badly and no other option for their livelihood they justified prostitution by saying that their "women came out to support their families and such practices became their identity".[249] Moreover they claimed that after independence, "Government of India did not do anything for them and whatever they have today is because of prostitution, so they can't leave prostitution".[250] In this way, questions of morality, values, legality, exploitation, etc. do not seem to bother them and they find nothing wrong with prostitution. Their acceptance of this way of life is so ingrained that many of them tend to view it as the essential occupation for the sustenance of the family. The history and origin of the practice of the women or girls taking to prostitution, the association of this practice with the community's self-perception and the causal element that may led to its evolution, its ritualistic aspect, impact of the practice on the women and girls the position, role and status of women in the community, self-image of the women, etc.

Geographically, the Bedias as a rural based community are dispersed in the border area of states of M.P., Rajasthan and U.P. Most of the Bedia women called 'Bernis' in the parlance of the business are functional in the city red-light areas like those of Agra, Allahabad, Bombay, Delhi, Kanpur, Meerut and Nagpur. Some of them also operate in their native villages. While the womenfolk prostitute, men of the community operate as pimps and procurers. They constitute the supportive structure on which the business rests. So, with passage of time, prostitution has become a caste phenomenon for their sex defined roles for attaining greater heights in, and through, prostitution. Bedia involvement in the business of prostitution does not end with the induction of their own girls into it. They enjoy both power and control over be brothels in the city red-light areas. They run brothels and draw economic benefits from the earnings of those prostitutes living in, and operating from their brothels. In this way, the community lives of the earnings of others forced to sell themselves. By way of boosting this aspect of their business involvement, Bedias indulge in the sale and purchase of girls from other castes and communities. Those girls forced into prostitution by the Bedias are called 'Lonchi'. Bedias are party to force that use inhuman means to compel these unfortunate girls to accept prostitution. For instance, they are usually running 'training centers' near their villages for conditioning this category of girls. In this way, Bedias form a part of a very well-organised system and network, which runs and manages the business of flesh trade. In fact, this community is so well established, that one generation hands over the rights of business to the next in the red-light areas. For next generations, it is therefore easier to get a strong hold in the trade environment. Not only this, some of the elder "Bernis" who were functional in the trade as prostitutes are presently holding high positions in their professional circles like secretaryship or presidentship to some music and dance society. Moreover, their "knowledge of the Pasto language" helps them in business. They use this language to communicate their trade secrets without the fear of being understood by others. It is evident that consumption of alcohol and pork are mandatory during occasions for renouncement and festivities and any celebration. Moreover, the women, particularly those in the red-light areas, addicted to smoking and drinking. Besides, marriage was a rare phenomenon in the past and even among the Bedia men but Bedia men married women from other castes like Kanjars by paying bride price. "Bedia women who get married may discontinue the work. However, that would mean a loss of revenue for the family and community. Probably to discourage that, the norm has been for Bedia men to pay a large bride-price for a Bedia bride. Hence, Bedia men usually marry women from outside communities".[251] Moreover, very few Bedia women are married, since a majority of them would be engaged in prostitution. It is said that only those Bedia girls were destined to marry who were ugly and unfit for prostitution. But, in the recent years, some Bedia girls are getting married, not because of the above-mentioned considerations, but as a result of awareness among some sections of the community. However, Bedia daughter-in-law are not allowed to go for prostitution. Conversely, those in prostitution are debarred from marriage. Bedias resolve disputes and quarrels within the community in their own 'panchayats' and do not seek help either from the police or administration. Someone from the community in the event of approaching the police is liable to be either penalised and boycott from Bedias.

Bedias are village-based community who migrate to the urban areas for the purpose of expansion of prostitution. However, at the village level, they are settled with some land and property, and are primarily agriculturists. Even though some have their own business or work as a casual labour. It is found that small section of Bedia men are employed with the government and police departments, banks, private organisations etc. Besides, few of them have been working as a medical and engineering professional. This, however, is one side of the story. Some families are comparatively poor. Their economical backwardness is mainly on account of bad ownership position and minimal or no involvement the trade. The life cycle of

Bedia women is divisible into two phases. The first is the preliminary phase comprises selection and trading of the girls while the second phase implies the actual beginning in the profession. However, the first phase is the process of training which is a gradual one and spread out over few years by which young girls are being trained into the foundational phase before they are able to exercise their own senses of maturity. In this way Bedia girls are conditioned slowly and by the time they develop acceptance for the caste occupation. Moreover, actual initiation and confirmation in the profession of prostitution is based on three phases and these are namely: (a) Debut of presentation, (b) Selection of the partner and (c) Honour granted and cultivation of trade. Firstly, the debut of presentation begins after successful completion of training the girls are introduced to "Mehfils" in the brothels of big cities at the age of 14 to 15 years and their formal induction into protection is marked by the "Nath Utrai' or Sar dhaki Ceremony. Here is a ceremonial initiation of girls soon after puberty in a ritual called Nath Utrai. Because of the normalcy of this practice, it is not viewed as prostitution but as a time-honoured tradition".[252] Secondly, the selection of the partner under which elders like mothers and aunts choose the man to partner her among those who have been attending the 'Mehfils' and his ability to pay is one of the major considerations determining his selection. Apparently, prices paid for the virgin very between Rs 25,000 to 50,000 rupees. It is an occasion for celebration (Jashn) and the fellow prostitutes from the neighbourhood and other members of the Bedia community join in the festival which lasted for 2-3 days. Thirdly, honour assigned and cultivation of trade in which everyone extends good wishes and blessings to the new candidate for her success and fulfilment in her life as a prostitute. This function serves the additional purpose of instilling a sense of pride in the girl towards the profession of prostitution she is going to enter.

Now the basic question arises here: what are the prospects of Bedia Women in the trade? From discussions it transpires that Bedia women do not tread any set path in the course of their lifetime in the trade. Three instinct alternatives came to notice. In the first situation, all Bedia women do not continue in the red-light areas for a lifetime. Those who do are the ones who have been able to rise to the position of 'nayika' or 'chaudhary' which are the equivalent of brothel keeper in the parlance of the business. There are the ones who hold offices in the different in the different societies and generally lay a leadership role. In the second situation, there are some who withdraw from active professional life and either return to their villages and moved out of the red-light area as to live in some respectable locality. They now live a mistress of some already married men who give them their monthly expenses. Insecurity looms average in the lives of these women because they are without any income of their own and become totally dependent on the money given by their partner. In this way, they develop emotional dependence on this relationship; contrary to what their training taught them in childhood. In the third situation, women are those who devote their whole life to the trade, but do not reach any positing in the trade hierarchy. In their old age some men of this kind lead a life of total misery devoid of any material or financial support.

Moreover, birth of a female child is greatly welcomed in Bedia community because a child with her potentiality to earn in the future for the family. As Jha and Sharma has rightly pointed out in "Caste and Prostitution in India: Politics of Shame and of Exclusion", "While India's loathing of daughters leads to more than a million female feticides each year, and the killing of thousands of new born girls, the Bedia are one community that wants girls. When a woman is pregnant, the family hopes it will be a girl. Not a boy. What makes the Bedias stance on girls different from that of the rest of India? It is their old tradition of inducting their daughters into prostitution. For long, women have served as the lifeline of the Bedia community".[253] There were cases of families whose economics status has experienced a great boost since one girl in the family took to the trade. In one particular instance, before the girl was in the trade the parents were causal labourers, but since she has been in it, they are living a life of economics sufficiency. A family's economic dependence on this source of income is great. In other words, while in the trade, a woman not only occupies an independent position but is also given more respect within the family as long as she continues to be in business. However, a woman's voluntary and premature withdrawal from the profession is not gracefully taken by the family as it means a set back to the family's income. As a result, woman who dissociates herself from trade and starts living with her family has to bear up with frequent taunts and occasional ill treatment from family members because she no longer earns. They are looked upon as a burden to the family. Moreover, women in the trade are treated at par with the male siblings and thereby equal share in the property along with their brothers. It must be mentioned in passing that, while members of this community do not feel any shame in drawing benefits from the caste occupation, although, they do not easily disclose their identity.

"Very few of the employed Bedias declare their caste background. They avoid use of the caste surname-instead they suffix their name with some more ambiguous surname like Singh. The women in this community play of role of bread earners more than the conventional role of mother or wife evolvement in the trade hampers with their role of mother. Keeping the business, which they do not like and they neither consider it proper for the children to be constantly exposed to the trade environment".[254] The above exposition clearly reveals that, Bedia women are not in prostitution by choice or preferences, but more on account of the pressure of the men in their society, who are basically lazy, alcoholics and inconsistent in their occupational perusals. Moreover, the men have come to believe in the concept of 'easy money' and enjoyment of life, and what can be better than have the letter without having to work for it while others sell themselves to provide for them. It has also emerged from the discussions that economic considerations and male domination are significantly responsible for the continuation of this tradition till today. Men have tried to attach legitimacy to their stand by using the plea that flesh trade is their traditional profession which has social sanction. Actually, their ulterior motive is to effortlessly gain money and in their pursuit of money, they are exploiting their women and silencing them whenever they make an attempt to raise a voice in protest. Therefore, at present economic capability of the women among the Bedias continues to determine their status in the community. In fact, they are held in high esteem till the time they are economically productive. It can be argue that, the female sex in this community has been reduced to objects or commodities with mere monetary value. However, the Bedias are organised and the processes of environment are so perfect that, prostitution is deeply rooted in their lives. It has been very difficult to make breakthrough in bringing about any change in attitude among them. Even though efforts have been made but very little results achieved because those efforts were quantitatively limited has not left any visible mark in the overall situation. Hence, sincere and substantial efforts of individuals and organisations working in this field need a boost to create the kind of attitudinal change that is essential. Moreover, their activities have not with stiff resistance because the community interpreted their intervention as threat to their source income. Despite all these, one must draw inspiration from those sections of Bedias who welcome change and launch consorted efforts to reach out the community and induce in them attitudinal change. Even at present some change is noticeable, though things are moving only because of the emphatic resistance from other section of the community who prefer to be the way they are rather than accept change for betterment. What is required is getting together people from government, society and the Bedia community to prevent the tradition that has dehumanised women. However, it can be argue that, intervention of agencies is likely to be more effective because they found to be more sensitive to the issue in question as compared to the local bodies (even the administration and public) for whom whole thing is an everyday affair, probably, not worthy of all hue and cry.

To sum up this chapter, I can say that, prostitution as a profession was practiced since the time of ancient India. Moreover, they enjoyed social acceptance while practicing bodily services. In fact, their role in political, social and religious sphere has been commendable and "therefore they were treated with respect of course". History bears that the famous socio-political treatise of Kautily's *Arthashastra* mentioned about "sexual entertainment to the public by means of trained Ganikas" and they were "controlled by the state and carried on by state-owned establishments". Further it can be argue that, "prostitution was a necessary evil" which the society required since the beginning to satisfy the sexual needs of rich class. But their condition becomes pathetic since Gupta era onwards. However, during medieval time, certain restrictions were imposed on prostitution but the practice was going on with some pause, but the overall situation of prostitutes was terrible and they were considered as a "luxurious commodity of the feudal class, the kings, high officials and the princes". Still, it can be argue that, since "early days of human history, woman's sexuality has been controlled by her nation state and state has facilitated" the "idea of providing sexual entertainment to the public", therefore, I can reach into the conclusion that since the beginning "women's sexuality was controlled by the state throughout Indian history". For instance, prostitution is old issue in our society as it considered a part of religious and cultural practices among some communities like Bedia tribe who has been engaging in singing, dancing and prostitution which is deeply rooted in their lives. Therefore, prostitution becomes a modern-day slavery which dehumanises and degraded the dignity of women. Despite several laws have been enacted from time to time to address this menace at international, regional and local level and incorporate them into mainstream development.

Notes

1. Alexis, A Aronowitz, *Human Trafficking, Human Miseries: The Global Trade in Human Beings* 4-5 (Praeger Publishers, USA, 2009.
2. Prostitution, New World Encyclopedia, *available at*: https://www.neworld. (Last visited July 17, 2017).
3. Sanighdha, S, "The sex worker Predicament: A Silent Wail", *available at*: info@probono-india.in, (Last visited July 17, 2017).
4. *Supra* note 2.
5. Aslam Mohammad, "When Prostitution was a symbol of high culture in elite circles of 19th century", Quartz India, *available at*: https://qz.com/india/1000432/ (Last visited Jun 7, 2017).
6. Kuppuram, "Chanakya on prostitution" 40, *Proceedings on the Indian History Congress* 215-219 (1979).
7. Tulsing Solwani, "Prostituion in Indian Society: Issues, Trends and Rehabilitation", *available at*: https://www.ugc.ac.in. (Last visited August 15, 2017).
8. Krithika Rajam, "How Devdasis went from having high social status to being sex slaves and child prostitutes" 2 *Human Rights Quarterly* 25-61 (2013).
9. Ashok, K Jain, *Socio- Economic Offences* 35-40 (Ascent Publications, Delhi, 2016).
10. Sen, S, Nair, PM, *"A Report on trafficking on women and children in India 2002-2003* 440 (*Institute of Social Sciences, NHRC & UNIFEM, India*; 2004)".
11. *Supra* note 1 at 4-5.
12. *Supra* note 1.

13. J.N. Pandey, *The Constitutional Law of India* 299-304 (Central Law Agency, Allahabad, 45th edn., 2008).
14. Sen, Sankar & Nair, P.M. *Trafficking in Women and Children in India* 191 (Orient Longman Pvt. Ltd., New Delhi, 2005).
15. *Supra* note 14 at 193.
16. *Supra* note 14 at 194-195.
17. Ghosh, S. K., *The World of Prostitution* 959 (A. P. H. Publishing Corporation, New Delhi, 1996).
18. *Supra* note 17 at 959-960.
19. May, Geoffrey, "Prostitution" XII, *Encyclopaedia of Social Sciences* (Macmillan Co., New York, 1936).
20. David L. Sills, 12, *International Encyclopaedia of Social Sciences*, (The Macmillan Co., NY, 1968).
21. Suppression of Immoral Trafficking Act, 1956 (104 of 1956), s. 2 (f).
22. Savita Bhatt, *Women and Human Rights* 193-194, (Altar Publishing House, New Delhi, 2010).
23. Supra note 22 at 194-195.
24. Saraswati Raju Iyer & N. Radha, "Women Trafficking in India: A Critical Analysis" 4, *Shanlax International Journal of Arts* 108-109 (2016).
25. *Supra* note 24
26. *Supra* note 24
27. *Supra* note 24.
28. *Supra* note 24.
29. *Supra* note 24.
30. *Supra* note 24.
31. *Supra* note 24.
32. *Supra* note 24.
33. Nag Moni, "Anthropological perspectives on prostitution and AIDS in India" 36 *Economic and Political Weekly* 4026 (2001).
34. Umesh Kr. Singh, *Women Crime & Punishment in Ancient India, Earliest Times to 1200 A.D.* 113 (Janki Prakashan, Patna, 2017).
35. *Supra* note 33 at 4026.
36. *Supra* note 36 at 1-2.
37. Y. B. Singh, "Roots of the Ganika-Culture of Early India" 74 *Annals of the Bhandarkar Oriental Research Institute* 181-190 (1993).
38. Shailendra, N S, *Ancient Indian History and Civilisation* 17-18 (New Age International Publications, India, 2nd edn., 1999).
39. Divyendu Jha & Tanya Sharma, "Caste and Prostitution in India: Politics of Shame and of Exclusion" 4 *Anthropology* 2-4 (2016).
40. Sukumari Bhattacharji, "Economic Rights of Ancient Indian Women", 26 *Economic and Political Weekly* 507-512 (1991).

41. Wendy Doniger, "The Kama Sutra: It Isn't All about Sex" 5 *The Kenyon Review* 18 (2003).
42. *Supra* note 41.
43. Mukherji Santosh Kumar, *Prostitution in India* 32 (Inter India Publications, Delhi, 1986).
44. *Supra* note 43.
45. *Supra* note 43.
46. Sukumari Bhattacharji, "Prostitution in ancient India" 15, *Social Scientist* 32-61 (1987).
47. Chandra Moti, *The World of Courtesans* 1 (Vikas Publishing House Pvt. Ltd, Delhi, 1973).
48. K. K. Mukherji & Deepa Das, *Prostitution in Metropolitan Cities of India, A Study by: Central Social Welfare Board* 16 (Samaj Bhavan, New Delhi, 1996).
49. Joseph Gathi, *Child Prostitution in India* 10 (Concept Building Company, New Delhi, 1998).
50. *Supra* note 49 at 11—15.
51. *Supra* note 47 at 22.
52. L K Khurana, *Ancient India* 26 (Laxmi Narayan Publication, Agra, 2001).
53. *Supra* note 47 at 22-23.
54. *Supra* note 33 at 3.
55. *Supra* note 46 at 33.
56. Sukumari Bhattacharji, "Prostitution in Ancient India" 15 *Social Scientist* 32-61 (1987).
57. *Supra* note 56 at 32.
58. *Supra* note 56 at 32-33
59. *Supra* note 56 at 32-33
60. *Supra* note 56 at 32-33
61. *Supra* note 32 at 32-61.
62. Sinha, S.N. & Basu, N.K., *History of Prostitution in India*, 10-13 (Cosmo Publications, New Delhi, 1994).
63. Mehta, Rama, *Socio-Legal Status of Women in India* 38 (Mittal Publication, Delhi, 1957).
64. *Supra* note 63 at 39-40.
65. Sikka, K. D., "Prostitution: Indian Perspectives and Realities" XLV *The Indian Journal of Social Work* 216 (1984).
66. Sinha,S. N., N. K. Bose, *History of Prostitution in Ancient India* 4 (Shree Balaram Prakasani, Kolkata, 2003).
67. *Supra* note 36 at 20.
68. Sinha, S.N. & Basu, N.K., *The History of Marriage and Prostitution* 10-28 (Khama Publishers, Delhi, 1992.
69. *Supra* note 37-39.

70. Westemarg, E., *History of Human Marriage* 7-52 (The Macmillan Company, New York, 1892).
71. *Supra* note 36 at 5.
72. *Supra* note 62.
73. *Supra* note 36 at 12.
74. Rooppreet, K. Sohal, *The Exploitative Nature of Prostitution and Sex Trafficking in India (*2013) (Unpublished Ph.D. thesis, Texas State University)
75. *Supra* note 74.
76. Sukumari Bhattacharji, "Prostitution in Ancient India" 15 *Social Scientist* 32-61 (1987).
77. *Supra* note 76.
78. Chandra Moti, *The World of Courtesans* 3 (Vikas Publishing House Pvt. Ltd. Delhi, 1973).
79. *Supra* note 78.
80. Sarkar, S. C., *Some Aspects of the Earliest Social History of India* 94 (Oxford University Press, London, 1928).
81. *Supra* note 80.
82. *Supra* note 80.
83. *Supra* note 42 at 4.
84. *Supra* note 78 at 5-18.
85. *Supra* note 78 at 5.
86. Sinha, S. N., N. K. Basu, *The History of Marriage & Prostitution* 29 (Khama Publishars, Delhi, 1992).
87. Supra note 86
88. *Supra* note 86 at 29.
89. *Supra* note 86 at 35-42.
90. Rozario, Rita, *Trafficking in Women and Children in India* 6 (Uppal Publications House, New Delhi, 1988).
91. Salla Sariola, *Gender and Sexuality in Selling Sex in Chennai* 59 (Routledge, London, 2010).
92. Umesh Kumar Singh, "Immoral Trafficking of Girls and Women in Ancient India" 68 *Proceedings of the Indian History Congress* 162-178 (2007).
93. *Supra* note 92 at 167.
94. *Supra* note 21 at 285.
95. Valmiki, Translated by Ramesh C Datt, *Ramayana* 127 (Vijaya Goyal Publisher, Delhi, 2018).
96. *Supra* note 96 at 164-166.
97. Adi Parva, Krishna Mohan Ganguli (trs.) *The Mahabharata* (1883-1896).
98. *Supra* note 97.
99. *Supra* note 97.
100. *Supra* note 99.

101. *Supra* note 99
102. *Supra* note 51 at 168-170.
103. *Supra* note 56 at CXXIII
104. Prabha Chandra Tripathy, *Crime Against Working Women* 24 (Vikas Publication, New Delhi, 2000).
105. *Supra* note 104 at 53.
106. Nagendra Kumar Singh, *Divine Prostitution* 14 (A.P.H. Publishing Corporation, New Delhi, 1997).
107. Sinha, S. N., N. K. Basu, *The History of Marriage & Prostitution* 30 (Khama Publishars, Delhi, 1992).
108. Dr. K.L. Khurana, *Ancient India* 26 (Laxmi Narayan Publication, Agra, 5th edn., 2001).
109. P.C. Sahoo, "THE ARTHA A STRA ON PROSTITUTION" 70 71 *Bulletin of the Deccan College Post-Graduate and Research Institute* 359-361 (2010).
110. *Supra* note 109 at 341.
111. *Supra* note 109 at 350.
112. Rozario, Rita, *Trafficking in Women and Children in India*, 7 (Uppal Publication House, New Delhi,1988).
113. *Supra* note 64 at 359-361.
114. *Supra* note 66
115. *Supra* note 66
116. *Supra* note 109 at 359-361.
117. G. Kuppuram, "CHANAKYA ON PROSTITUTION (Based on Arthasastra)" 40, *Proceedings of the Indian History Congress* 215-219 (1979).
118. *Supra* note 66
119. Chandra, Moti, *The World of Courtesans* 43-68 (Vikas Publishing House Pvt. Ltd. Delhi, 1973).
120. R. Shamasastry (ed.,) *Kautilyas Arthasastra*. 153 (The Government Press, Bangalore, 1915).
121. *Supra* note 70 at 155.
122. Walter R.Gove, *The Labeling of Deviance Evaluating Perspective* 4 (Sage Publication Inc., New York, 1975).
123. Chandra, Moti, *The World of Courtesans* 105 (Vikas Publishing House Pvt. Ltd. Delhi, 1973).
124. Sinha, S. N., N. K. Bose, *History of Prostitution in Ancient India* 238 (Shree Balaram Prakasani, Kolkata, 2003).
125. *Supra* note 122 at 243.
126. Sinha, S. N., N. K. Bose, *History of Prostitution in Ancient India* 238 (Shree Balaram Prakasani, Kolkata, 2003).
127. Ghosh, S. K., *The world of Prostitution* 674 (A. P. H. Pub., New Delhi, 1996).

128. Shadab Bano, "WOMEN PERFORMERS AND PROSTITUTES IN MEDIEVAL INDIA" *Proceedings of the Indian History Congress* 251-265 (2009-2010).
129. Chandra, Satish, *History of Medieval India* 12 (Orient Black Swan, New Delhi, 2007).
130. *Supra* note 129.
131. *Supra* note 77 at 251-265
132. Chandra, Satish, *History of Medieval India* 191 (Orient Black Swan, New Delhi, 2007).
133. Singh, Nagendra Kumar, *Divine Prostitution* 35 (A. P. H. Publishing Corporation, New Delhi, 1997).
134. *Supra* note 133.
135. Thomas, P., *Indian Women Through the Ages* 237 (Asia Publishing House, Bombay, 1964).
136. *Supra* note 135.
137. *Supra* note 81 at 35.
138. *Supra* note 81 at 36.
139. *Supra* note 81.
140. *Supra* note 77 at 251-252.
141. *Supra* note 77 at 251-265
142. Chandra, Moti, *The World of Courtesans* 194 (Vikas Publishing House Pvt. Ltd. Delhi, 1973).
143. *Supra* note 142 at 194-199.
144. Kambale, Uttam, *Devadasi ani Nagnapuja* (Marathi) 16 (Lokvangmaya Gruh Pvt. Ltd. Bombay, 1988).
145. *Supra* note 61 at 29.
146. Frazer, James George, *The Golden Bough: A Study in Magic and Religion* 385 (The Macmillan Company, New York, 1951).
147. *Supra* note 146.
148. Dubois Abbe, *Hindu Manners, Customs and Ceremonies* 585 (Oxford University Press, London, 1924).
149. *Supra* note 148 at 31.
150. Chakraborthy Kakolee, *Women as Devadasis: Origin and Growth of The Devadasi Profession* 30 (Deep and Deep Publication Pvt. Ltd., New Delhi, 2000).
151. Sinha, S. N., N. K. Basu, *History of Prostitution in India* 4 (Cosmo Publications, Delhi, 1994).
152. Chandra, Moti, *The World of Courtesans* 24 (Vikas Publishing House Pvt. Ltd. Delhi, 1973).
153. Mazumadar, B. P., *Socio-Economic History of Northern India* 372 (Firma K.L. Mukhophadhaya, Calcutta, 1960).
154. Trivadi, Harshad, *Scheduled Caste Women: Studies in Exploitation* 76-81 (Concept Publishing Company, New Delhi, 1977).

155. Mohammed Qasim Ferishta (ed.), *Tarikh-i Ferishta* 114 (Nawal Kishore, Lucknow, 1323).
156. *Supra* note 96 at 68.
157. *Supra* note 70 at 251-265.
158. Supra note 70 at 251-265.
159. Captain William (ed.), Abdul Qadir Badauni *Muntakhabu-t- Tawarikh* 249 (Nesolias and Munshi Ahmad Ali, Calcutta, 1865).
160. I.H. Siddiqui (tr.), *Waqiat-i-Mushtaqi* 67 (New Delhi, 1993).
161. H.A.R. Gibb (tr.), The travels of Ibn Batuta, *Rihla* 686 (Cambridge, 1956-71, Vol. III).
162. Mohammed Qasim Ferishta (ed.), *Tarikh-i Ferishta* 114 (Nawal Kishore, Lucknow, 1323)
163. *Supra* note 103 at 114.
164. Zia Barani (ed.), *Tarikh-i- Firozshahi* 51 (Sk. Abdur Rashid, Aligarh, 1957).
165. K.M. Ashraf, *Life and Conditions of the People of Hindustan 1200-1500 AD* 265 (Gyan Publishing House, Delhi, 2001).
166. S.C. Misra and M.L. Rahman (ed.), Sikandar Ibn Mohammad, *Mirat-i-Sikandari*, 247 (Baroda, 1961).
167. Badauni, 384, Vol. 1, 28 Niccolao Manucci, Storia do Mogol 189 tr. W. Irvine, (London, 1906-8, Vol. I).
168. Mukherji, Santosh Kumar, *Prostitution in India* 80 (Inter – India Publications, Delhi, 1986).
169. Elliot, H. M., *History of India as told by its own Historians: The Mohammedan Period* 111-112 (Trubner and Company, London, 1872).
170. Shashi Prabha Jain, Mamta Singh, *Violence Against Women* 162 (Radha Publications, Delhi, 2001).
171. Sewell, Robert, *A Forgotten Empire* 267 (London, 1924).
172. Dargah Quli Khan, *Muraqqa-i-Dehli* 32, ed. Nurul Hasan Ansari (Delhi, 1982).
173. *Supra* note 172.
174. Chitnis, K. N., *Socio – Economic History of Medieval India* 96 (Atlantic Pub., 2005).
175. Chakraborty, Dipanshu, *Atrocities on Indian Women* 19 (A. P. H. Publishing Corporation, New Delhi, 1999).
176. *Supra* note 175 at 27-35. 177
178. Blochmann, H. (Tr.), Abul Fazal, *Ain E Akbari* 43-44 (Oriental Books Reprints, New Delhi, 1977).
179. Darga Quli Khan, *Muraqqa-i-Dehli* 35-36, ed. Nurul Hasan Ansari, (Delhi, 1982).
180. Sinha, S. N., N. K. Basu, *History of Prostitution in India* 18 (Cosmo Publications, Delhi,1994).
181. Darga Quli Khan, Muraqqa-i-Dehli 36, Nurul Hasan Ansari (ed.) (Delhi, 1982).
182. *Supra* note 119 at 55-56.

183. *Supra* note 119 at 56-57.
184. Sundra, Raj M., *Prostitution in Madras: A Study in Historical Perspective* 13 (Konark Publisher Pvt. Ltd., Delhi, 1993).
185. Kincaid, Dennis, *British social life in India (1608 – 1937)* 26 (Routledge and Kegan Paul, India, 1938).
186. *Supra* note 185.
187. Carey, W. H., *Good Old Days of Honorable John Company* 456 (R. Combay and Co. Calcutta, 1906).
188. *Supra* note 123 at 68.
189. Sundra, Raj M., *Prostitution in Madras: A Study in Historical Perspective* 42 178. (Konark Publisher Pvt. Ltd., Delhi, 1993).
190. Poudel, Meena, *Traffic in Women: Violation of Women's Dignity and Fundamental Human Rights* 137 (Asian Conference on Traffic in Women, December 11 – 13, Seoul, Korea, 2018).
191. CATW, "Coalition Against Trafficking in Women", (2002), *available at:* http: www.catwintemational.org
192. Orhant, M. 2001. "Trafficking in Persons: Myths, Methods and Human Rights", 2001, *available at:* http://www.prb.org.
193. Samarasinghe, Vidyamali and Barbara Burton, *"Strategizing prevention: A critical review of local initiatives to prevent female sex trafficking"* 17 Development in Practice 51-64 (2007)
194. Robinson, Laurie Nicole, "The globalisation of female child prostitution: A call for reintegration and recovery measures" 5 *Indiana Journal of Global Legal Studies* 239-261 (1997).
195. Tulsing Sonwani & K. Davis, "Prostitution in Indian Society: Issues, Trends and Rehabilitation" 5 (2013). *Available at:* https://www.ugc.ac.in.
196. *Supra* note 195.
197. Arun Kumar Acharya, "Impact of Cultural and Religious Practices of Prostitution on the Trafficking of Women in India" 14 *Trayectorias* 95-114 (2011).
98. Tulsing Sonwani & K. Davis, "Prostitution in Indian Society: Issues, Trends and Rehabilitation" 5, (2013), *Available at*: https://www.ugc.ac.in.
199. *Supra* note 134 at 6.
200. *Supra* note 134 at 7.
201. Robinson, Laurie Nicole, "The globalisation of female child prostitution: A call for reintegration and recovery measures" 5 *Indiana Journal of Global Legal Studies* 239-261(1997).
202. Coalition Against Trafficking in Women - Asia Pacific, "Every woman has a right: Not to be prostituted", 31 *Off our Backs* 7-9 (2001).
203. *Supra* note 202.
204. *Supra* note 139 at 9.
205. *Supra* note 202.
206. *Supra* note 141 at 8.

207. Joffres, Christine., Mills, Edward., Joffres, Michel., Khanna, Tinku., Walia, Harleen., & Grund David., "Sexual Slavery without borders: trafficking for commercial sexual exploitation in India" 7-22 *International Journal for Equity in Health* 7-22 (2008).
208. *Supra* note 136 at 20.
209. *Supra* note 136 at 21.
210. *Supra* note 128 at 9.
211. *Supra* note 128 at 9-10.
212. *Supra* note 202.
213. Tulsing Sonwani & K. Davis, "Prostitution in Indian Society: Issues, Trends and Rehabilitation" 5-6 (2013) *Available at*: https://www.ugc.ac.in.
214. *Supra* note 213.
215. *Supra* note 213.
216. *Supra* note 213.
217. Poonam Pradhan Saxena, "Immoral Traffic in Women and Girls: Need for 178. Tougher Laws and Sincere Implementation" 44 *Journal of the Indian Law Institute* 504-533 (2002).
218. http://www.gaurdian.co.uk/Archive/Article.
219. *Supra* note 218.
220. Internet Crime Forum, Internet Relay Chat Sub. Group, Chat wise, Street Wise: Children and Internet Chat Services, March 2001.
221. Kaur, Karamjit, *More Internet Date Rapes* 44 (Straits Times, Singapore, 2001).
222. Arun Kumar Acharya, "Impact of Cultural and Religious Practices of Prostitution on the Trafficking of Women in India" 14 *Trayectorias* 94-114 (2011).
223. Usha Rana, Diwakar Sharma and Debarati Ghosh, "Prostitution in northern Central India: an ethnographical study of Bedia community" 7 *International Journal of Anthropology and Ethnology 2-* 3(2020).
224. *Supra* note 222 at 95-98.
225. Supra note 153 at 95-114.
226. Gathia, Joseph, *Child prostitution in India.* 35 (Concept Publishers, New Delhi, 1999).
227. *Supra* note 156 at 36.
228. Anuja Agrawal, "Situating the Law on Prostitution Sex Work in India" 2 *Indian Sociological Society* 3-20 (2018).
229. Russell & Hiralal, "Caste and Tribes of India", ASI 19, (1861).
230. Anuja Agrawal, *Chaste wives and prostitute sisters: Patriarchy and prostitution among the Bedias of India*, India 251 (Taylor and Francis Group, Routledge, 2008).
231. Usha Rana, Diwakar Sharma and Debarati Ghosh, "Prostitution in northern Central India: an ethnographical study of Bedia community", *International Journal of Anthropology and Ethnology 2-3(2020).*
232. *Supra* note 161.

233. Dipankar Gupta, *Caste in Question: Identity or Hierarchy? 225-228* (Sage Publications Ltd, New Delhi, 2004).
234. *Supra* note 160 at 251-255.
235. Anuja Agarwal, "Kinship and Trafficking the Case of the Bedia Community" 22 *Canadian Women Studies*131 (2003).
236. Agrawal, Anuja, *Migrant women and work* 12 (Sage Publication, New Delhi, 2012).
237. Ramsanehi, "Untitled article on Bedias- Bedia jati jangal se gaon mein baskar jarayam pesha se vaishyavriti ki ore tatha uske kuch niyam" 45 (Morena: Abhyudaya Ashram, New Delhi,1998).
238. The Times of India. (2017). The Bedia girls won't dance no more. https://timesofindia.indiatimes.com/.
239. Trafficking in Persons Report: India. (2018). https://www.state.gov/reports/2018.
240. Usha Rana, Diwakar Sharma and Debarati Ghosh, "Prostitution in northern Central India: an ethnographical study of Bedia community" 2 *International Journal of Anthropology and Ethnology 2-3 (2020).*
241. *Supra* note 160 at 260-265.
242. Arun Kumar Acharya, "Impact of Cultural and Religious Practices of Prostitution on the Trafficking of Women in India" 14 *Trayectorias* 102-105 (2011).
243. *Supra* note 172 at 104 178.
244. Moti, Chandra, *Studies in the cult of Mother Goddess in Ancient India 39-40* (Vikas Publications, Delhi, 2017).
245. *Supra* note 244.
246. Chakraborthy, Kakolee, *Women as Devadasis: origin and growth of the Devadasi profession* 170 (Deep and Deep Publications, Delhi, 2011).
247. *Supra* note 174 at 107.
248. Field Survey on "Bedia Community" of Agra District.
249. *Supra* note 247.
250. Usha Rana, Diwakar Sharma and Debarati Ghosh, "Prostitution in northern Central India: an ethnographical study of Bedia community" 3 *International Journal of Anthropology and Ethnology 6 (2020).*
251. Divyendu Jha and Tanya Sharma, "Caste and Prostitution in India: Politics of Shame and of Exclusion" 4 *Anthropology 2-4 (*2016).
252. Sahni, R, Shankar, VK, Apte, H, *Prostitution and Beyond: An analysis of sex work in India* 15 (Sage Publications India Pvt. Ltd, India, 2008).
253. Divyendu Jha and Tanya Sharma, "Caste and Prostitution in India: Politics of Shame and of Exclusion" 2 *Anthropology 4* (2016).
254. *Supra* note 160 at 251-255.

Chapter - 3

Inter State Trafficking in India

This chapter discusses about various dimensions of inter-state trafficking in India which has been the focus of debate across national, regional and international levels. Often trafficking understood as the "movement of persons" by the use of force, threat and violence etc. for certain exploitative purposes. In other words, trafficking in persons especially women and children for commercial sexual exploitation must be seen within the larger perspective of national and international trends. Since, trafficking in persons includes not only "trafficking in women and children" alone but takes into account the other forms of movement of persons such as "migration and smuggling" within and across borders. According to Salt & Stein, "migration is the movement of persons from one country to another by legal or illegal means".[1] Moreover, "it can be voluntary (with consent)" or involuntary (without consent) or forced migration comprising the displacement of persons due to natural disasters. For instance, people might migrate to seek economic opportunities to support their dependants, or to escape domestic violence. Besides migration, "smuggling in persons consists of the transport of persons, with their consent, to another country through illegal means".[2] Furthermore, "trafficking in persons resembles the smuggling of migrants which is the subject of a separate protocol but there are several important differences"[3] and these are namely:

Firstly, the "smuggling of migrants undertaken in dangerous and degrading conditions of migrants who have consented to the smuggling while trafficking victims have either never consented or if they did then their consent has been rendered meaningless by the coercive deceptive or abusive actions of the traffickers".[4]

Secondly, "smuggling ends with the arrival of the migrants at their destination, whereas trafficking involves the ongoing exploitation of the victims in some manner to generate illicit profits for the traffickers".[5]

Thirdly, victims of trafficking also tend to be more severely affected and greater need of protection against revictimisation and other forms further abuse than are smuggled migrants.

Lastly, smuggling is always transnational unlike trafficking and the victims of trafficking can be either taken to another country or simply moved from one place to another within the same country.[6]

In this way, "trafficking is exploitation in one form or the other without the consent of the victims. It includes forced and bonded labour within the sex trade, forced marriage and other slavery like practices".[7] In this way, trafficking is the "part of demand and supply chain which characterised by modes of movement across labour market". "Like any other commodity sold in the market, the trade in human trafficking has its own supply and demand sides. The supply side is composed of trafficked persons. These include men, women and children with the latter two making up the bulk. On the demand side come abusive employers and sexual exploiters (sexual buyers)".[8] Trafficking is affected by globalisation; however, the specific pattern of globalisation is accompanied by many side effects, uncertainties, and complexities in the field of illegal smuggling and trafficking of weapons, drugs, and humans across borders.

According to Jahangir, "The current era of human history is heavily influenced, and is perhaps even defined, by globalisation. This 'Triple I phenomenon i.e. internationalisation, interdependence, and interaction can be described in the simplest terms as the increasing volume and variety of cross-border flows of people, goods, services, capitals, and technologies across the globe".[9] However, there is also a "dark side" to this phenomenon.

Since the "positive effects of globalisation are coupled with negative ones and the growing volume and variety of worldwide cross-border exchanges of illegal migrants, explosive ideas, deadly weapons, and lethal diseases".[10] In other words, it can be argue that "trafficking and smuggling in migrants are the parts of "transnational organised crime". Evidence shows that, the opening of markets and borders due to globalisation has facilitated the movement and transport of people across countries which mean a larger number of immigrants. It has brought about a rapid growth of the informal sectors which led to a large number of illegal immigrants and as a result 90 percent of human trafficking incidents occurred in poor and underdeveloped states such as Bihar, Orissa and Jharkhand etc. However, data have been taken from 29 states and 7 union territories as the status prior to August 5, 2019.

For the sake of clarity and precision, I shall divide the present chapter into three parts. In Part I, I will analyse pattern of interstate trafficking flows from rural to urban centres, less developed to more developed states and the metropolitan cities like Delhi and Mumbai is the favourite destination place. It can be argue that despite of having various stringent laws and pervasive policies, interstate trafficking for sexual exploitation is on the rising trend. So, the inter-state trafficking can be efficiently address if the coordination among various agencies and the officials have to be made more sensitive towards the issues of human rights violations especially of those related to women and children. In part II, I will examine the pattern of transnational trafficking among neighbouring countries particularly Bangladesh and Nepal. Further it tries to discuss about the "supply and demand nexus of trafficking" and emphasizing on safe migration while separating between trafficking and illegal migration. In order to combat transnational trafficking, many countries have laws to prevent it since colonial times. Still many counties felt that, these provisions are inadequate to address transnational trafficking.

In part III, I will discuss about the pattern of cases concerning trafficking under "Immoral Trafficking Act and Indian Panel Code". It tries to seek that, India is considered as one of the major South Asian country where cases concerning trafficking have increasing at alarming level. Nearly 90 percent of India's trafficking cases are within the country and those who belong to disadvantaged socio-economic "states are being the most vulnerable to trafficking". In order to understand about sources, destination and transit for trafficking in India, it is very important to analyse the cases registered, arrested person and disposal of cases by police and court etc.

Coming to the basic issues which I am discussing in the above three parts, I would like to point out that, human trafficking can occur at local levels, within a state and trans-nationally and consider to be the fastest and growing activities of criminal organisation after arms and drugs. Moreover, it has been found that, "trafficking is the third largest criminal" and most lucrative "industry in the world". It may be called "the modern equivalent of slavery, threatening the dignity and security of millions of people throughout the world. Nearly, every country in the world and every state of India affected by this crime as a place of origin, transit or destination".[11] As Kapsetin argues, "When people consider slavery, they more than likely assume that it was abolished during the 19th century. Unfortunately, this is far from the truth. The truth is that slavery and the global slave trade continues to flourish up until this day. In fact, it is more likely that people are being trafficked across borders now than any point in the past. Contemporary slavery involves women and children being forced into servitude through violence and deprivation".[12] It is to be noted that "trafficking for commercial sexual exploitation of women in India" is becoming more and more rampant.

According to Jose & Sunitha, "United Nations has reported that up to 700,000 children were trafficked in Asia each year and about 100,000 of them were from India. As per another report, there are approximately 2.3 million women in prostitution in which a quarter of them are underage. There are over 1,000 red light districts all over India, where most working prostitutes are underage girls".[13] Further, "many studies in India have pointed that, India has emerged as an international supplier of trafficked women and children to South East Asia, the Gulf States and as well serves as the destination nation for girls and women trafficked for CSE from Nepal and Bangladesh. The trafficking for CSE is a highly profitable and low risk business that preys on vulnerable populations".[14] Besides, there is a substantial quantity of domestic trafficking from one state to another and within states has proved to be highly lucrative. Digal has rightly pointed out in his article entitled "India, World Hub in Human Trafficking", "It is terrible and shameless that a fair skinned, eight-year-old child can fetch US $2,500 a night. Underage, female prostitution in India is a billion-dollar industry".[15] With this brief remark regarding human trafficking; I shall come to the Part I of the chapter.

3.1. Pattern of Inter State Trafficking in India

Approximately 90% of trafficking is inside in India and those are the most disadvantaged social economic states are vulnerable to sex trafficking and forced or bonded labour. According to, "UN Office of Drugs and Crime (UNODC)", "South Asia, with India at its center is the fastest growing region for human trafficking. Millions of persons are trafficked domestically and internationally in India every year".[16] It has found that, "India is a source; destination and transit nation for both labour and sex trafficking. In India, 90 percent of trafficking occurs domestically (intra-state or inter- state), and 10 percent occurs across national border".[17] It can be argue that "sex tourism" is rampant across India particularly the "pink triangle" which includes the "Agra-Delhi-Jaipur Belt, as well as south and south-west India; Goa, Maharashtra (Mumbai), Karnataka, Kerala, Tamil Nadu and in Orissa. Moreover, Himachal Pradesh and Rajasthan are also Indian states where sex tourism is emerging. In India, sex tourism can be facilitated by travel agencies; hotels associated business and tour operators".[18] Recent studies have thrown light on the "root cause of trafficking, focusing both on the demand and supply sides of the situation. The key factors influencing the supply side of human trafficking are poverty, globalisation, social practices, natural disasters and governance".

On the other hand, factors like demand for labour in sectors like commercial sex work (CSW), brick factories etc. determine the demand side of trafficking".[19] "Given demand and supply interdependence, addressing both types of facts has been central to curbing trafficking in India".[20] Since the impact of trafficking on social, health and economic are the major causes of concern. More importantly social practices become the major hurdle for a survivor who faces difficulty while dealing with the "social stigma when rehabilitated back after trafficking. They are unable to integrate back into their communities".[21] While in economic impact, the survivor or trafficked victims debarred from the mainstream source of livelihood so they need external support to sustain themselves". "Moreover, there are significant health impacts of trafficking mentally and physically on the survivors. Trauma and depression after rehabilitation and prone to AIDs has been observed among the survivors or victims".[22]

As Santhosh Digal pointed out in "India: World Hub in Human Trafficking", "human trafficking in India is intra-country and it is centered in the poorest states of India such as Orissa, Jharkhand, Madhya Pradesh and Chhattisgarh".[23] Moreover out of total estimated victims of commercial sexual exploitations, "majority of the victims are trafficked first and then used as a commodity in sex trade. Eighty-five to ninety percent of Indias human trafficking is intra-national".[24] This means the nationality of the more than 90 percent victims is Indian and supplied in domestic market of the sex trade as and when there is a demand. "Most of the demand-supply chain in the sex trade went unnoticed because of the very nature of the trade is the clandestine".[25] However, the available data may not give the exact facts and figures but it can be used as to understand the enormity of the grievous crime of "trafficking for commercial sexual exploitation". Though the majority of the data on trafficking for commercial sexual exploitations are integrated both women and child, yet the interviews of the rescued victims reveal that the number of child in the brothel and other form of sexual exploitation is on the rise and there are a considerable number of children who are made victim in this illegal trade. It has been found that, a data shows that the highest demand in brothel is for children for sexual exploitation. Almost 62 percent of the victims confirmed that their sexual exploitations commenced even before they attain the age of 18 years. The youngest age for the sexual exploitations in the brothel found to be of 6 years".[26] According to Sen & Nair, "Andhra Pradesh, Bihar, Karnataka, Madhya Pradesh, Rajasthan, West Bengal, Uttar Pradesh and Maharashtra as the main states from where women and minor girls are being trafficked and they are the main source states for traffickers".[27] Furthermore, "the predominant destination for commercial sexual exploitation of these women and minor girls for which they have been trafficked are Maharashtra (Mumbai), West Bengal (Kolkata) and Delhi".[28] It has been found that, "trafficking in which women and children have been trafficked" comes from "Andhra Pradesh (25.9 per cent), Karnataka (15 per cent), West Bengal (12.5 per cent) and Tamil Nadu (12.3 per cent). In most states, intra-state trafficking is a common phenomenon".[29]

According to Nair, out of the total respondents or survivors, "79.5 percent were Hindus, 15.7 per cent were Muslims, 3.7 per cent were Christians and 1.1 per cent belonged to other communities. Just over a quarter of them, 25.1 per cent were from Scheduled Castes, 4.5 per cent from Scheduled Tribes, 22.1 per cent belonged to the other Backward Classes and 20.5 per cent to other communities. The rest were not able to specify the caste they belonged to. Thus, almost 52 per cent of the respondents came from socially deprived sections of society".[30] Thus, they are mostly socially from deprived sections of the society and most of them are also illiterate. "The other factors that contribute in making women more vulnerable to trafficking are low income of the family, ill-treatment or domestic violence in the in-laws house, sexual assault in in-laws house".[31] While discrimination against women and traditional "patriarchal thinking of male chauvinism are two major contributing factors in making girl child more vulnerable to trafficking".[32] Moreover, in the disturbed families surrounded with the problems of alcohol, drug, physical and sexual violence etc., "women and children easily fall prey in the lure of better life by traffickers through promising a good job in the city or becoming a faithful life partner".[33] Except Goa and Delhi, the major form of trafficking in every states enumerated above have been of intra-state trafficking. Within states the flow is from rural areas to urban centre. And in context of the inter-state trafficking, the source states are those that are less developed and poor whereas, the destinations are those that are comparatively developed and rich. The favourite destinations according to the study of Sen and Nair 2005, includes Delhi, Maharashtra (Mumbai), Uttar Pradesh and West Bengal. However, the source states include "Andhra

Pradesh, Bihar, Karnataka, Maharashtra, Rajasthan, Tamil Nadu, Uttar Pradesh and West Bengal"[34].

The following are the social aspects of inter-state trafficking such as tradition, male chauvinism, or patriarchy, migration and poverty and unemployment. First and foremost, in some communities, trafficking for prostitution has been practiced as a tradition, for example in Bedias, Bacchdra, Sansi, Kanjar and Nats or the Devadasi and Jogin tradition, which are still prevalent in some part of India and have the tacit support of family and society. Men of the community not even accept it but also resist any change in the mode of earning and living of the community[35]. Furthermore, women have been the victim of patriarchy, women in the said communities felt and treated better than that of the larger society outside. To earn a better living, they have moved on to Mumbai for work in beer bar as bar dance girls. However, the ban on the bar brings them back to same old place and profession. Secondly, the subordinate status of women prevented them to have access to education and economic security at par with men. The protracted dismal position of women in society seems to be a causal factor for lack of awareness among them. This further makes them to easily get trapped in the nexus for trafficking. Women are trafficked from Bengal, Assam, North Eastern States to Rajasthan, Haryana, Punjab, Delhi, and Mumbai through honey trapping, and false promise for marriages. Most of the times, they are forced into prostitution. Thirdly, migration from poor villages to developed urban areas for employment has been increasing manifold. The conditions in the urban areas are however, is not as per their expectation. The poverty of immigrants in the urban areas makes compel them to choose prostitution as meant to earn their living. It has been found that that due to inter-state trafficking high migration to Mumbai, Chandigarh, Gurugram. Delhi from Assam, West Bengal, Bihar and Jharkhand can be taken as example. Last and most important causes of inter-state trafficking of women are due to search of employment and that s why they are easy target for traffickers. They lure them for better employment and handsome salary. However, they are cheated most often and in turn they are ended up into prostitution.

Table 3.1: Human Trafficking Cases Reported under IPC in 2016-2018

S.No.	States/UTs	Cases Reported, 2016	% Share	Cases Reported, 2018	% Share
1.	Andhra Pradesh	239	2.94	240	9.7
2.	Arunachal Pradesh	2	0.02	3	0.1
3.	Assam	91	1.12	262	10.6
4.	Bihar	43	0.53	127	5.2
5.	Chhattisgarh	68	0.84	51	2.1
6.	Goa	40	0.49	55	2.2
7.	Gujarat	548	4.90	13	0.5
8.	Haryana	51	0.63	34	1.4
9.	Himachal Pradesh	8	0.10	6	0.2
10.	Jammu & Kashmir	0	0.00	1	0.0
11.	Jharkhand	109	1.34	373	15.1
12.	Karnataka	404	4.97	27	1.1
13.	Kerala	21	0.26	105	4.3
14.	Madhya Pradesh	51	0.63	63	2.6
15.	Maharashtra	517	6.36	311	12.6
16.	Manipur	3	0.04	3	0.1
17.	Meghalaya	7	0.09	24	1.0
18.	Mizoram	2	0.02	2	0.1
19.	Nagaland	0	0.00	0	0.0
20.	Odisha	84	1.03	75	3.0
21.	Punjab	13	0.16	17	0.7
22.	Rajasthan	1422	17.49	86	3.5
23.	Sikkim	1	0.01	1	0.0
24.	Tamil Nadu	434	5.34	8	0.3
25.	Telangana	229	2.83	242	9.8
26.	Tripura	0	0.00	2	0.1
27.	Uttar Pradesh	79	0.97	35	1.4
28.	Uttarakhand	12	0.15	29	1.2
29.	West Bengal	3579	44.01	172	7.0
30.	A & N Island	1	0.00	0	0.0
31.	Chandigarh	1	0.00	0	0.0
32.	D &N Haveli	0	0.00	0	0.0
33.	Daman & Diu	7	0.1	0	0.0
34.	Delhi	66	0.8	98	4.0
35.	Lakshadweep	0	0.0	0	0.0
36.	Punducherry	0	0.0	0	0.0
	Total States & UTs	**8132**	**100.0**	**2465**	**100.0**

Source: Crime in India, NCERB, Ministry of Home Affairs, 2016-2018.

The Table 3.1 shows that total human trafficking cases under IPC reported in 2016 was 8132 and in 2018 reduced to 2465, that is a reduction of 70 percent cases registered. The highest number of cases registered in 2016 was from West Bengal that is approximately 44 percent of all India cases reported. West Bengal was followed by Rajasthan with 1422 cases (17%) and Gujarat with 548 cases.

However, in 2018, highest number of cases reported from Jharkhand with 373 cases (15%) followed by Maharashtra which was 311 cases (12%) and Assam with 262 cases (10%).

Among in UTs in 2016, Delhi was reported 66 cases, Daman & Diu 7 cases and Andaman & Nicobar Island and Chandigarh, 1 case each. In 2018, 98 cases reported from UTs and all of them from Delhi only.

Table 3.2: Below 18 Years Victims Trafficked, 2016 & 2018

S.N.	States	Male (2016)	Female (2016)	Total (2016)	Male (2018)	Female (2018)	Total (2018)
1.	Andhra Pradesh	0	44	44	1	15	16
2.	Arunachal Pradesh	0	2	2	3	0	3
3.	Assam	34	96	130	23	164	187
4.	Bihar	183	13	196	529	10	539
5.	Chhattisgarh	60	78	138	45	56	101
6.	Goa	0	2	2	3	6	9
7.	Gujarat	137	348	485	0	1	1
8.	Haryana	5	8	13	3	23	26
9.	Himachal Pradesh	2	2	4	0	3	33
10.	Jammu & Kashmir	0	0	0	1	0	1
11.	Jharkhand	18	72	90	17	314	331
12.	Karnataka	113	219	332	3	5	8
13.	Kerala	18	65	83	40	105	145
14.	Madhya Pradesh	62	35	97	29	44	73
15.	Maharashtra	78	94	172	27	46	73
16.	Manipur	2	7	9	0	2	2
17.	Meghalaya	0	1	1	0	22	22
18.	Mizoram	0	2	2	2	0	2
19.	Nagaland	0	0	0	0	0	0
20.	Odisha	98	108	206	41	90	131
21.	Punjab	47	1	48	14	6	20

22.	Rajasthan	1823	696	2519	246	27	373
23.	Sikkim	0	1	1	0	2	2
24.	Tamil Nadu	122	195	317	5	3	8
25.	Telangana	0	7	7	4	4	8
26.	Tripura	2	4	6	0	1	1
27.	Uttar Pradesh	748	74	822	2	39	41
28.	Uttrakhand	1	2	3	6	12	18
29.	West Bengal	426	2687	3113	11	148	159
	Total States	**3979**	**4863**	**8842**	**1155**	**1148**	**2303**

Source: Crime in India, NCERB, Ministry of Home Affairs, 2016-2018.

In Table 3.2 shows that in 2016, highest number of victims below 18 years trafficked from West Bengal (3113) followed by Rajasthan (2519) and Uttar Pradesh (822). In 2018, highest number of victims from Bihar (539) followed by Rajasthan (373) and West Bengal (159). In 2016, highest number of males trafficked from Rajasthan (1823) followed by Uttar Pradesh (748) and West Bengal (426). Further in 2018, highest number of male victims trafficked from Bihar (529) followed by Rajasthan (346).

The highest number of female victims trafficked in 2016 from West Bengal (2687) followed by Rajasthan (696) and Gujarat (348). While in 2018, highest number of female victims trafficked from Assam (164) followed by West Bengal (148). However, it has been noticed that, there has been no victims trafficked below 18 years from Nagaland in 2016, 2018 and from Jammu and Kashmir in 2016.

Table 3.3: Above 18 Years Victims Trafficked, 2016 & 2018

S.N.	States	Male (2016)	Female (2016)	Total (2016)	Male (2018)	Female (2018)	Total (2018)
1.	Andhra Pradesh	0	311	311	0	351	351
2.	Arunachal Pradesh	0	1	1	1	0	1
3.	Assam	52	67	119	21	106	127
4.	Bihar	8	32	40	12	80	92
5.	Chhattisgarh	77	54	131	100	74	174
6.	Goa	0	84	84	0	93	93
7.	Gujarat	31	112	143	0	25	25
8.	Haryana	47	89	136	2	6	8
9.	Himachal Pradesh	0	113	113	0	13	13

10.	Jammu &Kashmir	0	0	0	0	0	0
11.	Jharkhand	7	58	65	24	78	102
12.	Karnataka	113	567	680	15	178	193
13.	Kerala	39	111	150	0	38	38
14.	Madhya Pradesh	4	19	23	13	19	32
15.	Maharashtra	1	972	973	24	698	722
16.	Manipur	3	9	12	0	3	3
17.	Meghalaya	0	7	7	0	2	2
18.	Mizoram	0	0	0	0	1	1
19.	Nagaland	0	0	0	0	0	0
20.	Odisha	173	133	306	57	64	121
21.	Punjab	1	1	2	2	7	9
22.	Rajasthan	56	279	335	0	6	6
23.	Sikkim	0	0	0	0	2	2
24.	Tamil Nadu	263	869	1132	16	12	28
25.	Telangana	22	361	383	118	373	491
26.	Tripura	3	1	4	1	0	1
27.	Uttar Pradesh	8	28	36	0	49	49
28.	Uttarakhand	2	18	20	0	40	40
29.	West Bengal	169	882	1051	7	96	103
	Total States	**1079**	**5178**	**6257**	**413**	**2414**	**2827**

Source: Crime in India, NCERB, Ministry of Home Affairs, 2016-2018.

Table 3.3 shows that in 2016, total victims of above 18 years trafficked was 6257 among them 1079 was male and 5178 (83%) was female. But in 2018, total victims above 18 years trafficked was reduced to 2827 (55%). Among them 413 (15%) was male and 2414 (85%) was female. In 2016, highest number of victims trafficked from Tamil Nadu was 1132 followed by West Bengal (1051) and Maharashtra (973). While in 2018, highest number of victims trafficked from Maharashtra (722) followed by Telangana (491) and Andhra Pradesh (351).

In 2016, the highest number of above 18 years male victims trafficked from Tamil Nadu (263) followed by Orissa (173) and West Bengal (196). Though in 2018, highest numbers of above 18 years victims are from Telangana (118) followed by Chhattisgarh (100) and Odisha (57). In 2016, highest number of female victims above 18 years was from Maharashtra (972) followed by West Bengal (882) and Tamil Nadu (869). While in 2018, highest number of female victims above 18 years trafficked from Maharashtra (698) followed by Telangana (373) and Andhra Pradesh (351). However, in 2016, there were no victims above 18 years was trafficked from Jammu & Kashmir, Mizoram, Nagaland and Sikkim. In 2018, from Jammu & Kashmir and Nagaland, not a single case reported.

Table 3.4: Total Victims Trafficked, 2016 & 2018

S.N.	States	Male (2016)	Female (2016)	Total (2016)	Male (2018)	Female (2018)	Total (2018)
1.	Andhra Pradesh	0	355	355	1	366	367
2.	Arunachal Pradesh	0	3	3	4	0	4
3.	Assam	86	163	249	44	270	314
4.	Bihar	191	45	239	541	90	631
5.	Chhattisgarh	137	132	269	145	130	275
6.	Goa	0	86	86	3	99	102
7.	Gujarat	168	460	628	0	26	26
8.	Haryana	52	97	149	5	29	34
9.	Himachal Pradesh	2	115	117	0	16	16
10.	Jammu & Kashmir	0	0	0	1	0	1
11.	Jharkhand	25	130	155	41	392	433
12.	Karnataka	226	786	1012	18	183	201
13.	Kerala	57	176	233	40	143	183
14.	Madhya Pradesh	66	54	120	42	63	105
15.	Maharashtra	79	1066	1145	51	744	795
16.	Manipur	5	16	21	0	5	5
17.	Meghalaya	0	8	8	0	24	24
18.	Mizoram	0	2	2	2	1	3
19.	Nagaland	0	0	0	0	0	0
20.	Odisha	271	241	512	98	154	252
21.	Punjab	48	2	50	16	13	29
22.	Rajasthan	1879	975	2854	346	33	379
23.	Sikkim	0	1	1	0	4	4
24.	Tamil Nadu	385	1064	1449	21	15	36
25.	Telangana	22	368	390	122	377	499
26.	Tripura	5	5	10	1	1	2
27.	Uttar Pradesh	756	102	858	2	88	90
28.	Uttrakhand	3	20	23	6	52	58
29.	West Bengal	595	3569	4164	18	244	262
	Total	**5058**	**10041**	**15099**	**1568**	**3562**	**5130**

Source: Crime in India, NCRB, Ministry of Home Affairs.

Table 3.4 depicts that the total number of victims trafficked in 2106 was 15099, among them 10041 was female (67%) and 5058 (33%) was male. While in 2018, total victims trafficked was 5130 which was reduced by 66%. Among them 3562 (69%) was female and 1568 (31%) was male. The highest number of male trafficked in 2016 was from Rajasthan (1879) followed by Uttar Pradesh (756) and West Bengal (595). While in 2018, highest number of male victims trafficked from Bihar (541) followed by Telangana (346) and Chhattisgarh (145).

In 2016, highest number of female trafficked was from West Bengal (3569) followed by Maharashtra (1066) and Tamil Nadu (1064). In 2018, highest female victims trafficked from Madhya Pradesh (744) followed by Jharkhand (392) and Telangana (377). However, highest total male and female in 2016 trafficked from West Bengal (4164) followed by Rajasthan (2854) and Tamil Nadu (1449). While in 2018 highest from Maharashtra (795) followed by Bihar (631) and Telangana (499). It has been found that, no victims trafficked in 2016 from Jammu & Kashmir and Nagaland, while in 2018 not a single case has been reported from Nagaland.

Table 3.5: Victims Trafficked Below 18 Years, 2016 & 2018 From UTs

S.N.	UTs	Male (2016)	Female (2016)	Total (2016)	Male (2018)	Female (2018)	Total (2018)
1.	A & N Island	0	0	0	0	0	0
2.	Chandigarh	0	1	1	0	0	0
3.	D &N Haveli	0	0	0	0	0	0
4.	Daman & Diu	0	1	1	0	0	0
5.	Delhi	144	46	190	432	99	531
6.	Lakshadweep	0	0	0	0	0	0
7.	Puducherry	0	0	0	0	0	0
	Total	**144**	**48**	**192**	**432**	**99**	**531**
	Total India	**3979**	**4863**	**8842**	**1587**	**1247**	**2834**

Source: Crime in India, 2016-2018, NCRB, Ministry of Home Affairs.

Table 3.5 exhibits regarding victims trafficked below 18 years in UTs in 2016 and 2018 shows that in 2016, highest number of victims trafficked was 192 among them 144 was male and 48 was female, while in 2018, total victims trafficked was 531 among them 432 was male and 99 was female. However, in 2016, out of 192 victims, 190 are from Delhi and 1 each from Chandigarh and Daman & Diu. But in 2018, all the 531 victims trafficked are from Delhi only.

Total number of victims trafficked within India including states and UTs in 2016 was 8842 among them 3979 was male and 4863 was female. While in 2018, total victims trafficked was 2834 among them 1587 was male and 1247 was female.

Table 3.6: Victims Trafficked Above 18 Years, 2016 & 2018 From UTs

S.N.	UTs	Male (2016)	Female (2016)	Total (2016)	Male (2018)	Female (2018)	Total (2018)
1.	A & N Island	0	5	5	0	0	0
2.	Chandigarh	0	0	0	0	0	0
3.	D &N Haveli	0	0	0	0	0	0
4.	Daman & Diu	0	9	9	0	0	0
5.	Delhi	27	47	74	69	58	127
6.	Lakshadweep	0	0	0	0	0	0
7.	Puducherry	0	0	0	0	0	0
	Total	**27**	**61**	**88**	**69**	**58**	**127**
	Total India	**1106**	**5239**	**6345**	**482**	**2472**	**2954**

Source: Crime in India, 2016-2018, NCRB, Ministry of Home Affairs.

Table 3.6 shows that in 2016, total number of victims trafficked above 18 years from UTs was 88 out of which 27 were male and 61 were female. While 2018, total victims trafficked from UTs was 127 out of which 69 were male and 58 were female. However, in 2016, only cases reported from Delhi and Andaman & Nicobar Island was 5 and 74 respectively but in 2108, no victims were trafficked from other UTs except Delhi which was 127.

Table 3.7: Total Victims Trafficked From UTs, 2016 & 2018

S.N.	UTs	Male (2016)	Female (2016)	Total (2016)	Male (2018)	Female (2018)	Total (2018)
1.	A & N Island	0	5	5	0	0	0
2.	Chandigarh	0	1	1	0	0	0
3.	D &N Haveli	0	0	0	0	0	0
4.	Daman & Diu	0	10	10	0	0	0

5.	Delhi	171	93	264	501	157	658
6.	Lakshadweep	0	0	0	0	0	0
7.	Puducherry	0	0	0	0	0	0
	Total	**171**	**109**	**280**	**501**	**157**	**658**
	Total India	**5229**	**10150**	**15379**	**2069**	**3719**	**5788**

Source: Crime in India, 2016-2018, NCRB, Ministry of Home Affairs.

Table 3.7 shows that, total victims trafficked from UTs in 2106 was 280, out of them 171 was male victims and 109 was female victims. While in 2018, total number of victims increases to 658 out of which 501 was male victims and 157 was female victims. However, in 2016, victims reported from Andaman & Nicobar Island (5), Chandigarh (1), Daman & Diu (10) and Delhi (264) but in 2018, all 658 victims are trafficked from Delhi only.

Table 3.8: Victims Rescued Below 18 Years From States, 2016 & 2018

S.N.	States	Male (2016)	Female (2016)	Total (2016)	Male (2018)	Female (2018)	Total (2018)
1.	Andhra Pradesh	0	44	44	1	15	16
2.	Arunachal Pradesh	0	0	0	3	0	3
3.	Assam	9	28	37	3	0	3
4.	Bihar	183	13	196	527	10	537
5.	Chhattisgarh	60	76	136	45	56	101
6.	Goa	0	2	2	2	7	9
7.	Gujarat	132	303	435	0	1	1
8.	Haryana	5	8	13	2	22	24
9.	Himachal Pradesh	2	2	4	0	0	0
10.	Jammu & Kashmir	0	0	0	1	0	1
11.	Jharkhand	4	27	31	13	90	103
12.	Karnataka	113	219	332	3	5	8
13.	Kerala	147	192	339	28	84	112
14.	Madhya Pradesh	975	1678	2653	31	41	72
15.	Maharashtra	78	94	172	25	49	74
16.	Manipur	2	7	9	0	2	2
17.	Meghalaya	0	1	1	0	5	5
18.	Mizoram	0	2	2	2	0	2
19.	Nagaland	0	0	0	0	0	0
20.	Odisha	96	96	192	41	90	131

21.	Punjab	33	1	34	12	3	15
22.	Rajasthan	5281	345	5626	346	27	373
23.	Sikkim	0	1	1	0	2	2
24.	Tamil Nadu	215	433	648	19	8	27
25.	Telangana	0	7	7	4	4	8
26.	Tripura	2	4	6	0	1	1
27.	Uttar Pradesh	772	80	852	2	39	41
28.	Uttarakhand	1	2	3	6	12	18
29.	West Bengal	397	1819	2216	23	131	154
	Total	**8507**	**5484**	**13991**	**1152**	**842**	**1994**

Source: Crime in India, 2016-2018, NCRB, Ministry of Home Affairs.

Table 3.8 shows that in 2016, victims rescued below 18 years was 13991 which was reduced to 1994 in 2018 which means reduction of 86% in recue victims. In 2016 male victims rescued was 8507 and female victims was 5484 whereas in 2018 male victims rescued are reduced to 1152 and female to 842. In 2016, highest male victims rescued from Rajasthan (5281) followed by Madhya Pradesh (975) and Uttar Pradesh (772). While in 2018, highest male victims rescued from Bihar (527) followed by Rajasthan (346) and Chhattisgarh (45).

However, in 2016, highest female victims rescued from West Bengal (1819) followed by Madhya Pradesh (1678) and Tamil Nadu (433). While in 2018, highest female victims rescued from Assam (138) followed by West Bengal (131), Jharkhand (90) and Odisha (90). In 2016, no victims rescued from Arunachal Pradesh, Jammu & Kashmir and Nagaland while in 2018 no victims rescucd from Himachal Pradesh and Nagaland.

Table 3.9: Victims Rescued Above 18 Years From States, 2016 & 2018

S.N.	States	Male (2016)	Female (2016)	Total (2016)	Male (2018)	Female (2018)	Total (2018)
1.	Andhra Pradesh	0	839	839	0	437	437
2.	Arunachal Pradesh	0	1	1	1	0	1
3.	Assam	20	35	55	13	99	112
4.	Bihar	8	32	40	12	73	85
5.	Chhattisgarh	75	54	129	100	74	174

6.	Goa	0	84	84	0	93	93
7.	Gujarat	31	111	142	0	25	25
8.	Haryana	23	72	95	1	5	6
9.	Himachal Pradesh	0	152	152	0	11	11
10.	Jammu & Kashmir	0	0	0	0	0	0
11.	Jharkhand	5	9	14	11	44	55
12.	Karnataka	113	567	680	15	178	193
13.	Kerala	96	179	275	1	45	46
14.	Madhya Pradesh	620	1544	2164	12	16	28
15.	Maharashtra	0	969	969	24	693	717
16.	Manipur	3	9	12	0	3	3
17.	Meghalaya	0	7	7	0	2	2
18.	Mizoram	0	0	0	0	1	1
19.	Nagaland	0	0	0	0	0	0
20.	Odisha	169	135	304	57	64	121
21.	Punjab	0	0	0	2	5	5
22.	Rajasthan	8	133	141	0	6	6
23.	Sikkim	0	0	0	0	2	2
24.	Tamil Nadu	375	1348	1723	16	22	38
25.	Telangana	0	348	348	118	381	499
26.	Tripura	3	1	4	1	0	1
27.	Uttar Pradesh	46	26	72	0	45	45
28.	Uttarakhand	1	18	19	0	40	40
29.	West Bengal	73	504	577	6	94	100
	Total	**1669**	**7177**	**8846**	**390**	**2458**	**2848**

Source: Crime in India, 2016-2018, NCRB, Ministry of Home Affairs.

Table 3.9 shows that total number of victims rescued from all the states above 18 years in 2016 was 8846 and it was reduced to 2848 which is the reduction of 68%. In 2016, total numbers of male and female above 18 years are rescued 1669 and 7177 respectively. It has been found that the highest number of victims rescued from Madhya Pradesh (620) followed by Tamil Nadu (375) and Odisha (169). While in 2018, highest number of victims rescued from Telangana (118) followed by Chhattisgarh (100) and Odisha (57).

In 2016, highest number of female victims above 18 years rescued from Madhya Pradesh (1544) followed by Tamil Nadu (1348) and Maharashtra (969). While in 2018, highest number of victims rescued from Maharashtra (693) followed by Andhra Pradesh (437) and Tamil Nadu (381). Though the total number of victims rescued from Tamil Nadu (1723) followed by Madhya Pradesh (2164) and Maharashtra (969). But in 2018, highest number of victims rescued from Maharashtra (717) followed by Telangana (499) and Andhra Pradesh (437). It has been noted that in 2016, no victims rescued from Jammu & Kashmir, Mizoram, Nagaland and Sikkim while in 2018 from Jammu & Kashmir and Nagaland only.

Table 3.10: Total Victims Rescued From States, 2016 & 2018

S.N.	States	Male (2016)	Female (2016)	Total (2016)	Male (2018)	Female (2018)	Total (2018)
1.	Andhra Pradesh	0	883	883	1	452	453
2.	Arunachal Pradesh	0	1	1	4	0	4
3.	Assam	29	63	92	29	237	266
4.	Bihar	191	45	236	539	83	622
5.	Chhattisgarh	135	130	265	145	130	275
6.	Goa	0	86	86	2	100	102
7.	Gujarat	163	414	577	0	26	26
8.	Haryana	28	80	108	3	27	30
9.	Himachal Pradesh	2	154	156	0	11	11
10.	Jammu & Kashmir	0	0	0	1	0	1
11.	Jharkhand	9	36	45	24	134	158
12.	Karnataka	226	786	1012	18	183	201
13.	Kerala	243	371	614	29	129	158
14.	Madhya Pradesh	1595	3222	4817	43	57	100
15.	Maharashtra	78	1063	1141	49	742	791
16.	Manipur	5	16	21	0	5	5
17.	Meghalaya	0	8	8	0	7	7
18.	Mizoram	0	2	2	2	1	3
19.	Nagaland	0	0	0	0	0	0
20.	Odisha	265	231	496	98	154	252
21.	Punjab	33	1	34	14	8	22
22.	Rajasthan	5289	478	5767	346	33	379
23.	Sikkim	0	1	1	0	4	4
24.	Tamil Nadu	590	1781	2371	35	30	65
25.	Telangana	0	355	355	122	385	507

26.	Tripura	5	5	10	1	1	2
27.	Uttar Pradesh	818	106	924	2	84	86
28.	Uttarakhand	2	20	22	6	52	58
29.	West Bengal	470	2323	2793	29	225	254
	Total	**10176**	**12661**	**22837**	**1542**	**3300**	**4842**

Source: Crime in India, 2016-2018, NCRB, Ministry of Home Affairs.

Table 3.10 shows that total victims rescued in 2016 was 22837 and it reduces to 4842 (i.e. reduction of 79%) in 2018. However, in 2016, total male victims rescued were 10176 while female victims rescued were 12661. But in 2018, total male victims rescued were 1542 and female victims rescued were 3300. In 2016, highest male victims rescued from Rajasthan (5289) followed by Madhya Pradesh (1595) and Uttar Pradesh (818) whereas in 2018 highest male victims rescued from Bihar (539) followed by Rajasthan (346) and Chhattisgarh (145).

In 2016, highest female victims rescued from Madhya Pradesh (3222) followed by West Bengal (2323) and Tamil Nadu (1781). But in 2018, highest female victims rescued from Maharashtra (742) followed by Andhra Pradesh (452) and Telangana (385). It is to be noted the total highest victims rescued in 2016 from Rajasthan (5767) followed by Madhya Pradesh (4817) and West Bengal (2793) whereas in 2018, total highest victims rescued from Maharashtra (791) followed by Bihar (622) and Telangana (507). Moreover, there have been no victims rescued from Jammu & Kashmir and Nagaland in 2016 and 2018 not a single victim rescued from Nagaland.

Table 3.11: Victims Rescued Below 18 Years from UTs, 2016 & 2018

S.N.	UTs	Male (2016)	Female (2016)	Total (2016)	Male (2018)	Female (2018)	Total (2018)
1.	A & N Island	0	0	0	0	0	0
2.	Chandigarh	0	1	1	0	0	0
3.	D &N Haveli	0	0	0	0	0	0
4.	Daman & Diu	0	1	1	0	0	0
5.	Delhi	144	46	190	304	60	364
6.	Lakshadweep	0	0	0	0	0	0
7.	Punducherry	0	0	0	0	0	0
	Total	**144**	**48**	**192**	**304**	**60**	**364**
	Total India	**8651**	**5532**	**14183**	**1456**	**902**	**2358**

Source: Crime in India, 2016-2018, NCRB, Ministry of Home Affairs.

Table 3.11 shows that the total number of victims rescued below 18 years from UTs in 2016 was 192 whereas in 2018, it was increased to 364 (i.e. 47% increases). In 2016, total male was 144 and female was 48. On the other hand, in 2018 total male was 304 and female was 60. Moreover, the data shows that, highest number of victims rescued below 18 years in 2018 and 2018 was from Delhi i.e. 190 and 364 respectively. In 2016, it has been noticed that, no victims below 18 years rescued from Andaman & Nicobar Island, Dadar & Nagar Haveli, Lakshadweep and Puducherry while in 2018, no victim were rescued from any UTs except Delhi.

Table 3.12: Victims Rescued Above 18 Years from UTs, 2016 & 2018

S.N.	UTs	Male (2016)	Female (2016)	Total (2016)	Male (2018)	Female (2018)	Total (2018)
1.	A & N Island	0	5	5	0	0	0
2.	Chandigarh	0	0	0	0	0	0
3.	D&N Haveli	0	0	0	0	0	0
4.	Daman & Diu	0	9	9	0	0	0
5.	Delhi	27	47	74	23	35	58
6.	Lakshadweep	0	0	0	0	0	0
7.	Puducherry	0	0	0	0	0	0
	Total	**27**	**61**	**88**	**23**	**35**	**58**
	Total India	**1696**	**7238**	**8934**	**413**	**2493**	**2906**

Source: Crime in India, 2016-2018, NCRB, Ministry of Home Affairs

Table 3.12 exhibiting that in 2016, total number of victims was rescued above 18 years from UTs were 88 and out of which 27 was male and 61 females. However, in 2018, total number of victims rescued was 58 (reduce by 34%) and out which 23 was male and 35 was female. In 2016, it has been noticed that there were 5 female victims rescued from Andaman Nicobar Island, 9 females from Daman & Diu and 74 victims rescued from Delhi among them 27 was male and 47 was female victims, while rest of the UTs have not rescued any victims. In 2018, only 58 victims were rescued from Delhi and out of them 23 was male and 35 was female, however rest of the UTs have not rescued any victims.

Table 3.13: Total Victims Rescued From UTs, 2016 & 2018

S.N.	UTs	Male (2016)	Female (2016)	Total (2016)	Male (2018)	Female (2018)	Total (2018)
1.	A & N Island	0	5	5	0	0	0
2.	Chandigarh	0	1	1	0	0	0
3.	D &N Haveli	0	0	0	0	0	0
4.	Daman & Diu	0	10	10	0	0	0
5.	Delhi	171	93	264	327	95	422
6.	Lakshadweep	0	0	0	0	0	0
7.	Puducherry	0	0	0	0	0	0
	Total	**171**	**109**	**280**	**327**	**95**	**422**
	Total India	**10347**	**12770**	**23117**	**1869**	**3395**	**5264**

Source: Crime in India, 2016-2018, NCRB, Ministry of Home Affairs.

Table 3.13 showing that, total number of victims rescued from UTs in 2016 was 280, out of them 171 was male and 109 was female. While in 2018, total victims rescued from UTs was 422 and out of them 327 was male and 95 was female. However, data shows that there have been no victims rescued from Puducherry and Lakshadweep in 2016. But in 2018, all the victims were rescued from Delhi only.

Table 3.14: Purpose of Human Trafficking From States, 2016 & 2018

S.N.	States	Sexual Exploitation for Prostitution (2016)	Total Persons (2016)	Sexual Exploitation for Prostitution (2018)	Total persons (2018)
1.	Andhra Pradesh	736	883	353	453
2.	Arunachal Pradesh	0	1	0	4
3.	Assam	51	92	52	266
4.	Bihar	43	236	73	622
5.	Chhattisgarh	35	265	12	275
6.	Goa	86	86	88	102
7.	Gujarat	117	577	5	26
8.	Haryana	27	108	1	30
9.	Himachal Pradesh	141	156	5	11
10.	Jammu & Kashmir	0	0	0	1
11.	Jharkhand	2	45	18	158
12.	Karnataka	429	1012	24	201
13.	Kerala	20	614	7	158
14.	Madhya Pradesh	585	4817	5	100
15.	Maharashtra	1020	1141	726	791
16.	Manipur	3	21	1	5

17.	Meghalaya	8	8	0	7
18.	Mizoram	2	2	1	3
19.	Nagaland	0	0	0	0
20.	Odisha	11	496	0	252
21.	Punjab	0	34	5	22
22.	Rajasthan	30	5767	3	379
23.	Sikkim	1	1	3	4
24.	Tamil Nadu	1087	2371	11	65
25.	Telangana	314	355	335	507
26.	Tripura	0	10	0	2
27.	Uttar Pradesh	25	924	46	86
28.	Uttarakhand	13	22	40	58
29.	West Bengal	155	2793	68	254
	Total	**4980**	**22837**	**1882**	**4842**

Source: Crime in India, 2016-2018, NCRB, Ministry of Home Affairs.

Table 3.14 showing that, the total person trafficked in 2016 was 22837 and out of them 4980 victims trafficked for sexual exploitation for prostitution (i.e. 22%). While in 2018, total person trafficked was reduced to 4842 (79%) out of which 1882 victims trafficked for sexual exploitation for prostitution (39%). It has been found that in 2016, highest number of victims trafficked for sexual exploitation for prostitution was from Tamil Nadu (1087) followed by Maharashtra (1020) and Madhya Pradesh (582). On the other hand, in 2018, the highest number of victims trafficked for prostitution was from Maharashtra (729) followed by Andhra Pradesh (353) and Telangana (335).

Table 3.15: Purpose of Human Trafficking From UTs, 2016 & 2018

S.N.	UTs	Sexual Exploitation for Prostitution (2016)	Total persons (2016)	Sexual Exploitation for Prostitution (2018)	Total persons (2018)
1.	A & N Island	5	5	0	0
2.	Chandigarh	0	1	0	0
3.	D &N Haveli	0	0	0	0
4.	Daman & Diu	10	10	0	0
5.	Delhi	24	264	40	422
6.	Lakshadweep	0	0	0	0
7.	Puducherry	0	0	0	0
	Total UTs	**39**	**280**	**40**	**422**
	Total India	**4980**	**23117**	**1922**	**5264**

Source: Crime in India, 2016-2018, NCRB, Ministry of Home Affairs.

Table 3.15 exhibiting that the purpose of trafficking for sexual exploitation for prostitution form UTs in 2016 was 39 (14%) out of 280 victims of trafficking. While in 2018, out of 422 victims trafficked, only 40 (10%) was trafficked from prostitution. In 2016, total victims from states and UTs trafficked for the purpose of prostitution was 22%, while in 2018, victims trafficked for prostitution was 37%. It has been noticed that there has been not a single victim was trafficked for prostitution form Dadar & Nagar Haveli, Lakshadweep and Puducherry in 2016 and 2018.

3.2. Pattern of Transnational Trafficking

Human trafficking is borderless and organised offenses which involve multiple numbers of violators and abusers. In other words, "human trafficking is one of the most debated areas of transnational criminal law and the number of countries criminalising trafficking in persons".[36] "Trafficking in persons for labour" as well as "sexual exploitation" considered as the "modern-day slavery" and a "human rights violation that constitutes a crime against the individual and the State". "It is a deplorable human rights violation" that occurs worldwide and empirically it has been the international and transnational agenda since a century. Transborder "trafficking of human particularly women and children" across neighbouring countries is a matter of concern since it violates fundamental rights to live with dignity. According to a 2008 report on human trafficking, "trafficking from neighbouring countries such as Nepal and Bangladesh accounts for about 10 percent of India's trafficking into brothels, while 89 percent of the crime takes place internally".[37] "An alarming trend is reported in South-Central Asia: girls trafficked into the sex trade are increasingly younger. The average age of girls trafficked into India from Nepal has decreased from 14–16 years to 10–14 years, with girls as young as 8–9 years being sold at auctions in Mumbai and other Indian cities. It is estimated by police that more than 15,000 children and women are taken out of Bangladesh every year; NGOs estimate that between 160,000 and 250,000 Nepalese girls and women are forced to work in India's brothels. Young girls from Pakistan and Sri Lanka are also trafficked into Indian brothels".[38]

The pattern of transnational trafficking has been a major problem in India and its neighbouring countries. According to Nair, "Transborder trafficking of women and children from Bangladesh to India is an issue which has drawn the attention of all concerned. Trafficking is an offence under the laws of both Bangladesh and India".

"Therefore, trafficking carry out their operation in the most clandestine manner so as to avoid direction, especially by the Bangladesh Rifles (BDR) and civil police meaning in the Bangladesh borders as well BSF and other police agencies in India manning the Indian border. These agencies have, no doubt, played an effective role in preventing trafficking. However, trafficking continues to take place despite their efforts and trafficked victims are pushed into exploitative situation in which they usually remain unnoticed and unheard".[39] According to Alex, "Within South-Central Asia, India and Pakistan serve as the major destination points for children and women trafficked from Bangladesh and Nepal, the major countries of origin in South-Central Asia. India and Pakistan also serve as transit countries for trafficking to the Middle East. Exploitation occurs in the sex industry as well as other labour markets".[40] "In Sri Lanka, children are trafficked for the purpose of commercial sex and domestic work, and also as child soldiers. Between the beginning of 2002 and the end of 2007, UNICEF reported the 6,248 cases of child recruitment by the Liberation Tigers of Tamil Eelam (LTTE)".[41]

Globally, it has been identified as the "third largest source of profit for organised crime, followed by arms and drug trafficking which has been generating billions of dollars annually".[42] According to Saxena, "The movement of young girls and women from Bangladesh and Nepal into Indian brothels is very common and there is further movement of these women to the Middle East as well as other destinations for flesh trade is not rare at times of hardship, this starts out as illegal migration and ends up as trafficking".[43] Moreover, such "migration occurs in the backdrop of supply and demand in the sending and receiving countries". "The supply side is associated with structural inequality, poverty, illiteracy and lack of opportunities for livelihood, whereas the demand rises from the need of cheap labour in the destination".

"Often women from the poorer countries like Bangladesh and Nepal are at risk of exploitation and are trafficked to the neighbouring country like India".[44]

Many of SAARC countries have trafficking laws to prevent trafficking since colonial times; however, they felt that such laws unable to address trafficking properly and incorporating new laws for transnational trafficking by passing of legislations are the need of an hour. For instance, "Article 23 of the Constitution of India", Article 20 of the Constitution of Nepal and Article 18 and 34 of the Constitution of Bangladesh contained provisions prohibiting trafficking in forced labour. Furthermore, the "law of crimes of India namely, the Indian Penal Code, (IPC) 1860 have several provisions for trafficking and forced prostitution." "Imprisonment up to ten years and fine is provided for kidnapping or abduction of a woman with intent to marry her by force or to force her into illicit intercourse or to compel her directly or indirectly to go from a place for this purpose".[45] More importantly, "When the girl happens to be a minor, even inducing her by any means to go from any place for this purpose is punishable. Importing into India a girl below 21 years with intent or knowledge for this purpose will incur the same penalty".[46]

It has been found that due to open border between Bangladesh and India, many times the trafficking victims hardly recognised by the "border security forces". For instance, Bengali girls from India send to Bangladesh and vice versa and then selling them to brothels where they find themselves helpless and event they are force to work against their will. However, "it is important to consider that trafficking of women has been rarely referred to as an issue of individual security both in academic research and policy intervention" and such form of immoral trafficking of women need to be addressed by individual nation and legislative measure has to be taken collectively to preserve women's dignity effectively. It has been argue that, the wide prevalence of trafficking across SAARC region, many of these laws are not satisfactory to address trafficking. Instead a "complete code dealing with different forms of trafficking, law is scattered across different legislations" among neighbouring countries.

Table 3.16: Indian Citizen's Victim of Human Trafficking Rescued From States/UTs, 2016 & 2018

S.N.	States/UTs	Male (2016)	Female (2016)	Total (2016)	Male (2018)	Female (2018)	Total (2018)
1.	Andhra Pradesh	0	882	882	1	452	453
2.	Arunachal Pradesh	0	1	1	4	0	4
3.	Assam	29	63	92	29	237	266
4.	Bihar	191	44	235	466	80	546
5.	Chhattisgarh	135	130	265	145	124	269
6.	Goa	0	85	85	2	86	88
7.	Gujarat	163	403	566	0	16	16
8.	Haryana	28	78	106	3	27	30
9.	Himachal Pradesh	2	154	156	0	11	11
10.	Jammu & Kashmir	0	0	0	1	0	1
11.	Jharkhand	9	36	45	24	134	158
12.	Karnataka	217	780	997	18	145	163
13.	Kerala	202	355	557	29	129	158
14.	Madhya Pradesh	1595	3222	4817	43	57	100
15.	Maharashtra	78	1040	1118	48	680	728
16.	Manipur	5	16	21	0	4	4
17.	Meghalaya	0	8	8	0	7	7
18.	Mizoram	0	2	2	0	1	1
19.	Nagaland	0	0	0	0	0	0
20.	Odisha	265	231	496	98	154	252
21.	Punjab	33	1	34	14	8	22
22.	Rajasthan	5276	483	5759	346	33	379
23.	Sikkim	0	1	1	0	4	4
24.	Tamil Nadu	585	1773	2358	35	30	65
25.	Telangana	0	355	355	122	380	502
26.	Tripura	0	0	0	0	1	1
27.	Uttar Pradesh	815	105	920	2	84	86
28.	Uttarakhand	2	20	22	6	50	56
29.	West Bengal	468	2295	2763	29	225	254
30.	A & N Island	0	5	5	0	0	0
31.	Chandigarh	0	1	1	0	0	0
32.	D &N Haveli	0	0	0	0	0	0
33.	Daman & Diu	0	8	8	0	0	0
34.	Delhi	171	86	257	325	63	388
35.	Lakshadweep	0	0	0	0	0	0
36.	Puducherry	0	0	0	0	0	0
	Total	**10269**	**12663**	**22932**	**1790**	**3222**	**5012**

Source: Crime in India, 2016-2018, NCRB, Ministry of Home Affairs.

Table 3.16 shows that total Indian victims rescued under human trafficking in 2016 was 22932 while in 2018, it was reduced to 5012. Out of them in 2016, 10269 was male and 12663 was female while in 2018, it was 1790 male and 3222 was female. However highest number of victims rescued in 2016 was from Rajasthan (5759) followed by Madhya Pradesh (4817) and West Bengal (2763). While in 2018, highest victims rescued from Bihar (546) followed by Telangana (502) and Andhra Pradesh (453). Besides states, among UTs the highest number of victims has been rescued in 2016 as well as 2018 from Delhi i.e. 257 and 388 respectively.

Table 3.17: Sri Lankan Citizen's Victim of Human Trafficking Rescued From States/UTs, 2016 & 2018

S.N.	States/UTs	Male (2016)	Female (2016)	Total (2016)	Male (2018)	Female (2018)	Total (2018)
1.	Andhra Pradesh	0	0	0	0	0	0
2.	Arunachal Pradesh	0	0	0	0	0	0
3.	Assam	0	0	0	0	0	0
4.	Bihar	0	0	0	0	0	0
5.	Chhattisgarh	0	0	0	0	0	0
6.	Goa	0	0	0	0	0	0
7.	Gujarat	0	0	0	0	0	0
8.	Haryana	0	0	0	0	0	0
9.	Himachal Pradesh	0	0	0	0	0	0
10.	Jammu & Kashmir	0	0	0	0	0	0
11.	Jharkhand	0	0	0	0	0	0
12.	Karnataka	0	0	0	0	0	0
13.	Kerala	38	0	38	0	0	0"
14.	Madhya Pradesh	0	0	0	0	0	0
15.	Maharashtra	0	0	0	0	0	0
16.	Manipur	0	0	0	0	0	0
17.	Meghalaya	0	0	0	0	0	0
18.	Mizoram	0	0	0	0	0	0
19.	Nagaland	0	0	0	0	0	0
20.	Odisha	0	0	0	0	0	0
21.	Punjab	0	0	0	0	0	0
22.	Rajasthan	0	0	0	0	0	0
23.	Sikkim	0	0	0	0	0	0

24.	Tamil Nadu	0	0	0	0	0	0
25.	Telangana	0	0	0	0	0	0
26.	Tripura	0	0	0	0	0	0
27.	Uttar Pradesh	0	0	0	0	0	0
28.	Uttarakhand	0	0	0	0	0	0
29.	West Bengal	0	0	0	0	0	0
30.	A & N Island	0	0	0	0	0	0
31.	Chandigarh	0	0	0	0	0	0
32.	D &N Haveli	0	0	0	0	0	0
33.	Daman & Diu	0	0	0	0	0	0
34.	Delhi	0	0	0	0	0	0
35.	Lakshadweep	0	0	0	0	0	0
36.	Puducherry	0	0	0	0	0	0
	Total	**38**	**0**	**38**	**0**	**0**	**0”**

Source: Crime in India, 2016-2018, NCRB, Ministry of Home Affairs.

Table 3.17 shows that in 2016, highest and only state from where Sri Lankan nationals victims of human trafficking rescued was from Kerala and all the 38 victims are male. On the other hand, in 2018 no Sri Lankan nationals' victims of human trafficking were rescued. However, there has been no Sri Lankan victim rescued under human trafficking from UTs both in 2016 and 2018.

Table 3.18: Nepal's Citizen's Victim of Human Trafficking Rescued From States/UTs, 2016 & 2018

S.N.	States/UTs	Male (2016)	Female (2016)	Total (2016)	Male (2018)	Female (2018)	Total (2018)
1.	Andhra Pradesh	0	0	0	0	0	0
2.	Arunachal Pradesh	0	0	0	0	0	0
3.	Assam	0	0	0	0	0	0
4.	Bihar	0	1	1	73	3	76
5.	Chhattisgarh	0	0	0	0	0	0
6.	Goa	0	1	1	0	3	3
7.	Gujarat	0	0	0	0	3	3
8.	Haryana	0	0	0	0	0	0
9.	Himachal Pradesh	0	0	0	0	0	0
10.	Jammu & Kashmir	0	0	0	0	0	0
11.	Jharkhand	0	0	0	0	0	0

12.	Karnataka	9	0	9	0	38	38
13.	Kerala	3	0	3	0	0	0
14.	Madhya Pradesh	0	0	0	0	0	0
15.	Maharashtra	0	4	4	1	11	12
16.	Manipur	0	0	0	0	0	0
17.	Meghalaya	0	0	0	0	0	0
18.	Mizoram	0	0	0	0	0	0
19.	Nagaland	0	0	0	0	0	0
20.	Odisha	0	0	0	0	0	0
21.	Punjab	0	0	0	0	0	0
22.	Rajasthan	7	0	7	0	0	0
23.	Sikkim	0	0	0	0	0	0
24.	Tamil Nadu	0	0	0	0	0	0
25.	Telangana	0	0	0	0	0	0
26.	Tripura	0	0	0	0	0	0
27.	Uttar Pradesh	3	1	4	0	0	0
28.	Uttarakhand	0	0	0	0	1	1
29.	West Bengal	0	4	4	0	0	0
30.	A & N Island	0	0	0	0	0	0
31.	Chandigarh	0	0	0	0	0	0
32.	D & N Haveli	0	0	0	0	0	0
33.	Daman & Diu	0	0	0	0	0	0
34.	Delhi	0	5	5	2	32	34
35.	Lakshadweep	0	0	0	0	0	0
36.	Puducherry	0	0	0	0	0	0
	Total	**22**	**16**	**38**	**76**	**91**	**167**

Source: Crime in India, 2016-2018, NCRB, Ministry of Home Affairs.

Table 3.18 highlights that, the total number of victims from Nepal rescued in 2016 was 38 among them 22 were male and 16 were female. But in 2018, total number of victims rescued was increased to 167 among them 76 was male and 91 was female. However, in 2016, the highest number of victims was rescued from Karnataka and all 9 victims were male. While in 2016, highest number of victims rescued from Bihar that was 76 out of them 73 was male and 3 was female followed by Karnataka that was 38 victims and all of them was female. Among UTs in 2016, 5 victims rescued and all are female from Delhi.

While in 2018, victims rescued from UTs increase to 34 among them 32 was female.

Table 3.19: Bangladesh Citizen's Victim of Human Trafficking Rescued From States/UTs, 2016 & 2018

S.N.	States/UTs	Male (2016)	Female (2016)	Total (2016)	Male (2018)	Female (2018)	Total (2018)
1.	Andhra Pradesh	0	1	1	0	0	0
2.	Arunachal Pradesh	0	0	0	0	0	0
3.	Assam	0	0	0	0	0	0
4.	Bihar	0	0	0	0	0	0
5.	Chhattisgarh	0	0	0	0	0	0
6.	Goa	0	0	0	0	2	2
7.	Gujarat	0	0	0	0	0	0
8.	Haryana	0	1	1	0	0	0
9.	Himachal Pradesh	0	0	0	0	0	0
10.	Jammu & Kashmir	0	0	0	0	0	0
11.	Jharkhand	0	0	0	0	0	0
12.	Karnataka	0	2	2	0	0	0
13.	Kerala	0	3	3	0	0	0
14.	Madhya Pradesh	0	0	0	0	0	0
15.	Maharashtra	0	18	18	0	18	18
16.	Manipur	0	0	0	0	0	0
17.	Meghalaya	0	0	0	0	0	0
18.	Mizoram	0	0	0	0	0	0
19.	Nagaland	0	0	0	0	0	0
20.	Odisha	0	0	0	0	0	0
21.	Punjab	0	0	0	0	0	0
22.	Rajasthan	7	0	0	0	0	0
23.	Sikkim	0	0	0	0	0	0
24.	Tamil Nadu	0	0	0	0	0	0
25.	Telangana	0	0	0	0	4	4
26.	Tripura	3	1	4	0	0	0
27.	Uttar Pradesh	0	0	0	0	0	0
28.	Uttrakhand	0	0	0	0	1	1
29.	West Bengal	0	5	5	0	0	0
30.	A & N Island	0	0	0	0	0	0
31.	Chandigarh	0	0	0	0	0	0

32.	D &N Haveli	0	0	0	0	0	0
33.	Daman & Diu	0	2	2	0	0	0
34.	Delhi	0	0	0	0	0	0
35.	Lakshadweep	0	0	0	0	0	0
36.	Puducherry	0	0	0	0	0	0
	Total	**3**	**33**	**36**	**0**	**25**	**25**

Source: Crime in India, 2016-2018, NCRB, Ministry of Home Affairs.

Table 3.19 shows that total victims from Bangladesh rescued from different states and UTs in 2016 was 36 and out of them 33 was female and only 3 was male. While in 2018, total number of victims rescued was 25 and all of them were female. However, in 2016, highest number of victims rescued from Maharashtra that was 18 and all of them were female only. Where as in 2018, highest from Maharashtra and all of them were female. From UTs, 2 females were rescued from Daman & Diu in 2016 but it has been found that not a single Bangladeshi's victim was rescued in 2018 from UTs.

Table 3.20: Victims of Other Nation's Rescued Under Human Trafficking From States/UTs, 2016 & 2018

S.N.	States/UTs	Male (2016)	Female (2016)	Total (2016)	Male (2018)	Female (2018)	Total (2018)
1.	Andhra Pradesh	0	0	0	0	0	0
2.	Arunachal Pradesh	0	0	0	0	0	0
3.	Assam	0	0	0	0	0	0
4.	Bihar	0	0	0	0	0	0
5.	Chhattisgarh	0	0	0	0	6	6
6.	Goa	0	0	0	0	9	9
7.	Gujarat	0	11	11	0	7	7
8.	Haryana	0	1	1	0	0	0
9.	Himachal Pradesh	0	0	0	0	0	0
10.	Jammu & Kashmir	0	0	0	0	0	0
11.	Jharkhand	0	0	0	0	0	0
12.	Karnataka	0	4	4	0	0	0
13.	Kerala	0	13	13	0	0	0
14.	Madhya Pradesh	0	0	0	0	0	0

15.	Maharashtra	0	1	1	0	33	33
16.	Manipur	0	0	0	0	1	1
17.	Meghalaya	0	0	0	0	0	0
18.	Mizoram	0	0	0	2	0	2
19.	Nagaland	0	0	0	0	0	0
20.	Odisha	0	0	0	0	0	0
21.	Punjab	0	0	0	0	0	0
22.	Rajasthan	1	0	1	0	0	0
23.	Sikkim	0	0	0	0	0	0
24.	Tamil Nadu	0	13	13	0	0	0
25.	Telangana	0	0	0	0	1	1
26.	Tripura	2	4	6	1	0	1
27.	Uttar Pradesh	0	0	0	0	0	0
28.	Uttarakhand	0	0	0	0	0	0
29.	West Bengal	2	19	21	0	0	0
30.	A & N Island	0	0	0	0	0	0
31.	Chandigarh	0	0	0	0	0	0
32.	D &N Haveli	0	0	0	0	0	0
33.	Daman & Diu	0	0	0	0	0	0
34.	Delhi	0	2	2	0	0	0
35.	Lakshadweep	0	0	0	0	0	0
36.	Puducherry	0	0	0	0	0	0
	Total	**5**	**68**	**73**	**3**	**57**	**60**

Source: Crime in India, 2016-2018, NCRB, Ministry of Home Affairs.

Table 3.20 exhibits that, total victims rescued from under human trafficking in 2016 from other nations, different states and UTs were 73, among them 68 were female and 5 were male. While in 2018, total victims were 60 and among them 57 was female and 3 was male. While in 2016, highest number of victims rescued from West Bengal was 21 and among them 19 was female and 2 was male. However, in 2018, highest number of victims rescued from Maharashtra and all 33 victims were female. But in 2016 from UTs, 2 female victims rescued from Delhi whereas in 2018, no victims rescued other nations rescued from any UTs.

Table 3.21: Total Profile of India and other National's Victims Rescued Under Human Trafficking from States/UTs, 2016 & 2018

S.N.	States/UTs	Male (2016)	Female (2016)	Total (2016)	Male (2018)	Female (2018)	Total (2018)
1.	Andhra Pradesh	0	883	883	1	452	453
2.	Arunachal Pradesh	0	1	1	4	0	4
3.	Assam	29	63	92	29	237	266
4.	Bihar	191	45	236	539	83	622
5.	Chhattisgarh	135	130	265	145	130	275
6.	Goa	0	86	86	2	100	102
7.	Gujarat	163	414	577	0	26	26
8.	Haryana	28	80	108	3	27	30
9.	Himachal Pradesh	2	154	156	0	11	11
10.	Jammu & Kashmir	0	0	0	1	0	1
11.	Jharkhand	9	36	45	24	134	158
12.	Karnataka	226	786	1012	18	183	201
13.	Kerala	243	371	614	29	129	158
14.	Madhya Pradesh	1595	3222	4817	43	57	100
15.	Maharashtra	78	1063	1141	49	742	791
16.	Manipur	5	16	21	0	5	5
17.	Meghalaya	0	8	8	0	7	7
18.	Mizoram	0	2	2	2	1	3
19.	Nagaland	0	0	0	0	0	0
20.	Odisha	265	231	496	98	154	252
21.	Punjab	33	1	34	14	8	22
22.	Rajasthan	5284	483	5767	346	33	379
23.	Sikkim	0	1	1	0	4	4
24.	Tamil Nadu	585	1786	2371	35	30	65
25.	Telangana	0	355	355	122	385	507
26.	Tripura	5	5	10	1	1	2
27.	Uttar Pradesh	818	106	924	2	84	86
28.	Uttarakhand	2	20	22	6	52	58
29.	West Bengal	470	2323	2793	29	225	254
30.	A & N Island	0	5	5	0	0	0
31.	Chandigarh	0	1	1	0	0	0

32.	D &N Haveli	0	0	0	0	0	0
33.	Daman & Diu	0	10	10	0	0	0
34.	Delhi	171	93	264	327	95	422
35.	Lakshadweep	0	0	0	0	0	0
36.	Puducherry	0	0	0	0	0	0
	Total	**10337**	**12780**	**23117**	**1869**	**3395**	**5264**

Source: Crime in India, 2016-2018, NCRB, Ministry of Home Affairs.

Table 3.21 shows that total profile of victims rescued under human trafficking in 2016 was 23117 while in 2018, it was 5264 and among them in 2016, 10337 was male and 12780 was female. At the same time, in 2018, 1869 was male and 3395 was female. In 2016, highest number of victims rescued from Rajasthan (5767) followed by Madhya Pradesh (4817) and West Bengal (2793) while in 2018, highest number of victims rescued from Maharashtra (791) followed by Bihar (622) and Telangana (507). However, in 2016, highest male victims rescued from Rajasthan (5284) and female victims from Madhya Pradesh (3222). On the other hand, in 2018, highest male victims rescued from Bihar (539) and female victims from Maharashtra (742). Furthermore, it is to be noted that among UTs highest victims rescued from Delhi both in 2016 and 2018 that is 264 and 422 respectively.

Table 3.22: Nation-wise Profile of Victims Rescued Under Human Trafficking, 2016 & 2018

S.N.	Countries	2016	2018
1.	India	22932	5012
	Male	10269	1790
	Female	12663	3222
2.	Sri Lanka	38	00
	Male	38	00
	Female	00	00
3.	Nepal	38	167
	Male	22	76
	Female	16	91
4.	Bangladesh	36	25
	Male	03	00
	Female	33	25

5.	Others	73	60
	Male	05	03
	Female	68	57
	Total	**23117**	**5264**

Source: Crime in India, 2016-2018, NCRB, Ministry of Home Affairs.

Table 3.22 shows that in 2016, total 22932 numbers of Indian victims were rescued and while in 2018 only 5012 Indian victims rescued that is 77% reduction in rescue cases. On the other hand, in 2016, female rescue victims are account for 55% while in 2018 female rescue victims account for 64%. It is to be noted that, Sri Lankan victims rescued and all of them were male while almost all Bangladeshi victims were female.

3.3. Pattern of Cases under Immoral Trafficking Act

Generally trafficking is considered as one of the severe crimes whereby human beings are trafficked beyond boundaries and jurisdictions. It is a human rights violation since women are being forced into servitude through violence and various forms of coercion. According to Reanda, "Trafficking in the form of prostitution is a slavery in which the alienation of the person is far more reaching than with slavery in its usual sense, where what is alienated is labor not intimacy".[47] He further says, "Once entered, prostitution result in a state of servitude which may be maintained through overt coercion and physical abuse but is more frequently the result of emotional blackmail, economic deprivation, marginalisation and the loss of identity".[48] It makes clear that "forced prostitution" is not easy for prostitute to leave rather it maintained by enforcing violence and misuse upon the victim. It can be argue that once a person coerced for prostitution is not deprived of his/her fundamental rights only but he/she is also degraded to slaves in society in 21st century.

According to Ministry of Women and Child Development, "India has estimated the number of persons specifically for the purpose of commercial sexual exploitation to be around 2.8 million, an increase of 22% from the past".[49] Furthermore, "majority of trafficked persons across India are young women or children who have been forced into the sex trade as a result of poverty, often before the age of 18".[50] It has found that the main reason behind "increasing demand for younger children and virgins in India, partly due by the fear of contracting the HIV/AIDS virus from girls and women who are not virgins. When the fear of contracting HIV/AIDS is leading to the sexual exploitation of young children and virgins in India, not only is this painfully absurd but also unjust.

"Young children should not have to sacrifice their human dignity and respect to feed the needs and desires of peoples who are utilising and exploiting their bodies".[51] In order to prevent such inhuman cases, we need to implement laws properly "at the same time law enforcement officers have to equip" with modern technology and training to deal with traffickers and to do justice with the victims.

To address cases concerning trafficking, "India utilises the instrument of "law which was embodied in the Suppression of Immoral Traffic in Women and Girls Act" 1956 (SITA). In other words, "SITA was enacted under Article 35 of the Indian Constitution with the object of inhibiting or abolishing trafficking in women and girls".[52] Further this act was amended several times and renamed as a "Immoral Trafficking Act, 1956" or "IT (P) Act, 1956". Moreover, this "act was passed in 1956 and was enforced in India in 1958. The passage of this act was the result of India being a signatory to the United Nations International Convention for the Suppression of Traffic in Persons passed in 1950".[53] Its purpose is to "abolish traffic in women and girls for prostitution" and therefore, "penalised brothel keeping, pimping, procuring, detention of a woman or girl for prostitution and seduction of a woman in custody".[54] According Gary, "in order to prevent and combating human trafficking, requires a holistic approach by all stakeholders and integrated actions on prosecution, prevention and protection".[55]

Even though trafficking is prohibited in the "Constitution of India" and more importantly IT (P) Act, prohibits the brothels, criminalisation of earnings through sex work, and gave power to the police to conduct raids, expulsion, rescue and rehabilitation, protective homes for sex workers and establishment of special courts for speedy justice.

Despite of these provisions, "India becomes a source, destination and transit country for human trafficking primarily for commercial sexual exploitation and forced labour, and with the falling sex ratio, trafficking for marriage is becoming another pull factor for trafficking of women and girls".[56] It can be argue that, India has unable to implement IT (P) Act in letter and spirit and to maintain the obligation of several anti-trafficking covenants and laws because women and children still have been trafficking for the sake of prostitution and forced labour. Now it practiced as a matter of routine which can be explore from data which I am going to discuss and analyse below.

Table 3.23: State-wise Breakup of Cases Registered Under IT(P) Act, 2016 & 2018

S.N.	States	2016	2018
1.	Andhra Pradesh	186	152
2.	Arunachal Pradesh	0	0
3.	Assam	65	37
4.	Bihar	50	49
5.	Chhattisgarh	17	15
6.	Goa	3	7
7.	Gujarat	76	34
8.	Haryana	59	43
9.	Himachal Pradesh	7	10
10.	Jammu & Kashmir	1	1
11.	Jharkhand	0	9
12.	Karnataka	323	179
13.	Kerala	113	4
14.	Madhya Pradesh	20	40
15.	Maharashtra	303	200
16.	Manipur	0	0
17.	Meghalaya	2	2
18.	Mizoram	3	0
19.	Nagaland	0	1
20.	Odisha	38	10
21.	Punjab	64	6
22.	Rajasthan	56	62
23.	Sikkim	0	0

24.	Tamil Nadu	432	386
25.	Telangana	240	81
26.	Tripura	0	2
27.	Uttar Pradesh	50	27
28.	Uttarakhand	11	0
29.	West Bengal	87	97
	Total	**2206**	**1454**

Source: Crime in India, 2016-2018, NCRB, Ministry of Home Affairs.

Table 3.23 shows that, total number of cases registered in 2016 was 2206 which reduces to 1454 cases in 2018 under IT(P) Act that is reduction of 35% from 2016 and 2018. It has found that Tamil Nadu was worst affected state in 2016 as well as 2018 with 432 and 386 cases registered respectively. In 2016, Tamil Nadu was followed by Karnataka (323), Maharashtra (303), Telangana (240) and Andhra Pradesh (186) while in 2018; Tamil Nadu was followed by Maharashtra (200), Karnataka (179), Andhra Pradesh (152) and West Bengal (97). It has been noticed that no case was reported both in 2016 and 2018 from Arunachal Pradesh, Manipur and Sikkim.

Table 3.24: UTs-wise Breakup of Cases Registered Under IT(P) Act, 2016 & 2018

S.N.	UTs	2016	2018
1.	A & N Island	0	0
2.	Chandigarh	0	0
3.	D & N Haveli	0	0
4.	Daman & Diu	4	0
5	Delhi	4	1
6.	Lakshadweep	0	0
7.	Puducherry	0	4
	Total UTs	**8**	**5**
	Total India	**2214**	**1459**

Source: Crime in India, 2016-2018, NCRB, Ministry of Home Affairs.

Table 3.24 shows that total number of cases registered in 2016 and 2018 under IT(P) Act in UTs reduced from 8 to 5 that is reduction of 38% from 2016 to 2018. In 2016, Daman & Diu and Delhi reported 4 cases each but in 2018, Delhi reported 1 case and Puducherry increase from 0 cases in 2016 to 4 cases in 2018. However, Andaman & Nicobar Island, Chandigarh, Dadar & Nagar Haveli, and Lakshadweep have not reported any case both in 2016 and 2018.

Table 3.25: Cities-wise Breakup of Cases Registered Under IT(P) Act, 2016 & 2018

S.N.	Cities	2016	2018
1.	Ahmadabad	11	14
2.	Bengaluru	152	80
3.	Chennai	205	236
4.	Coimbatore	41	51
5.	Delhi	4	1
6.	Ghaziabad	0	0
7.	Hyderabad	63	3
8.	Indore	8	7
9.	Jaipur	10	10
10.	Kanpur	1	0
11.	Kochi	14	0
12.	Kolkata	5	35
13.	Kozhikode	1	0
14.	Lucknow	3	4
15.	Mumbai	26	63
16.	Nagpur	125	18
17.	Patna	28	0
18.	Pune	34	14
19.	Surat	20	0
	Total Cities	**751**	**538**

Source: Crime in India, 2016-2018, NCRB, Ministry of Home Affairs.

Table 3.25 shows that cases registered in 2016 and 2018 under IT(P) Act in 19 important cities was 751 and 538 respectively i.e. reduction of 28% cases from 2016 to 2018. The worst affected cities both in 2016 and 2018 was Chennai with 205 and 236 cases respectively followed by Bengaluru with 152 and 80 cases respectively. While Ghaziabad reported no case both in 2016 and 2018 as well as Kanpur, Kochi, Kozhikode, Patna and Surat reported no cases in 2018.

Table 3.26: State-wise Human Trafficking Cases (IPC), 2016 & 2018

S.N.	States	2016	%	2018	%
1.	Andhra Pradesh	239	2.94	240	9.7
2.	Arunachal Pradesh	2	0.02	3	0.1
3.	Assam	91	1.12	262	10.6
4.	Bihar	43	0.53	127	5.2
5.	Chhattisgarh	68	0.84	51	2.1
6.	Goa	40	0.49	55	2.2
7.	Gujarat	548	4.90	13	0.5
8.	Haryana	51	0.63	34	1.4
9.	Himachal Pradesh	8	0.10	6	0.2
10.	Jammu & Kashmir	0	0.00	1	0.0
11.	Jharkhand	109	1.34	373	15.1
12.	Karnataka	404	4.97	27	1.1
13.	Kerala	21	0.26	105	4.3
14.	Madhya Pradesh	51	0.63	63	2.6
15.	Maharashtra	517	6.36	311	12.6
16.	Manipur	3	0.04	3	0.1
17.	Meghalaya	7	0.09	24	1.0
18.	Mizoram	2	0.02	2	0.1
19.	Nagaland	0	0.0	0	0.0
20.	Odisha	84	1.03	75	3.0
21.	Punjab	13	0.16	17	0.7
22.	Rajasthan	1422	17.4	86	3.5
23.	Sikkim	1	0.0	1	0.0
24.	Tamil Nadu	434	5.34	8	0.3
25.	Telangana	229	2.82	242	9.8
26.	Tripura	0	0.0	2	0.1
27.	Uttar Pradesh	79	0.97	35	0.4
28.	Uttarakhand	12	0.19	29	1.2
29.	West Bengal	3579	44.0	172	7.0
	Total	**8057**	**99.1**	**2367**	**96.0**

Source: Crime in India, 2016-2018, NCRB, Ministry of Home Affairs.

Table 3.26 shows that, human trafficking cases reduced by around 70% from 8075 cases in 2016 to 2367 cases in 2018. In 2016, worst affected state was West Bengal with 3579 cases account for 44% of cases reported in India followed by Rajasthan 1422 cases (17.49%),

Gujarat 548 (4.9%), Maharashtra 517 (6.36%), Tamil Nadu 434 (5.34%) respectively. In 2018, Jharkhand was the worst affected states with 373 cases account for 15.1% cases of India followed by Maharashtra 311 (12.6%), Assam 262 (10.6%), Telangana 242 (9.8%) and Andhra Pradesh 240 (9.7%) cases respectively.

Table 3.27: UTs-wise Human Trafficking Cases (IPC), 2016 & 2018

S.N.	UTs	2016	% Share	2018	% Share
1.	A & N Island	1	0.0	0	0.0
2.	Chandigarh	1	0.0	0	0.0
3.	D &N Haveli	0	0.0	0	0.0
4.	Daman & Diu	7	0.1	0	0.0
5.	Delhi	66	0.8	98	4.0
6.	Lakshadweep	0	0.0	0	0.0
7.	Puducherry	0	0.0	0	0.0
	Total UTs	**75**	**0.9**	**98**	**4.0**
	Total India	**8132**	**100.0**	**2465**	**100.0**

Source: Crime in India, 2016-2018, NCRB, Ministry of Home Affairs.

Table 3.27 shows that, human trafficking cases registered in UTs in 2016 was 75 cases but in 2018 cases increase to 98 that is almost 23% increase in human trafficking cases registered under Indian Panel Code. However, in 2016, out of 75 cases, Delhi alone reported 66 cases while in 2018, all 98 cases reported from Delhi only. In 2016, Daman & Diu reported 7 cases and Andaman & Nicobar Island and Chandigarh reported 1 case each.

Table 3.28: Disposal of Persons Arrested for Crime Against Women Under IT(P) Act, 2016 & 2018

S.N.		2016	2018
1.	Person Arrested	5177	4237
	Male	3780	2964
	Female	1397	1273
2.	Person Charge Sheeted	4371	3546
	Male	3181	2453
	Female	1190	1093
3.	Person Convicted	723	540
	Male	563	383
	Female	160	157

4.	Person Discharged	1149	19
	Male	844	15
	Female	305	4
5.	Person Acquitted	33	1184
	Male	13	949
	Female	20	235

Source: Crime in India, 2016-2018, NCRB, Ministry of Home Affairs.

Table 3.28 shows that person arrested under IT(P) Act in 2016 was 5177 but in 2018 it was 4237 that is reduction of 18%. In 2016 male accounts for 3780 (73%) and female account for 1397 (27%), while in 2018 male account about 2964 (70%) and female account 1273 (30%). However, it has been noticed that person charge sheeted in 2016 was 4371 among them male account for 3181 (73%) and female 1190 (27%). But in 2018, 3546 persons charge sheeted among them male account for 2453 (69%) and female 1093 (31%), from 2016 to 2018 person charge sheeted is reduced by 19%.

In 2016, total number of persons convicted was 723 whereas 540 persons convicted in 2018 which was the reduction of 25%, out of them male account for 563 (78%) and female 160 (22%) in 2016 while in 2018 male account for 383 (71%) and female 157 (29%). Furthermore, person discharged in 2016 was 1149 but in 2018 rescued by 98% to 19 only. Out of them in 2016, male account for 844 (73%) and female 305 (27%). While in 2018, male account for 15 (79%) and female 4 (21%).

Table 3.29 shows that, total number of cases for investigation in 2016 was 3280 which was reduced to 2683 cases in 2018 that is the reduction of 18%. In 2016, cases ended as final report was only 1 but in 2018, it was increased to 5 i.e. 80% increase. However, cases ended as mistake of fact or law in 2016 was 5 which was increase to 13 cases in 2018 i.e. increase by 61%. It has been found that the cases dismissed due to insufficient evidences etc. in 2016 was 35 but in 2018 decrease to 31 cases i.e. reduction of 11%.

Table 3.29: Police Disposal of Crime Against Women Under IT(P) Act, 2016 & 2018

S.N.		2016	2018
1.	Total Cases for Investigation	3280	2683
2.	Cases ended as Final Report	1	5
3.	Cases ended as Mistake of Fact or Law	5	13
4.	Cases true but Insufficient Evidences etc.	35	31
5.	Cases Charge Sheeted	1921	1279
6.	Total Cases Disposed off by Police	1965	1328
7.	Charge Sheeting Rate	97.8	96.3
8.	Pending Percentage	40.1	50.5

Source: Crime in India, 2016-2018, NCRB, Ministry of Home Affairs.

Cases charge sheeted was 1921 which reduced to 1279 in 2018 i.e. reduction of 33%. On the other hand, cases disposed off by police in 2016 was 1965 which reduced to 1328 in 2018 i.e. reduction of 22%. Moreover, data also shows that, charge sheet rate in 2016 was 97.8% but in 2018, it was 96.3%. It is to be noted that, pending percentage in 2016 was 40.1% but it was 50.5% in 2018.

Table 3.30: Court Disposal of Crime Against Women Under IT(P) Act, 2016 & 2018

S.N.		2016	2018
1.	Total Cases for Trial	8895	9136
2.	Cases Disposed off Without Trial	27	25
3.	Cases Convicted	329	299
4.	Cases Discharged or Acquitted	525	555
5.	Cases in which Trial Completed	854	854
6.	Cases Disposed off by Courts	881	879
7.	Conviction Rate	38.5	35.0
8.	Pendency Percentage	90.1	90.4

Source: Crime in India, 2016-2018, NCRB, Ministry of Home Affairs.

Table 3.30 exhibits that cases on trial in 2016 was 8895 which was increased by 3% to 9136 in 2018. While cases disposed off without trial in 2016 was 27 but in 2018, it was 25 i.e. reduction of 7%. Further in 2016, cases in which conviction made was 329 but in 2018, only 299 conviction i.e. reduction of 9%. The data showing that, cases discharged or acquittal made in 2016 was 525 and in 2018, it was 555 i.e. increased by 5%. Interestingly, both in 2016 and 2018, there have been 854 cases in which trial was complete. However, cases disposed off by courts in 2106 was 881 while in 2018, it was 879 which was almost same. In 2016, conviction rate was 38.5% and in 2018, conviction rate was 35%. It has also been observed that the pendency rate in 2016 was 90.1% while in 2018, it was 90.4%.

To sum up this chapter, I can conclude that, India is the 7th largest country of the world, having 2.5% of land area and about 1.3 billion population only after China. Moreover, India's density of population varies from state to state; for instance, Bihar is densely populated state with 1106% per square kilometer while Arunachal Pradesh only has 17% per square kilometer. In the same way, resources, literacy rate, etc. of the state also differ from one state to another state. The geographical location of the state is also one of the causes for human trafficking. For instance, the highest number of trafficking cases reported in 2016 was from West Bengal followed by Rajasthan, while in 2018, highest trafficking cases reported from Jharkhand followed by Maharashtra. As far as sex ratio is concern, West Bengal reported 947 females per thousand males (17th rank), Rajasthan 926/1000 (21st rank), Jharkhand 877/1000 (31st rank) and Maharashtra 925/1000 (22nd rank). It makes clear that, the above states having very poor sex ration. Furthermore, literacy rate of West Bengal is 76.3% (19th rank), Rajasthan 66.1% (33 rank), Jharkhand 66.4% (32 rank) and Maharashtra 82.3% (12th rank). If we talk about per capita income of all these four states then West Bengal (21st rank), Rajasthan (23rd rank), Jharkhand (29th rank) and Maharashtra (7th rank). The patter of trafficking also depends upon, the geographical location, economy and other factors of the neighboring countries. For instance, most of trafficked victims from Sri Lanka were male because there was an ethnic conflict in Sri Lanka between Tamils and Sinhalis. At the same time, trafficked victims from Nepal and Bangladesh mostly are female because the economic situation. However, in both the country is poor and per capita incomes of these countries are less than India.

NOTES

1. John Salt and Jeremy Stein, "Migration as a Business: The Case of Trafficking" 35 International Migration 469-494 (1997).
2. Supra note 1 at 485-486.
3. Supra note 1 at -494.
4. Jahangir Arasli, "The Rising Wind: Is the Caucasus Emerging as a Hub for Terrorism, Smuggling, and Trafficking?" 6 Connections 5-26 (2007).
5. Supra note 4.
6. Supra note 4.
7. Supra note 4 at 24-25.
8. Makonen Getu, "Human Trafficking and Development: The Role of Microfinance" 23 Transformation 142-156 (2006).
9. Supra note 4 at 5.
10. Supra note 4 at 25-26.
11. Kapstein Ethan B, "The new global slave trade" 85 Foreign Affair 103-115 (2006).
12. Supra note 9 at 104.
13. Vetticattil, J., & Krishnan, S. "Study unearths reality of sex trade in India: low caste, poor women lured into prostitution-World", 2002.
14. Joffres, Christine., Mills, Edward, Joffres, Michel, Khanna, Tinku, Walia, Harleen, & Grund, David. "Sexual Slavery without borders: trafficking for commercial sexual exploitation in India" 7 International Journal for Equity in Health 1-22 (2008).
15. Supra note 12 at 20.
16. Alexis, A. Aronowitz, Human Trafficking, Human Misery: The Global Trade Human Beings 77-79 (Library of Congress, London, 2009).
17. Asia Foundations, "Human Trafficking in India: Dynamics, Current Efforts and Intervention Opportunities", (March, 2010).
18. Supra note 12 at 23.
19. Supra note 12 at 22-23.
20. Supra note 14 at 103.
21. Swaniti Initiative, "State of Human Trafficking in India and Existing Government Mechanisms" available at: http://www.swaniti.com. (Last visited July 25 2019).
22. Supra note at 19.
23. Digal, Santosh, "India, World Hub in Human Trafficking" 2010, available at: http://www.asianews. (Last visited January 2019).
24. Human trafficking a serious organised crime: CBI chief, TIMES OF INDIA, May 12, 2009, available at: http://articles.timesofindia.indiatimes.com/ (Last visited January 2019).
25. Ministry of Women and Child Development, India Country Report to Prevent and Combat Trafficking and Commercial Sexual Exploitation of Children and Women 4 (2017)
26. Supra note 23.

27. Sen, S. and P. M. Nair, A Report on Trafficking in Women and Children in India 2001–2003 150 (Institute of Social Sciences, National Human Rights Commission & UNIFEM, New Delhi, 2004).
28. Supra note 25 at 50.
29. Supra note 25 at 51.
30. Supra note 25 at 52-53.
31. Supra note 25 at 54-55.
32. Hameed, S., S. Hlatshwayo, E. Tanner, Human Trafficking in India: Dynamics, Current Efforts and Intervention Opportunities for the Asia Foundation, 2010, available at: http://asiafoundation.org. (Last visited July 10, 2018).
33. Nair, P.M, Trafficking Women and Children for Sexual Exploitation: Handbook for Law Enforcement Agencies in India 176 (United Nations Office on Drugs and Crime: New Delhi, 2007).
34. Supra note 31 at 170.
35. Supra note 31 at 182.
36. Paulette Lloyd & Beth, A. Simmons, *Framing for a New Transnational Legal Organization: The Case of Human Trafficking, Transnational Legal Orders* 400, 423 (Terence C. Halliday & Gregory Shaffer eds., 2015).
37. Government of India, India Country Report: Prevent and Combat Trafficking and Sexual Exploitation of Children and Women (Ministry of Women and Child Development, 2008).
38. Alexis, A. Aronowitz, *Human Trafficking, Human Misery: The Global Trade Human Beings* 77-79 (Library of Congress, London, 2009).
39. Nair, P. M. and S. Sankar, *Trafficking in Women and Children in India* 128 (Orient Longman, New Delhi, 2005)
40. Alexis, A. Aronowitz, *Human Trafficking, Human Misery: The Global Trade Human Beings* 77-79 (Library of Congress, London, 2009).
41. *Supra* note 37.
42. M. Bashir Uddin, "Human Trafficking in South Asia: Issues of Corruption and Human Security" 2 *International Journal of Social Work and Human Services Practice,* 18-27 (2014).
43. Poonam Pradhan Saxena, "Immoral Trafficking in Women and Girls: Need for Tougher Laws and Sincere Implementation" 44 *Journal of the Indian Law Institute* 504-533 (2002).
44. Asian Development Bank, "Combating trafficking of women and children in South Asia: Regional synthesis paper for Bangladesh, India and Nepal. Manila, (2002).
45. 360, The Indian Panel (IPC) Code, 1860.
46. 366 B, The Indian Panel (IPC) Code, 1860.
47. Reanda Laura, "Prostitution as a human rights question: Problems and prospects of United Nations action" 13 *Human Rights Quarterly* 202-228 (1991).
48. *Supra* note 47.

49. Government of India, India Country Report: Prevent and Combat Trafficking and Sexual Exploitation of Children and Women (Ministry of Women and Child Development, 2017.

50. *Supra* note 49.

51. Joffres Christine Mills, "Sexual Slavery without borders: trafficking for commercial sexual exploitation in India" 7 *International Journal for Equity in Health* 7-22 (2008).

52. Beotra, B. R., *The Suppression of Immoral Traffic in Women and Girls* Act, 1956 *(with State Rules).* Revised by Devinder Singh (Law Book Co., India, 1981)

53. D'Cunha, Jean, "Prostitution in a patriarchal society: A critical review of the SITA Act" 22 *Economic and Political Weekly* 1919-1925 (1987).

54. *Supra* note 53 at 1919.

55. Mr. Gary Lewis, "Protocol on Inter State Rescue and Post Rescue Activities Relating to Persons Trafficked for Commercial Sexual Exploitation", 2007, UNODC *available at:* https://www.*un.org. (Last visited September 15 2018).*

56. Thomas, Sarasau Esther, "Responses to Human Trafficking in Bangladesh, India, Nepal and Sri Lanka- Legal and Policy Review" 26 (United Nations Office on Drugs and Crime: New Delhi, 2011).

Chapter - 4

Legislation and Law Enforcement

"One should not under-estimate implementation problems despite law reform. Often, it is not the law that is at stake, but the practice"
(UN Commission on Human Rights)

This chapter focuses on legislation and law enforcement to identify, prosecute and prevent human "trafficking of women for commercial sexual exploitation". In order to discuss about legislation and legal measures to be enacted in concurrence with trafficking one may refer to measures whereby trafficking is legally regulated. For example, through criminalisation or to measures whereby the law enforcement system in a country is made responsive to the problems of trafficking, or to measures whereby the victims of human rights violation are provided with effective legal remedies. It can be argued that cases of trafficking not only cross national and international borders but it also appears at the street level and local law enforcement agencies generally are the first to come into contact with this "clandestine crime". In this way, "law enforcement agencies play an important role in identifying and responding to human trafficking cases". Therefore, it is very important to know about how international conventions, legislations, and various law enforcement agencies are sufficient to address the needs of "trafficking victims".

In order to combat trafficking, various government throughout the world including "India utilises the instrument of law to deal with violence against women in the realm of prostitution and sex trafficking". It can be argued that, during 19th century, feminist activism is considered to be initial attempts to combat international trafficking in women for prostitution. Moreover, the issue of white slave trade has become the matter of attention which has been brought to the fore by the feminists. For example the "International Convention for Suppression of White Slave Traffic, adopted in 1910, bound its signatories to severely punish any person who hired, abducted or enticed for immoral purposes any woman under the age of twenty-one, or used violence, threats, fraud or any compulsion on a woman over twenty-one to accomplish the same purpose, even if he or she committed the acts constituting the offence in different countries".[1] Even though the issues of forced prostitution came under the purview of domestic jurisdiction; it was not covered under this international convention.

Furthermore, after "World War I, the League of Nations enacted "The International Convention for the Suppression of the Traffic in Women and Children and it was ratified by a substantially larger number of States than were the earlier conventions.[2] Subsequently, after World War II, "The Universal Declaration on Human Rights adopted in 1948[3] paved the way for several legislations which would be enacted later such as "The United Nations International Convention for the Suppression of the Traffic in Persons and of the Exploitation of the Prostitution of Others of 1949 which came into force in 1951.[4] More importantly, the convention focused on punishing procurers, brothel owners and persons exploiting prostitution. However, the clauses for its enforcement were weak since it afforded little protection to the rights of trafficked women and ignored the socio-economic causes of trafficking for prostitution.

India is a signatory to various international conventions related to suppression of trafficking and accordingly enacted various laws but fail to implement these laws properly due to lack of political will as well as inefficient and lack of manpower in law enforcement agencies. Besides various laws for combating trafficking, there has been "millions of women are being trafficked and exploited on a daily basis. In other words, "if protecting the trafficked victims had been one of the priorities in India, would there be fewer women who are sexually exploited today? Even though, the trafficking in human being is "prohibited in the Constitution of India as fundamental rights according to Article 23 and it also had forbidden all forms of forced labour. "Despite this prohibition, India is a source, destination and transit country for human trafficking primarily for commercial sexual exploitation and forced labor, and with the falling sex ratio, trafficking for marriage is becoming another pull factor for trafficking of women and girls.[5]

In many cases, "men are marrying women and then selling their wives to traffickers in exchange of money. In this context, people are essentially taking the institution of marriage as a joke in order to fulfill their monetary gains.[6] However, it is argued here that "the government of India has made some progress in law enforcement to combat human trafficking but concerns still exist.[7] Even though, the — Trafficking in Persons Report has highlighted that the central and the state governments have attempted to initiate many initiatives to raise awareness about sex trafficking, but little progress has been made.[8]

For the sake of clarity and precision, I shall divide the present chapter into four parts. In Part I, I will examine the chronological global efforts to combat trafficking "from the beginning when the issue of white slave trade in the western world. Furthermore, I will also try to discuss about various international conventions which leads to various enactment in India laws. In Part II, I will try to discuss in detailed about Indian legislation pertaining to "trafficking for commercial sexual exploitation of women such as "Indian Panel Code, "CrPC", "Immoral Trafficking (Prevention) Act, 1956, etc. to provide an overview of "how law enforcement agencies are responding to trafficking and emphasizing the implications of this response for trafficking victims. In part III, I will discuss about enforcement of law and various procedure including various enforcement agencies such as police, judiciary and special agencies in order to address trafficking problems. It also examines various procedural and special laws related to trafficking issue. In Part IV, my attempt is to discuss push forward the debate whether prostitution should be legalised or criminalised. However, it tries to debate various pros and cons concerning legalisation of prostitution in India.

Coming to the basic issues which I am discussing in the above four parts, I would like to point out that at the present time, "the size of the sex industry continues to grow in India due to various reasons but one of the many factors that is contributing to this growth is the fact that people are still not aware or educated enough on how their daughters and children are being deceived and tricked into the sex industry. This is a major issue which needs governmental attention.[9]

Moreover, the government of "India has continued to debate on proposed amendments to the Immoral Trafficking (Prevention) Act to give trafficking victims greater protections and also to get rid of Section 8, which is used to criminalise sex trafficking victims[10]. As PM Nair has rightly pointed out "a trafficked person could be a male or a female of any age who has been trafficked for commercial sexual exploitation (CSE) in a brothel or any place where CSE takes place.[11] It provides "punishment even for an attempt to traffic a person."

Therefore, this law comes into question before the person is physically trafficked.[12] In this way the "IT (P) Act is a legislation which provides strength and power to the law enforcement delivery agencies to combat and prevent trafficking.[13] Further, this "legislation has been enacted since 1956 and it has been amended by the Indian parliament twice, in 1978 and also in 1986 and focused upon prevention, but for various reasons, such as ignorance and a lack of understanding of these provisions, the different provisions of this law are not being used and are also misused and abused.[14] Now it can be argued that if IT (P) Act would have enforced in such a manner where the "legislation is seriously taken into consideration without the lack of ignorance and proper understanding of various provisions", it can be said that this "legislation can be powerful in eradicating the commercial sexual exploitation of women." With this brief remark regarding IT (P) Act as legislation for the prevention of human trafficking; I shall come to the Part I of the chapter.

4.1. International Conventions to Combat Trafficking for Commercial Sexual Exploitation

The initial attempt to combat international trafficking of women for prostitution was initiated by feminist activists. In other words,

Nineteenth-century feminist activism may be regarded as one of the major earliest attempts to combat international trafficking in women for commercial sexual exploitation. For instance, the issue of white slave trade has become the matter of attention which has been brought to the fore by the feminists. In Britain, there was a Contagious Diseases Act, under which women identified as prostitutes were subjected to numerous internal examinations and those found to be infected were sent to a special hospital ward for whores. However, the campaigns of feminists led to the Acts repealed in 1883. According to Donald J. Guy, "Since the nineteenth century, trafficking in women and girls for prostitution has attracted great attention. Information about the so-called white slave trade – initiated by British reports on the abduction of English women to continental brothels and the sexual slavery of European females in South America – spread rapidly during the 1870s and led to the formation of the first anti-trafficking movement. At the end of the nineteenth and beginning of the twentieth century's efforts to prevent and combat trafficking in persons resulted in the organisation of a series of conferences and the passage of national laws and international conventions.[15] "The International Convention for Suppression of White Slave Traffic, adopted in 1910, bound its signatories to severely punish any person who hired, abducted or enticed for immoral purposes any woman under the age of twenty-one, or used violence, threats, fraud or any compulsion on a woman over twenty-one to accomplish the same purpose, even if he or she committed the acts constituting the offence in different countries.[16] Even though the issues of trafficking were dealt by the conventions of 1904 and 1910 but these conventions did not include persons who detained women in brothels. Since the issue of forced prostitution came under the purview of domestic jurisdiction, it was not covered under this international convention.

Furthermore, after World War I (1914-1918), the League of Nations got involved in making efforts at international level as against the trafficking of women and children for prostitution. As Paul Knepper has rightly pointed, "the League of Nations strengthened the legal instruments aimed at the suppression and prevention of international crime.[17] "The League's member states agreed in Article

23 of the Covenant of the League to entrust the League with the general supervision over the execution of agreements with regard to the traffic in women and children and the traffic in opium and other dangerous drugs.[18] During 1921, "The International Convention for the Suppression of the Traffic in Women and Children under the auspices of the League retained the focus on trafficking.[19] "In 1921– in cooperation with anti-traffic voluntary organisations -it first addressed the recruitment of persons for purposes of prostitution by approving the International Convention for the Suppression of the Traffic in Women and Children. In subsequent years, the League and its anti-traffic committee contributed to perfecting a global prohibition regime against international sex trafficking and the direct or indirect recruitment for prostitution against international sex trafficking and the direct or indirect recruitment for prostitution that endures to this day.[20]

Now the convention was "ratified by a substantially larger number of states than were the earlier conventions. The white slave traffic now changed into traffic in women and children.[21] At this time, "states were encouraged to take legislative and administrative measures for the protection of immigrating women and children. "Also an advisory committee was established on the traffic in women and children[22] to secure the implementation of the convention by the states that would have to report it periodically. The victims, thus, are totally dependent on the exploiters. "A special body of experts was commissioned to engage in fact finding mission on the traffic in women and children in selected countries of West Asia, Europe, North America and South America[23]. They found it very difficult to distinguish or separate international trafficking with commercialised forced prostitution within a nation. They came to conclusion that the "existence of licensed houses is undoubtedly an incentive to traffic both at national and international level[24]. That was further reaffirmed by the subsequent body of experts who study on the "similar issue in Asia and the Far East.[25] They found that the profit is sole base on which the "business of forced prostitution thrives.[26]

Besides, they condemned the "forced prostitution or business of prostitution more strongly than prostitution itself for the two primary reasons, first, it is at the pleasure of third party and second, there is no one in abroad whom the trafficked victims can rely upon.[27] Moreover, a significant step was taken "with the signing of the International Convention on the "Suppression of the Traffic in Women of Full Age", in 1933. This convention extended the scope of punishable acts that had previously been criminalised only with regard to minors to women of age, and declared that even the consent of the woman would not exempt the offender from penalty. Preparatory acts, attempts and the actual procurement of adult women for immoral purposes in another country would be punishable.[28] During 1937, "League of Nations drafted a convention with the inputs from these two fact finding missions. "The draft was designed in a way so as to it consolidated the earlier treaties and secure international co-operation in the abolition of brothels as well as the prosecution and punishment of brothel owners and managers[29].

Hence, it was to be a first of its kind of treaties that counter the practice of prostitution which underlies trafficking. Prostitution was taken as an effect of trafficking and vice versa. Thus, the "existence of brothel is no longer purely a domestic issue as it is the center of the system of trafficking".[30] "The overall goal of the consolidated convention which never opened for signatures due to the outbreak of World War II was to abolish regulation of prostitution by any party, repress third party profiteering from prostitution, and rehabilitate the female victims.[31] Moreover, the "outbreak of World War II prevented its approval, but many of the ideas included in the draft convention were taken up by the United Nations in 1949.[32]

After World War II (1939-1945) the "Universal Declaration on Human Rights adopted in 1948, led by Eleanor Roosevelt, envisaged three parts to the postwar human rights enterprise: a set of general principles; the codification of those principles into law; and practical means of implementation.[33] The UNDHR paved the way for several legislations which would be enacted later. Moreover, it set out a charter of rights for "all people, irrespective of nationality, race, caste, sex, religion, colour, or any other status. It accorded all individuals the right to life, liberty and security, and the right not to be held in slavery or servitude, among other rights.[34] All the desirable drafts of consolidated convention of 1937 and other earlier conventions' protocols that were taken into account to produce, the "Convention for the Suppression of the Traffic in Persons and of the Exploitation of the Prostitution of Others of 1949 which came into force in 1951.[35] This convention focused on punishing procurers, brothel owners and persons exploiting prostitution. However, the clauses for its enforcement were weak. It afforded little protection to the "rights of trafficked women and ignored the socio-economic causes of trafficking for prostitution.[36] Moreover, "the prostitution and the accompanying evil of the traffic in persons for the purpose of prostitution are incompatible with the dignity and worth of the human person and endanger the welfare of the individual the family and the community."[37]

According to "Article 1 of the Convention for the Suppression of the Traffic in Persons and of the Exploitation of the Prostitution of Others categorically stated that, "The parties of convention agreed upon to (a) punish any person who, to gratify the passions of another, procures, entices or leads away, for purposes of prostitution, another person, even with the consent of that person[38]; (b) "exploits the prostitution of another person, even with the consent of that person.[39] According to article 2 of this convention, "They agreed upon to punish any person who: (a) Keeps or manages, or knowingly finances or takes part in the financing of a brothel; (b) Knowingly lets or rents a building or other place or any part thereof for the purpose of the prostitution of others.[40] It deters the trafficking across borders and extradition be made possible among themselves to punish the culprits. In case, extradition is not made or possible then, the state has to bring them before the law of court when they came back home country. Therefore, it is stringent upon traffickers so as the trafficking and business of prostitution could be curbed or prohibited totally. As it was concluded by the UN studies that the brothels existed partly because of the women supplied to them through international trafficking, trafficking would not cease unless brothels were abolished. Though the convention of 1949 took an abolitionist approach with respect to brothels, it did not prohibit prostitution *per se*. Also, the convention equates trafficking with prostitution, and entirely disregarded the aspect of the consent of persons involved in sex work.

Though the convention under article 5, make trafficked women to participate in the proceeding against the offenders, they are limited in procedural rights of the women. As the right would be made available only if the national law allowed it. According to the convention, "In cases where injured persons are entitled under domestic law to be parties to proceedings in respect of any of the offences referred to in the present Convention, aliens shall be entitled upon the same terms as nationals.[41] In this manner the victims of trafficking would be repatriated if they wished, or if their "expulsion is ordered in conformity with law. This may make women without legal resident status likely to be expelled from a country. Therefore, the state from which the victim was repatriated would be even less likely to pursue criminal prosecution against the pimps or brothel owners in the absence of the victim. Thus, the root cause of prostitution is not addressed completely; rather they are focused merely on the conduit. However, the parties agreed upon to supervise the employment agencies, particularly those who deal in the employment of women and children. It helps prevent "women and children from being exposed to the danger of prostitution.[42] States have to issue public warning on the dangers of trafficking and accordingly they have to ensure supervision of all the centers of transportations like airports, railway stations, and other points of entry and departure in order to prevent trafficking.

The victims of prostitution have to be provided proper rehabilitation and social adjustment by the State. Moreover, the State has to provide them education whether public or private, health, social, economic and other related services. However, in conflict between the international laws derived from the convention and the domestic law of the State, a situation of anomaly arises. The differences of national laws or the lack of conformity to the international laws on human rights violations might be due to two reasons. First, the notion of international laws was still relatively less pervasive and the second, the perception of keeping off from undue interferences in the domestic laws by the intergovernmental organisations deemed essential. The enforcement mechanisms of the convention were weak. The parties are required to send annually the reports on the domestic laws and regulations that were in conformity with the convention to the "UN Secretary General to give effect to the provisions of the convention.[43] And Secretary General was directed to publish and send this communication to all the UN members and non-members who had been invited by the UN to ratify the convention.

This is what the convention provided in the name of implementation and enforcement mechanisms. It did not establish any independent supervisory body which would have the authority to question the States' reports, issue recommendations to them on the basis of those reports, or receive and act "on petitions brought by victims of trafficking alleging that a State had failed to try to eliminate trafficking.[44] "In 1974, however, the Economic and Social Council of the United Nations (ECOSOC) decided that the parties to the 1949 convention should submit regular reports on the situation in their countries regarding slavery and trafficking to the UN Sub-Commission on Prevention of Discrimination and Protection of Minorities.[45] "United Nations Human Right Commissions Sub-Commission's Working Group on Contemporary Forms of Slavery reviews these reports, but is not empowered to take action on them."[46] Besides the conventions discussed above, "anti-slavery treaties also cover trafficking for prostitution." The Slavery Convention, 1926, amended by the Protocol of 1953, defines slavery as the status or condition of a person over whom any or all of the powers attaching to the right of ownership are exercised[47] and it also agreed upon that "slave trade includes all acts involved in the capture, acquisition or disposal of a person with intent to reduce him to slavery; all acts involved in the acquisition of a slave with a view to selling or exchanging him; all acts of disposal by sale or exchange of a slave acquired with a view to being sold or exchanged, and, in general, every act of trade or transport in slaves."[48] The parties to the 1926 convention committed themselves to "prevent and suppress the slave trade and to bring about the complete abolition of slavery in all its forms."[49] They undertook "to adopt the necessary measures in order that severe penalties may be imposed in respect of' infractions of laws and regulations that give effect to the 1926 Convention's purposes."[50] In terms of enforcement mechanisms, this convention had many flaws in common with the 1949 convention. The requirement of reporting was very general, and no supervisory body was established to "monitor the implementation and enforcement of the convention's provisions."[51] Like the parties to the 1949 convention, the parties to the 1926 convention were to submit to the "UN Sub-Commission on Prevention of Discrimination and Protection of Minorities"[52] regular reports on the measures taken by them to implement the treaty.

Furthermore, "the 1926 anti-slavery convention was supplemented in 1956 by the Supplementary Convention on the Abolition of Slavery, the Slave Trade and Institutions and Practices similar to Slavery." The latter covered slavery-like practices and brought the 1926 Convention into the UN system.[53] "Article 1(c) of the supplementary convention on Abolition of Slavery defined slavery as any institution or practice whereby: (i) a woman, without the right to refuse, is promised or given in marriage on payment of a consideration in money or in kind to her parents, guardian, family or any other person or group[54] or (ii) "the husband of a woman, his family, or his clan, has the right to transfer her to another person for value received or otherwise[55]; or (iii) "a woman on the death of her husband is liable to be inherited by another person[56]. Article 1(d) added, "any institution or practice whereby a child or young person under the age of 18 years is delivered by either or both of his natural parents or by his guardian to another person, whether for reward or not, with a view to the exploitation of the child or young person or of his labour.[57] Moreover, unlike 1926 "anti-slavery convention, 1956 "supplementary convention on abolition of slavery obligatory to State parties to "impose domestic criminal sanctions on individuals who involve in selling women, exploiting "children for bonded labour and forced prostitution. Unfortunately, the provisions of this convention were weak as those of the 1949 convention on trafficking.

Moreover, the States were to "cooperate with each other and with the United Nations to give effect to the treaty's provisions. The 1956 convention contained a mild mechanism for reporting, similar to that of the 1926 convention. The States simply undertook to send the UN Secretary-General copies of any laws, regulations and administrative measures enacted or put into effect to implement the provision of this Convention.[58] As per this convention, the "Secretary-General would then communicate the information received through this process to all the State parties as well as to Economic and Social Council (ECOSOC) for consideration and for any further recommendations that ECOSOC might make on the abolition of slavery.[59] However, it can be argue that like earlier treaties, this convention contained no provisions for monitoring implementation, reviewing the information submitted by the States and making recommendations, or receiving petitions alleging violations of the convention.

Besides anti-slavery conventions, International Labour Organisation has formulated conventions for the "abolition of forced labour or sexual exploitation. According to Marley S. Weiss, "Human trafficking is widely referred to as the slavery of our times or modern- day slavery. The International Labour Organisation (ILO) has estimated that over a ten-year period, 20.9 million people—roughly three out of every one thousand people worldwide—have been victims of forced labour or sexual exploitation.[60] Moreover, "ILO enacted two conventions related to eradication of trafficking for prostitution and these are namely; (a) "Forced Labour Convention (No. 29), adopted in 1930, and the Abolition of Forced Labour Convention (No. 105), adopted in 1957.[61] The state parties to both the conventions decided to eradicate and penalize the "practice of forced labour." In both conventions, forced labour is defined as all work or service which is exacted from any person under the menace of any penalty and for which the person has not offered himself voluntarily.[62] This definition can be interpreted in such a way which can be applicable also for trafficked person. "The Committee of Experts on the Application of Conventions and Recommendations has identified the use of children for prostitution as one of the worst forms of forced labour."

"Consequently, the focus of the ILO's efforts in this area has been on trafficking in children."[63] Hence, the mechanisms for supervision and enforcement under the ILO system include a requirement of reporting as well as the provision of advisory services. According to the Constitution of the ILO, "the state parties must submit reports to the International Labour Office regarding the measures they have taken to give effect to any ILO convention they have ratified etc."[64] Every year, the "Director-General of ILO has to present a summary of the States' reports to the International Labour Conference."[65]

"The Convention on the Elimination of All Forms of Discrimination Against Women (CEDAW),[66] 1979 is another treaty that can be instrumental to pursue government to eradicate trafficking for sexual exploitation. According to Article 6 of the convention direct the state members to take all essential steps including laws to eradicate all type of trafficking for commercial sexual exploitation. As per "International Covenant on Civil and Political Rights, CEDAW touches upon the action of private parties. If inadequate measures or no measures at all are taken to eliminate trafficking by either the State or private actors, the State is considered to have violated its treaty obligations. Even though Article 2 of the convention better defines the measures provided for whereas Article 6 of the convention unable to define about measures which could be "appropriate, while Article 2 sets out a general framework of steps to be taken by the State parties. Earlier, there was no procedure allowing for individual complaints alleging violation of the convention's provisions. Such a protocol, however, was proposed later. At its 1996 session, "the UN Commission on the Status of Women recommended to Economic and Social Council (ECOSOC) that it renews the mandate of the working group on the elaboration of a draft optional protocol to the convention. "On October 6, 1999 an Optional Protocol on the Right to Petition was adopted by the General Assembly and this protocol gives individuals and groups of women the right to complain to the committee on CEDAW.[67] The process of making complaints is called the communication procedure.

After a complaint has been made, the "committee can conduct inquiries into the abuse of women's human rights in the countries that are party to the Optional Protocol[68]. This is known as the inquiry procedure. It is to be noted that the Optional Protocol calls upon all member states to the "CEDAW convention to sign, ratify or accede to the Protocol as soon as possible."

According to Article 18 of CEDAW, "the state parties undertake to report periodically on the legislative, judicial, administrative and other measures they have taken to give effect to the convention's provisions, and on the progress, they have made.[69] The first report is due a year after the treaty enters into force within a given State. The

State must report every four years thereafter. Of all the human rights conventions with some competence to examine trafficking, CEDAW is the one that has given the maximum attention to the matter, primarily, but not exclusively, under the Article 6 provision on trafficking. A review of CEDAW reports from 1987 through 1995 reveals that the committee paid significant attention tó trafficking, examining as it did the periodic reports submitted by the parties. The convention contains specific provisions "related to the trafficking." The "appropriate measures required by Article 6 to stop trafficking should be read in conjunction with the requirement in Article 5 which directs the parties to modify the social and cultural patterns of conduct of men and women in order to eliminate stereotypes regarding inferiority or superiority with respect to men or women."[70] It is apparent from the members' reports that they see the connection between Articles 5 and 6. The link between violence against prostitutes and the need to alter social and cultural patterns of prejudice was made in the "CEDAW committee's General Recommendation 19 on Violence Against Women, issued in 1993."[71] In 1992 the Committee adopted general recommendation 19 on violence against women asking states that traditional attitudes perpetuate widespread practices involving violence or coercion. These attitudes also contribute to the propagation of pornography and the depiction and other commercial exploitation of women as sexual objects rather than as individuals.

"This in turn contributes to gender-based violence."[72] It addresses the causes and effects of trafficking and exploitation of the prostitution of women by showing the link between trafficking for prostitution and violence against trafficked women. Stating that poverty and unemployment increase opportunities for trafficking in women and new form of sexual exploitation such as sex tourism has emerged and these practices are incompatible with the notion of women having equal access to rights and with respect for their rights and dignity. They put women at special risk of violence and abuse."[73] As a result, vulnerable situation not only increase opportunities for trafficking but also "force them into prostitution." Since their status may be vulnerable, the general recommendation also noted that these women tend to be marginalised and are thus more vulnerable to violence. This means that they need greater legal protection. Kapstein has rightly said in "The New Global Slave Trade".

Slavery was abolished during the 19th century unfortunately this is far from truth because slavery and the global slave trade continue to flourish up until this day. In fact, it is more likely that people are being trafficked across borders now than any point in the past. Contemporary slavery involves women and children being forced into servitude through violence and deprivation.[74] Furthermore, Reanda also pointed out, "enforced prostitution is considered to be a slavery-like practice. This distinction has been formalised under international law. The exploitation of prostitution was equated with slavery and an international convention was drawn under the United Nations. These instruments regard prostitution as a human rights violation only if it involves exploitation and coercion.[75] Therefore, when a human being is enforced into prostitution, one is not only being deprived of their basic human rights, but they are also degraded to slaves in society. "Approximately 800,000 women and children are trafficked each year across the international borders and 80 per cent of these individuals end up in forced sex work."[76] Human trafficking for CSE is a gross violation of human rights and has been described as a modern form of slavery.[77]

In order to provide for effective legislation to prevent and combat trafficking in persons, especially women and children., UNO adopted the Protocol to Prevent, Suppress and Punish Trafficking in Persons, Especially Women and Children in 2000 to supplement the United Nations Convention against Transnational Organised Crime.[78] The central idea is that the countries of origin, transit and destination should adopt a comprehensive international approach to prevent trafficking, punish the traffickers and protect the victims of trafficking. Furthermore, the protocol provides for the repatriation of the victims of trafficking and places the responsibility for this on the States from and to which the victim is travelling. There has been number of international as well as regional convention on trafficking for example "SAARC Convention on Preventing and Combating Trafficking in Women and Children for prostitution provides that the judicial authorities in the member states should ensure the confidentiality of the child and women victims.[79] To prevent trafficking, victims should also provide with proper counseling and legal aid.

Therefore, it can be argue that in addition of all the above conventions, there are various international and regional treaties and convention to eradicate trafficking but the burden of implementation lies on state parties and it depend upon the political will of different governments. However, it can be argue that the practice of prostitution with reference to adults is not prohibited under "international standards and States are not required to punish persons engaged in prostitution. Yet, international treaties and conventions, starting with the UN Convention of 1949 have equated "trafficking and prostitution", and the growing concern about sex work and prostitution can be attributed to their association with trafficking. In the light of the fact that prostitution, can be with or without consent, and that traffic in persons includes a wide range of exploitative practices, the main focus of international action needs to be on punishing the entire gamut of acts that fall under traffic in persons, including those in forcing a person to engage in prostitution. It has been found that in most countries it is not illegal to engage in sexual activity for monetary gain; however, the laws that exist make it almost impossible to do so and criminalise all activities associated with it. Evidence shows that in most of European countries, prostitution is not punishable, but the act of soliciting is. For example, in countries like Germany, Holland and Denmark, the laws accept female sex work "as long as sex workers ply their trade in designated areas and fulfill other requirements such as licensing and payment of taxes.

4.2. National Legislations to Combat Trafficking for Commercial Sexual Exploitation

India is sovereign, socialist, secular, democratic, republic and people of India adopted constitution for themselves. According to provision of the Constitution, we chose our representatives who enact laws to govern our country. Part III of the Constitution deals about fundamental rights for individuals whereby Article 23 of the Constitution of India, "prohibits traffic in human beings and forced labour and includes all forms of trafficking in persons and their use as commodities for the purpose of exploitation.[80] In the same way various Sections' in different legislations deals with issue of trafficking directly and indirectly for instance, Indian Panel Code (IPC), Immoral Trafficking (Prevention) Act, 1956 etc. In this part, I am trying to discuss these laws and their implementation to eradicate trafficking for commercial sexual exploitation.

4.2.1. The Indian Panel Code

Indian Panel Code (IPC) which was enacted before SITA is often used to deal with crime related to human trafficking. Among these provisions, some directly deal with human trafficking and several others are deals with associate crime. Although in this part, I am going to discuss only main provisions related to human trafficking given in Indian Panel Code. According to "Sections 366A and 366B were inserted in 1923, the IPC in order to comply with India's international obligations as a signatory to the International Convention for the Suppression of the Traffic in Women and Children, 1910.[81]

According to "Article 3 of the Convention, the States party should take necessary steps to incorporate within their legislations the necessary steps to punish procurers or persons who use force or violence to entice women and girls under 21 (even with consent) for immoral purposes.[82] Besides, "provisions of these sections are framed more with the desire of safeguarding the public interest of morality than the chastity of one particular woman.[83] Subsequently, to this convention,

> "India signed the 1922 Convention of the League of Nations. Both sections were introduced to punish international sale and purchase of persons for prostitution. Section 366A is aimed chiefly at procurers of minor girls who by any means whatsoever, induce any minor girl under the age of 18, to go from any place or to do any act with intent that such girl may be, or knowing that it is likely that she will be, forced or seduced to illicit intercourse with another person.[84]

Besides, "any reason given by the accused to move the girl from one place to another constitutes inducement. An accused cannot plead that he bona fide believed that the minor girl was over the prescribed age.[85] In other words, "a person merely accompanying a woman going out to ply her profession of sex work, even if she has not attained the age of 18 years does not commit an offence under Section 366 A.[86] It is mentioned that also, "persons giving encouragement or rendering assistance to a woman or prostitute offering herself promiscuously for money to customers cannot be said to have committed an offence under the section.[87] While "Section 366 B deals with the phenomenon of inter country trafficking which aims to punish the person who imports a girl under 21 from any country outside India with the intent that she may be or likely that she will be forced or seduced to illicit intercourse.[88] Moreover, this Section has been mentioned three important ingredients which are namely; firstly, "the accused imported a girl into India from any country outside India or from Jammu and Kashmir, secondly "the girl was under 21 and thirdly the "importation of the girl was with the intention that she will be forced or seduced to illicit intercourse.[89]

> "The Criminal Law (Amendment) Act, 2013 substituted Section 370 from new Sections 370 and 370A. Section 370 Trafficking of Person-Whoever, for the purpose of exploitation, (a) recruits, (b) transports, (c) harbours, (d) transfers, or (e) receives, a person or persons, by- firstly, using threats or secondly, using force or any other forms of coercion or thirdly, by abduction or fourthly, by practicing fraud or deception or fifthly by views of power or sixthly by inducement including the giving or receiving of payments or benefits in order to achieve the consent of any person having control over the person recruited, transported, harboured, transferred or received, commits the offence of trafficking .[90]

For the above crime, punishment varies from minimum rigorous "imprisonment for seven years to maximum life imprisonment i.e. natural life and shall also be liable to fine. Furthermore, "Section 370A exploitation of trafficked person. Whoever knowingly or having reason to believe that a minor has been trafficked, engages such minor for sexual exploitation in any manner, shall be punished with rigorous imprisonment for a term which shall not be less than five year but which may extend to seven years and shall also be liable to fine.[91]

While, "Section 371 covers with habitual dealing in slaves. Under it, whoever habitually imports, exports, buys, sells, traffics or deals in slaves is punishable with imprisonment for life.[92] It may point out that, this "Section can be very useful to target the organised groups of persons who have been indulging in traffic in persons for any or specifically for the purpose of Commercial Sexual Exploitation. While, "Sections 372 and 373 deals with the selling and buying of minors for the purpose of prostitution. Furthermore, this Sections states that,

> "Whoever sells, lets to hire, or otherwise disposes of any person under the age of eighteen years with intent that such person shall at any age be employed or used for the purpose of prostitution or illicit intercourse with any person or for any unlawful and immoral purpose, or knowing it to be likely that such person will at any age be employed or used for any such purpose, shall be punished with imprisonment of either description for a term which may extend to ten years, and shall also be liable to fine.[93]

However, it has been provided that, "the age of the person being sold for immoral purposes was raised from 16 to18 in 1924. For instance, if a girl under 18 years is disposed of to a prostitute or brothel manager, a presumption will arise that the person disposing of such a girl has done so with the intention mentioned in this section.[94]

4.2.2. Juvenile Justice (Care and Protection of Children) Act[95]

According to this, "child victims of trafficking and commercial sexual exploitation are protected under this Act. Moreover, "Section 2 (d) (vi) & (vii) of the Act defines a child in need of care and protection as a child who is being or is likely to be grossly abused tortured or exploited for the purpose of sexual abuse or illegal acts, and a child "who is found vulnerable and is likely to be inducted into drug abuse or trafficking.[96]

4.2.3. Suppression of Traffic in Women and Girls Act, 1956 (SITA)[97]

This legislation for the suppression of forced movement of women and girls into prostitution has undergone three stages of development. When it was initially enforced in 1956, its main focus was to criminalise the machinery around prostitution. It provided definitions of prostitution and prostitute. It was gender- specific and covered only women and girls. The next stage was the amendment of the Act in 1978.

The main development was the deletion of the definition of a prostitute and some procedural changes. The third stage in 1986, led to the change in the name of the Act too.[98]

4.2.4. The Immoral Traffic (Prevention) Act, 1978[99]

This Act was marked by vital changes in order to make more effective by changing the definition of prostitution. It is to be noted that certain procedural changes were also incorporated in this Act by stressing on offences committed against children. Despite of changes, "Act still lacks the definitions of trafficking and trafficker.[100] Moreover, "the bill was before the Parliament for over two years and was passed six years after India ratified the 1949 UN Convention for the purpose of suppression of prostitution as also for the other attendant evils.[101] In order to prevent trafficking, "Indian State felt the need for a Central Act, which would lay down a uniform procedure for the purpose of checking if not completely eradicating the evils associated with prostitution. Moreover, its aim was to have a uniform law which would be more effective in eradicating this evil.

"Prostitution per se was not made illegal under the law on grounds that would be in conflict with Article 19(g)[102] of the Constitution that gives all citizens the right to practice any profession.[103] Instead, the "legislators sought other measures to check if not eradicate the evil of prostitution.

"In a particular case, it was stated that the Act defines the term prostitute as a woman who offers her body to indiscriminate sexual intercourse especially for hire.[104] It is to be point out that, "the 1956 Act was gender specific and it recognised the traffic for prostitution in women as well as children only. However, "the SITA was amended in 1978 and renamed as the Suppression of Immoral Traffic in Women and Girls (Amendment) Act, 1978.[105] This Act has included, words conveyance in the definition of brothel and new definitions and amendments in the previous definitions of corrective institution, magistrate and protective home were incorporated."[106] While in relation to "Section 4 which deals with punishment for living on the earnings of prostitution, clause (2) was added, stating that any person over 18 who lives with or is in habitual company or exercises control or acts as a pimp of a prostitute is an offender."[107] Furthermore, "Section 7 was amended and made more stringent thus criminalizing the activity of any woman or girl who carries on prostitution as well as the person with whom such prostitution is carried out on in any premises within the vicinity of a public place. Various other amendments were made in the provisions for special police officers and other procedures.[108]

4.2.5. The Immoral Traffic (Prevention) Act, 1986[109]

This Act was last amended in 1986 to make it gender-neutral while incorporating various provisions concerning specific to offences against children. The Act introduced three categories of victims-minors, majors and children. Moreover, this Act defined, "a child as a person who has not completed the age of sixteen years; a minor as a person who has completed the age of sixteen years but has not completed the age of eighteen years and a major as a person who has completed the age of eighteen years.[110] It is to be noted that, "this was an important departure from the gender- specific definitions in the 1956 Act. And other amendments included certain procedural additions such as the appointment of a Trafficking Police Officer under Section 13 (4), medical examination of the rescued person under Section 15 (5A), the provision, under Section 15 (6A), for women police to accompany SPOs during a search.

Moreover the "Act altered the definition of prostitution from promiscuous sexual intercourse for hire to the sexual exploitation or abuse of persons for commercial purposes. In order to prove the offence various high courts have been given several guidelines in the following manner; (a) "Prosecution cannot be expected to give direct evidence and that they can give circumstantial evidences held in State of Mysore v Susheela.[111] (b) "To prove that a woman is a prostitute, indiscriminate and plural sexuality on her part has to be proved. But this does not require the evidence of more than one customer if the proven facts entitle the court to infer that she carries on prostitution held in Bai Radha v State of Gujarat[112] (c) "To prove indiscriminate sexuality, evidence of more than one customer is required held in T. Jacob v State of Kerala.[113]

"The essential component of the offence is promiscuous sexual intercourse, thus, proof of one sexual intercourse is inadequate. The courts have held that if several acts cannot be proved directly, there has to be material showing that the person is in the habit of indulging in promiscuous sexual intercourse held in Ved Prakash v State.[114] As per "Section 3 of the Act, punishment for keeping a brothel or allowing one's premises to be used as a brothel.[115] "It states that any person who keeps or manages, or acts or assists in the keeping or management of a brothel would be punished on first conviction with rigorous imprisonment for 1 to 3 years and also with fine not exceeding Rs 2000. In the event of a second or subsequent conviction the punishment is rigorous imprisonment for 2 to 5 years and fine not exceeding Rs 2000.[116] Moreover in "1986 sub section 2A was inserted in section 3 which lays down the presumption that unless proved contrary, "the tenant or occupier knowingly allowed the premises to be used as a brothel, if a report is published about the premises found to be used as a brothel as a result of a search made under the Act.[117] While, "Section 4 stipulates the punishment for living on the earnings of prostitution. It has a gender bias since it speaks of those compelling her prostitution. It targets pimps and others who bring customers, receive a share of the illegitimate income and live on it[118].

It also states that, "any person above the age of 18 can be an offender and may be punished with imprisonment for a term which may extend to 2 years or fine up to Rs 1000 or both.[119] Even though its states, "in the context of a child or a minor a term not less than 7 years and not more than 10 years.

> "Under Section 5 any person who induces or procures a woman with or without her consent for prostitution is punishable with rigorous imprisonment for a term of not less than 3 years and not more than 7 years and a fine not exceeding Rs 2000. If this offence is committed against the will of the person or a minor then the

imprisonment is for a term not less than 7 years and not exceeding 14 years. "The punishment for an offence in the context of a child may extend to life imprisonment.[120]

Furthermore, "Section 6 refers to the crime of detaining any person with or without their consent in premises where prostitution is carried out. It targets brothel owners and others who detain a person for the purpose of sexual exploitation for monetary gain.[121] It is to be noted that, "Section 7, makes prostitution in the vicinity of public places an offence and premises which are within 200 meters of any place of religious worship, educational institution, hostel, hospital, nursing home and other public place as notified by the commissioner of police or magistrate.[122] "Section 8 deals with seducing or soliciting for the purpose of prostitution and if prostitution is said to mean sexual exploitation for commercial purposes then the Section should target the exploiter or the person who solicits for clients on behalf of the exploited.[123] There have been various judgments which clarified specifically which is evident in the "Case of Re Kamala clearly held that mere flirtation or attempts to attract the opposite sex would not constitute an offence as soliciting had the essential import of an oral entreaty or persuasion used to achieve the object of prostitution.[124]

"Section 9 provides for punishing the seduction of girls who are in the custody of guardians or those in a position of authority or charge, where these persons use the women or girls for prostitution with a view to making gains for themselves[125]. But in 1978, the "punishment for the offence was increased from 1 to 3 years, to a term of not less than 7 and extending to life or 10 years and a fine.[126] Further an important amendment made in 1986 which was the "provision for the appointment of a trafficking police officer by the Central Government to deal with inter-state trafficking under Section 13 (4).[127] Moreover, "Section 18 states that the magistrate can order for the closure of any place that is in public vicinity and is being used as a brothel or for prostitution.[128]

While, "Section 19 allows a person who is carrying on or is being made to carry on prostitution to apply for being kept in a protective home or to be provided care and protection of the Court.[129]

> "Section 20 allows the removal of a prostitute from any place under the orders of a magistrate. The definition of the term prostitute' is not clear and the section could only refer to the removal of the exploiter or the one who sexually exploits for monetary gain from the place in question. However, in the implementation of the section, the term is taken to mean the woman/man who engages in sexual intercourse for a monetary gain. Punishments according to the legislators were provided according to the gravity or degree of deliberation and with the degree of harm that the particular wrong is likely to cause or caused to the person concerned in the first instance and to the society in general.[130]

In order to deal with legislation on trafficking, "the legislature and judiciary have often adopted a moral position that is detrimental to the cause of providing justice to commercially sexually exploited persons. "It is embedded in the conceptual mistake of interlinking trafficking with sex work. Moreover, there have been various "deliberations of the Courts in many cases seems to consider the sexually exploited person as a menace to society than a victim of a crime and very few landmark cases have viewed exploited person as a human being who entitled to basic human rights, dignity and freedom from exploitation. Moreover, important cases have raises several questions concerning women's lives who has been trap in the trafficking. "The judges did not think it fit to look at the problem in a legal framework, but took into account the socio-economic ramifications of the problem as well.[131] Besides, "important cases that led to a on the living conditions of persons in engaged in prostitution and the question of providing alternate sources of income to such persons is the Gaurav Jain v Union of India.[132] However, "there were significant problems with this judgment by which persons who involved in prostitution were referred as fallen women instead of treating such persons as perpetrators of crime.

Moreover, "the judgment looked upon them as victims requiring special attention and care which was mentioned in judicial orders which has provided for "rehabilitation of prostitutes." The Calcutta High Court in Shefali Banarjee case held that the legislation being a social legislation had a double objective and it was both penal and ameliorative as the legislature not only wanted to prevent trafficking but also wanted to provide for the rehabilitation of prostitutes.[133] It makes clear that, "if the penal provision were to be invoked, the ameliorative measures enjoined by the same provision were also to be invoked as in Vishal Jeet v Union of India, the court held that nothing would be achieved by punishing the victims of this malady but that results would be achieved if law enforcing bodies were to take action against all erring persons such as the pimps, brokers and brothel keepers.[134]

Recently, various amendments proposed in "Immoral Traffic (Prevention) Act, 1956 to strengthen the Act according to the need of an hour. Some important suggestions I have discussed below:

1. The definition of child in Section 2 (aa) will change and 16 years will be replaced by 18 years. Now child will be consider a person under 18 years of age.
2. Section 2 (k), a new clause will be added which will define, "Trafficking in Persons."
3. Under Section 3 (1) along with the word 'keeps' or 'manages' words 'acts' or 'assist' added and the punishment will be enhanced in "first conviction from rigorous imprisonment for not less than one years and not more than three years and also fines up to Rs. 2000 to not less than three years with fine up to Rs 10000[135]. And in case of subsequent conviction from rigorous imprisonment not less than 2 years and not more than 5 years[136] and also "fine up to Rs. 2000 to rigorous imprisonment not less than 7 years and also fine up to 2 lakh rupees.[137]
4. In Section 7 (1A) in place of "respect of child or minor replace by term "respect of a person less than 18 years.
5. In Section 10 (a) in place of "offence under Section 7 or 8 replace by "offence under Section 7 only and in place of "detention in corrective institutions not more than 5 years replace by "detention in corrective institutions not more than 7 years.
6. In Section 13 (2) suggested addition in place of "not below the rank of an inspector of police replace by "not below the rank of a sub-inspector/ inspector of police.

7. The Section 13 (3) (b) in place of may replace by "shall."
8. The proposed amendment also suggested deletion of various provisions like Section 2 (ca), 2 (cb), 8 etc.

   This amendment is proposed by "Ministry of Women and Childhood Development and recently Cabinet proposed to make "National Investigation Authority (NIA) as nodal agency for the investigation in the cases related to human trafficking.

4.3. Enforcement of Law

The police are the primary agency of law enforcement in India. The police as a law enforcement agency are the domain of the state government. Though different states have their own Acts governing the law enforcement agencies, most of them are based on the Police Act of 1861.Moreover, the Indian Police Act provides the following charter of "duties for the police:

1. "Obey and execute all orders and warrants lawfully issued by any competent authority.
2. Collect and communicate intelligence affecting the public peace.
3. "Prevent commission of offences and public nuisances.
4. Detect and bring offenders to justice.
5. "Apprehend all persons whom he is legally authorised to apprehend and for whose apprehension sufficient grounds exist.

"There is also a code of conduct for the law enforcement agency.[138] Procedurally, criminal law is mainly governed by the "Code of Criminal Procedure, 1973 (CrPC)" and "Indian Evidence Act 1872." However, special procedures have been prescribed from time to time, taking into account changes in legislation and in the police as an organisation. A number of special and local laws have been passed to deal with crimes emerging in the changing socio-economic scenario. One such social legislation is the "Immoral Traffic (Prevention) Act, 1956.

"The CrPC makes a distinction between cognizable and non-cognizable offences. "A cognizable offence is one under which a police officer can arrest without a warrant. The first schedule of the CrPC lists all offences in the IPC and mentions whether they are cognizable or non-cognizable.[139] It is to be noted that all offences under the IT (P) Act are cognizable.

Moreover, the process of criminal justice starts with the filling of the First Information Report (FIR). "Information given telephonically and recorded in the diary of a police station is also regarded as an FIR."[140] Section 154 of the CrPC provides the procedure to be followed by the police while recording information. "The FIR itself is not a substantive piece of evidence and can only be used to start an investigation."[141] "Criminal proceedings started against the accused on the basis of an FIR which does not contain any definite accusation amounts to an abuse of the process of the court and are liable to be quashed.[142] "In a case where the names of a few accused were not mentioned by the investigation officer despite the fact that their names were known to the informer, the accused were given the benefit of the doubt."[143] Besides above, the police are also obliged to undertake investigations in cases referred to them by a Magistrate. Further, they empowered to require the attendance of witnesses by issuing an order in writing. But they cannot make women and persons below the age of 15 years come to the police station. This has been upheld by the Supreme Court in the case of "Nandini Satpathy v. P.L. Dani."[144]

The police can examine the witnesses orally and record their statements under Section 161. They cannot force a person to make any statement that is incriminating, and any attempt to do so is a violation of the fundamental rights given in the Constitution. Moreover, the person being examined or interrogated can demand the presence of his lawyer during the period of investigation. However, the statements made to the police are not signed and cannot be used for corroboration, except to for the "purpose of contradicting a prosecution witness."[145] A person is free to make any statement of his free will and "no police officer or any other person in authority can induce, or cause the inducement of a wrongful statement." A police officer may search, or cause to be searched any premises, "if he fined any reasonable grounds to believe that such an act is a necessity" etc.

4.3.1. Special Procedure under it (P) Act, 1956

"The Act provides for Special Police Officers (SPO) to be appointed by the state government to deal with cases under this Act, especially in areas specified by the state government. The SPO shall not be below the rank of an inspector of police.[146] Moreover, the District Magistrate may empower retired police or military officers to be an SPO. Subordinate officers assist the SPO and the state government may also attach a "non-official advisory body of up to five social welfare workers including women wherever possible. For instance, the Delhi administration, vide notification F.5/67/88/Home (P)/ESTT dated 14/12/88, has appointed all ACPs working as sub-divisional police officers, SHOs and all ACPs of the crime branch, Palam Airport and the Railways as SPOs within the territory of Delhi.

There has been a special provision to deal with cases of sexual exploitation committed in more than one state, the Central Government has empowered the Trafficking Police Officer (TPO) to exercise powers and discharge functions in relation to the whole of India.[147]Arrests can be made without warrant under this Act only by an SPO or under his guidance or with his prior approval. In cases where such an arrest is made by a subordinate officer, it must be reduced to writing. In fact, a sub-inspector can make such an arrest without an order in an emergency, but he must inform the SPO at the earliest. "The SPO/TPO is empowered to enter any premises or undertake a search without a warrant and remove all the persons from there. However, the following rules must be followed.[101]

Moreover, he should have reasonable grounds to "believe that an offence under this act has been or is being committed. They must record the reasons for undertaking a search. Two or more respectable inhabitants of the area, including a woman must be present during the search.[102] The presence of a woman witness is mandatory. "Noncompliance makes the search illegal and prosecution fatal.[148] Moreover such type of search is considered to be illegal[149] and the accused is not liable for conviction under "Section 4 (1), i.e., punishment for living on the earning of prostitution.[150] Section 15 of the Act does not give arbitrary power to the SPO and it provides for immediate scrutiny of the officer's action by the magistrate, hence it is not "unconstitutional on the grounds of providing unbridled power to SPOs.[151] Several high courts have held also reiterated that the powers granted to an SPO cannot be utilised to conduct a search in disregard of elementary decencies, even when a prostitute is involved, since such an act amounts to "outraging the modesty of a woman or girl.[152]

4.3.2. The Central Bureau of Investigation (CBI)

The CBI is involved in anti-trafficking initiatives under Section 13 of the IT (P) Act in three types of cases:

1. Those referred by High Courts - here the CBI is obliged to take an action in the case/ initiate an investigation.
2. These referred by the State Government – here the CBI examines the merits of the case and states whether it wishes to take it up.
3. Anti-corruption cases that are referred directly to the CBI.

Moreover, the involvement of the CBI in relation to the IT(P)Act came after a case filed by Revati Rao in the Delhi High Court in 1999 (Cr WP 869/98). This case is related to the kidnapping of a child. It has been seen that following the failure of the local police in dealing with the case, the party moved the High Court which ordered the CBI to inquire into the matter. Still in relation to the above case, the Delhi High Court directed, the CBI in 1999, to collate and collect data relating to kidnapping cases from all states and Union Territories. The CBI has been filing status reports in the High Court since 1999. It was made the nodal agency for dealing with cases related to kidnapping for ransom, begging and trafficking for a range of exploitative purposes. After about a year of the Delhi High Court order, the Criminal Intelligence Cell was established in the CBI in 2001. It is headed by the Superintendent of Police who reports to a Deputy Inspector General and who further reports to an Inspector General of Police.

However, the CBI is not the investigative agency in all kidnapping cases. It cannot take *suo moto* action in cases; unless a particular State has given blanket permission to the CBI to investigate its cases. At present, about 14 states have given such permission to the CBI and if the CBI gives some information to a state police unit, it is not obligatory for the unit to act on it. It is also not obligatory for it to send a report to the CBI on the action taken. When the CBI receives new information, it attempts to find links with the already existing data. It also sends the information to the local police in the area where the person/gang operates. "As a result of the establishment of the Criminal Intelligence Cell, all officers above the rank of Inspector were designated Trafficking Police Officers in a notification dated 28/8/2001, under Section 13(4), IT (P) Act. To supplement the data collated by the CBI, the Bureau of Police Research and Development has been asked to research basic statistics related to (a) the time when kidnapping ordinarily takes place; (b) the average age of the kidnappers; (c) the average age of kidnapped persons; (d) the caste- wise break-up and the socio-economic profile of kidnapped persons, and so on.

Recently, "Union Cabinet approved the Draft on Trafficking of Persons (Prevention, Protection and Rehabilitation) Bill 2018.[153] "The proposed legislation addresses the issue of trafficking from the point of view of prevention rescue and rehabilitation and main provisions are as follows. "The National Investigation Agency (NIA) will act as the nodal authority for probing cases of human trafficking. The bill also proposes a punishment of life imprisonment for repeat offenders. Aggravated forms of trafficking include trafficking for the purpose of forced labour begging trafficking by administering chemical substance or hormones on a person for the purpose of early sexual maturity would carry a jail term of seven to 10 years.[154]

> "Trafficking of a woman or child for the purpose of marriage or under the pretext of marriage or after marriage would carry a punishment of at least 10 years in jail which can be extended to life imprisonment with a fine of Rs 1 lakh. The draft Bill also moots three years in jail for abetting, promoting and assisting trafficking. The proposed legislation recommends a national anti-trafficking relief and rehabilitation committee which would be headed by Secretary WCD Ministry.[155]

Moreover, the "Bill provides for interim relief immediately to victims within 30 days to address their trauma and further appropriate relief within 60 days from the date of filing of charge sheet. The NIA will receive financial aid under Nirbhaya fund for safety of women in order to set up a cell for investigating human trafficking.[156]

4.3.3. Adjudication of Law in India

Section 4 of the Cr.P.C. stipulates that all offences under the IPC as well as under other laws shall be investigated, inquired into and tried by the procedure contained in the provisions of the code. The Cr.P.C. also leaves scope for special enactments to be subjected to special procedures. The machinery for law adjudication in India is headed by the Supreme Court. There are, in each states and union territories High Courts. The judiciary in the states functions under their respective High Courts. Article 227 of the Constitution empowers the High Courts to issue orders, directions and guidelines for the general administration of the lower courts. The hierarchy of courts in India is as follows namely; (a) "The Supreme Court, (b) The High Courts, (c) Courts of Session, (d) Court of Judicial, Magistrates of First Class/ Metropolitan Magistrates, (e) Court of Judicial Magistrates of Second Class/Metropolitan Magistrates, and (f) Executive Magistrates.

Furthermore, the Supreme Court has three-fold jurisdiction. First, it has original jurisdiction over disputes between the Centre and states, and between two or more states; second, appellate Jurisdiction in Constitutional, civil and criminal matters; and third, advisory jurisdiction over matters referred to by the President of India. Besides Supreme Court, the high courts have civil, criminal and writ jurisdiction. While the session's courts have jurisdiction over all matters except writ jurisdiction. However, a death sentence passed by the session's court is subject to confirmation by the High Court. The Assistant Sessions Judges may pass any sentence under the law except for the death sentence, imprisonment for life and for a term exceeding 10 years. The courts of the Chief Judicial Magistrates/Chief Metropolitan Magistrate may pass any sentence of imprisonment of up to seven years. "The court of the Magistrate of the first class / Metropolitan Magistrate may pass a sentence of imprisonment of up to three years, or a fine of up to Rs 5000, or both. "The court of the magistrate of the second class may pass a sentence of imprisonment of up to a year, or a fine not exceeding Rs. 1000, or both.

Amendments made to the CrPC in 1973 not only ensured the independence of the judiciary, but also separated the wing of the prosecution from that of the police. Sections 24 and 25 of the Code expressly make a provision for the appointment Public Prosecutors (PPs) and Assistant Public Prosecutors (APPs). At the level of the High Court, the Central and state governments appoint the public prosecutor and one or more additional public prosecutors in consultation with the High Court. The Central government also appoints prosecutors at the district level. The state government appoints PPs and APPs at the district level either from the panel of names prepared by the District Magistrate in consultation with the sessions judge or from the regular state cadre of prosecuting officers if it exists. The basic criterion for eligibility is a standing of seven years as an advocate. The code also provides for the appointment of APPs at the district level by the state government to prosecute cases at Magistrate courts. The Central government may also make such appointment. However, "the jurisdiction of courts under the IT (P) Act is clearly mentioned in the Schedule of the Act."[157] It specifies that Magistrate' in the context mean a Magistrate upon whom power has been conferred under the specific section of the Act. Section 22 of the Act points out that, no court inferior to that of a metropolitan magistrate or a judicial magistrate of the first class is empowered to try offences under Sections 3, 4, 5, 6, 7 and 8 of the IT (P) Act.[158]

While Sections 15 (5) and 16 (2) are safeguards against the arbitrary exercise of power by SPOs and TPOs. "Magistrates have a crucial role to play in this regard. Sections 15 and 16, which refers to search without warrant and rescue of persons, have to be read in conjunction with Section 17. This says that it is for the Magistrate to decide whether to "send a rescued person to a protective home or make arrangements for her interim custody."[159] Although, the Act contains no specific provision to the effect, the Magistrate has the power to make an order for the interim "custody of rescued persons when an inquiry is needed to decide upon the matter.[160] Moreover, when there is nothing to show that the rescued person was involved in sex work and the offence was registered under Section 366 of the IPC and not under any of the provisions of IT (P) Act, "Sections 15 to 17 cannot be invoked for justifying an order remanding a woman to a state home.[161] It is to be noted that, Sub-section 5 of Section 17 provides that a Magistrate may summon a panel of five respectable persons, three of whom shall (wherever possible) be women, to assist him in discharging his functions under the section. For instance, in a case decided by the Allahabad High Court, it was held that the Magistrate may summon a panel' should be taken to mean that he must do so. Since, no panel had been constituted in the case, the judgment was held null and void."[162]

4.3.4. State Protective Homes

Protective homes run and established by state governments under four separate legislations to provide safe houses for victims of Commercial Sexual Exploitation. These are Section 21of the IT (P) Act, 1956, "The Women's and Children's Institutions (Licensing) Act, 1956 (WCIL Act), "The Orphanages and Other Charitable Homes (Supervision and Control) Act, 1960 (OCHSC Act) and "The Juvenile Justice (Care and Protection of Children) Act, 2000. According to "Section 10(b) of the Women's and Children's Institutions (Licensing) Act, 1956 (WCIL) does not apply to "any protective home established under the Suppression of Immoral Traffic in Women and Girls Act, 1956. While Section 3(b) of the Orphanages and Other Charitable Homes (Supervision and Control) Act, 1960 (OCHSC) contains the same provision. However, the homes established under both Acts can house persons who have been victims of abuse. Both the WCIL and OCHSC Acts specify laws pertaining to the licensing of institutions, including the grant and revocation of licences. The OCHSC Act, in addition specifies laws regarding the powers and functions of the board of control, the recognition of homes and the management of recognised homes. Moreover, Section 21(2) of the I T (P) Act states that after the Act comes into force, no person or no authority other than the state government shall establish or maintain any protective home. It further sets out the procedures to be adopted for issuing a license, besides specifying the period for which a license may be valid and the conditions under which it may be revoked. In addition, Article 21(2) deals with the powers of the state government in the matter of the transfer of inmates to other homes, and so on.

Recently Uttar Pradesh Government created Anti Human Trafficking Units (AHTUS). It is integrated task force to prevent and eradicate trafficking in persons especially women and children. This unit includes police officials, Women and Child Welfares Department of the State and Local NGOs. The funding for this force is provided by the Central Government. This unit is developed data based including anti-trafficking portal. In Uttar Pradesh till now 35 AHTU were formed each for number of districts; for instance, Agra Unit includes Mathura, Aligarh, Hathras and Eta.

4.4. Debate Concerning Prostitution: Legalisation and Criminalisation

As a matter of fact, trafficking for the purposes of prostitution is one of the debatable issues under the purview of women's dignity and their basic rights to be human. For instance, a debate is going on across India since a long time which compels us to think that either prostitution legalised or criminalised? In order to discuss about debate concerning legalisation and criminalization, it is very important to understand about the legalisation and criminalisation of prostitution in different countries vis-vis Indian legal system. According to Jean D'Cunha, "Three systems of prostitution-related laws have been formulated and applied in various parts of the world: the prohibitionist system, the tolerationist system and the system of legalised prostitution.[163] For her, the prohibitionist system perceives prostitution as immoral and aims at its eradication, while the tolerationist system rests on the assumption that prostitution is as old as human civilisation itself and state introduce some mechanisms of control over prostitution.[164] She also pointed out that, "the legal tradition grounded the assumption that prostitution is a necessary social evil required to safeguard women against male sexual aggression and to protect the family structure, and must hence be legalised.[165] Moreover, it has been found that, on the issue of prostitution concerning legalisation and criminalization, the world is divided into three groups namely; the first, group of countries where prostitution is banned or illegal if anyone is found to be indulged in this profession, she/he will be liable for punishment according to the establish law of the land. For instance, Afghanistan, China, Cuba, Egypt, Iran, Iraq, South Africa etc. While the second group of countries where prostitution is not a crime and government recognised it as a profession. Moreover, this profession is regularised by specific laws. For example, Argentina, Austria, Brazil, Belgium, UK, Italy, Israel etc. The third group of countries are those where prostitution is limited legal and restricted to some specific areas; for example; India, USA, Bulgaria, Australia etc.

Before discussing about legalisation and criminalisation of prostitution, it is worth to mention here about various approaches concerning prostitution. In fact, "most writers suggest that there are broadly four possible legal positions on sex work which encapsulate the range of legal options.[166] According Anuja Agrawal, "The first and most extreme of these positions is prohibition or complete criminalisation where all aspects of sex work and actors, including sex workers, are criminalised. This position assumes that all acts of prostitution are immoral and criminal.[167] She has also pointed "a second position on sex work is somewhat ambiguous and targets trafficking, pimping, procuring, soliciting and renting premises for prostitution. In the dominant version of this position all aspects of sex work are criminalised although sex workers themselves are not. This position is referred to as tolerationist or abolitionist depending upon whether it is ideologically grounded in the view that prostitution is the oldest profession; a necessary evil (tolerationist) or if it is based on the understanding that it is a form of sexual violence; women are its victims and should not be further victimized (abolitionist). Further she argues about, "A third position can be referred to as legalisation as it seeks to do away with anti-sex work laws and makes special rules regulating sex work. It is a means of regulating sex work and can vary in its forms. It is also often grounded in the views which see prostitution as the oldest profession, as a necessary evil, or as a safety valve which channelizes male sexual needs. This approach also prominently addresses concerns regarding spread of diseases particularly, sexually transmitted ones.[168]

Finally, she suggested about, "A fourth position on sex work espouses complete decriminalisation, where all special anti-sex work laws are repealed and sex work is left to be regulated by other laws applicable to all citizens. This position derives from the view of prostitution as a form of work which may be undertaken by women (or men) in different conditions; it also suggests that sex workers are not necessarily victims but agents.[169] Moreover, "when talking of legal measures to be adopted in conjunction with trafficking one may refer to measures whereby trafficking is legally regulated, for example through criminalisation or to measures whereby the law enforcement system in a country is made responsive to the problem of trafficking, or to measures whereby the victims of human rights violations are provided with effective legal remedies.[170] Therefore, it is an imperative to explore and examine various approaches related to prostitution which gives us more insight about the current issue:

1. **Criminalisation approach:** This approach refers that, prostitution is immoral therefore, it should be criminalised. Furthermore, it can be argue that, "in pursuance of this end, it bans prostitution *per se*, criminalising the activities of all categories of people involved in prostitution, i.e., brothel-keepers, pimps, procurers, clients and prostitutes.[171] Moreover, it divided into three sub-parts and these are namely; abolitionists, tolerations or crime control and illegal migration approach are as follows:
   (a) **Abolitionists Approach**[172]: "It regard prostitution as a form of exploitation and work towards strategies aimed at freeing society from prostitution. There are two groups advocating abolitionists view are the "moralists and the women's groups." The latter regard prostitution as a form of slavery which no woman would opt for whereas the moralists[173] believes that, women/persons engaged in prostitution as morally wrong or fallen' and feel that society should be denied access to this evil. They uphold the prohibition of prostitution, which would entail punishing the prostitute for soliciting clients, and so on. The women's groups, too, advocate the abolition of prostitution on the ground that it constitutes a violation

of the human rights of the women. "This approach is similar to the approach of the United Nations set forth in the 1949 UN Convention.[174]

(b) Toleration or the Crime Control Approach: The advocates of this approach view prostitution fundamentally in the context of criminality. They believe that stronger legislations and heavier punishments are required to penalise and detect traffickers so as to curb the crime. When the repressive strategy is adopted under this approach, stronger legislations and heavier punishments are recommended, so as to curb the crime. Thus, the primary aim is to combat prostitution, making the protection of the victims a secondary consideration.

(c) Illegal Migration Approach: This approach aims at regulating the illegal immigration of persons. The repressive strategy under this approach advocates stricter immigration laws, visa regulations and border controls, especially for women and children. Punishing and deporting illegal migrants also form a part of this strategy. This strategy is likely to have the impact of enhancing the power and role of middlemen, besides raising the level of corruption among the border police and immigration officials. An empowering strategy, in contrast, would reduce the power and role of the middlemen and traffickers by strengthening the migrants' rights and giving them more options.[66] "The empowering strategy, on the other hand, aims to control the crime by supporting the interests of the victims and raising their level of self-confidence.[175]

2. Labour Approach: This approach is set within the framework of the labour market, the workers' rights and their conditions of work, the areas of work that could be categorised or recognised as work, the problem of domestic unemployment, and the policies regarding migrant workers. Under this approach, a repressive strategy attempts to control the flow of migrants into the home labour market. This is likely to result in the exploitation of the illegal migrants and promote corruption in the market. An empowerment strategy, however, recognizes the contribution of the migrant labourers, regularise the rights of these workers (including migrant women in all sectors), educates the migrants about their rights, facilitates their organisation, and provides them with safe and just working conditions. This strategy strengthens the legal status and rights of the migrants, besides enhancing their efficiency and productivity in the host country. It also reduces the role of middlemen.[176]

3. **Decriminalisation Approach:** This approach regards sex work as a personal choice and aims at complete decriminalisation of voluntary sex work. It aims to protect the sex worker from exploitation or revictimisation by the state actors, especially the law enforcement agencies. Another aim is to prevent the activities of sex workers from going underground. The decriminalisation approach is sometimes divided on the lines of whether it is the sex worker or the entire sex industry that should be decriminalised, the latter being a more widely accepted from of the approach.
4. **Legalisation Approach:** The advocates of this approach regard sex work as a profession and believe that to protect sex workers from exploitative working conditions, it is important to legalise the profession. This would mean the strengthening of labour rights, and the provision of proper working conditions and better healthcare. Various strategies, including the following, are adopted under this approach; (a) Licensing, zoning and mandatory check-ups, (b) Under this approach, the empowerment strategy focuses on labour rights, women's rights and legal rights to curb exploitation. By including sex work in the economic sector, the strategy enables sex workers to lobby for a clean and healthy environment. The drawback of such legalisation is that it might result in shielding of the exploitation of sex workers. (c) The legalisation of migration is another aspect of this approach. This strategy seeks to prevent illegal migration and thus curb trafficking.

4.4.1. Criminalisation Verses Legalisation

Today, the global sex panic around sex work and trafficking has fostered prostitution law reform worldwide. While the normative status of sex work remains deeply contested, abolitionists and sex work advocates alike display an unwavering faith in the power of criminal law; for abolitionists, strictly enforced criminal laws can eliminate sex markets, whereas for sex work advocates, decriminalisation can empower sex workers.[177] As far as India is concern where prostitution is not illegal per se but activities such as pimping, maintaining brothels, prostitution in hotels and vicinity of public places are prohibited. In other words, in India, prostitution is partly legal. With the growing conscience of the society, civil society and many nongovernmental organisations demanding legalisation of prostitution in India and hence gave birth to the debate whether prostitution should be legalised or criminalised. Both the party put their views in support of their demand; for instance, those who are in support of criminalisation of prostitution in India argued that this profession reduces the dignity and sanctity of women to a mere object of sex. According to Martha Nussbaum,

> "Prostitution, we now see, has many features that link it with other forms of bodily services such as a factory worker, domestic servant, night club singer and artists. It differs from these other activities in many subtle ways, but the biggest difference consists in the fact that it is, today, more widely stigmatised. Since singer and factory workers no longer get told that they are unacceptable in polite society. Even the artist has won respect as a skilled professional. What is the difference about prostitution? Two factors stand out as sources of stigma. One is the prostitution is widely held immoral; the other is that prostitution is frequently bound up with gender hierarchy, with ideas that women and their sexuality need male domination and control, and the related idea that women should be available to men to provide an outlet for their sexual desire. The immortality view would be hard to defend today as a justification for the legal regulation of prostitution, and perhaps even for its moral denunciation. People thought prostitution was immoral because they thought prostitutes as a dangerous figure whose whole career was given over to lust. But female lust was

commonly seen as bad and dangerous, so prostitution was seen as bad and dangerous.[178]

It makes clear that as long as prostitution is stigmatized people are injured by that stigmatisation in order to criminalise prostitution. Besides, "there are various arguments that have been made to support criminalisation; firstly, prostitution involves health risk and risk of violence, secondly prostitution has no autonomy, her activities are controlled by others, thirdly, prostitution involves the invasion of one's intimate bodily space, fourthly, prostitution makes it harder for people to form relationship of intimacy and commitment, fifthly, prostitute alienates her sexuality on the market, she turns her sexual organs and acts into commodities, sixthly, the prostitutes activity is shaped by and in turn perpetuates male dominance of women, seventh, prostitution is a trade that people do not enter by choice, therefore, the bargains people make within it should not be regarded as real bargains[179]. Furthermore, in contrary to criminalisation of prostitution, there is another viewpoint which emphasizes on decriminalisation of prostitution which "would wipe out the stigma of immorality and criminality attached to prostitutes and prostitution."[180] Moreover, this view, "seeks to recognize prostitution as a legitimate business, subjecting owners and managers of prostitution establishments to business and labour laws and not to criminal law. It likewise advocates the removal of all criminal sanctions against prostitutes.[181] Still in order to support the legalisation of prostitution in India, "it is necessary to examine the arguments advanced in favour of legalisation of prostitution in the following manner, firstly, prostitution is often women's occupational choice, secondly, prostitution allows a woman freedom, financial autonomy, and the right to sexual self-determination, thirdly, prostitution facilitates unionisation of prostitutes for welfare facilities and better work conditions, fourthly, legalisation wipe out the stigma of immortality and criminality.[182]

Therefore, it can be argue that, both legalisation and criminalisation have its own pros and cons and both viewpoint may lead to some extreme which ultimately violate the basic right of the women which given by our constitution. Therefore, in my opinion, instead of criminalisation or legalisation, we should focus on legal reforms along with proper rehabilitation and provide them alternative job opportunities so that they can live better life and earn livelihood without exploitation.

To sum up this chapter, I can conclude that, the international communities have taken various steps in order to eradicate trafficking for prostitution because of gravity of the nature of the crime. At the same time various national legislation were also enacted to fight this menace. Moreover, it can be argue that, due to ineffective and lack of training of law enforcement of agencies, this problem aggravated day by day. Even though, from time to time, various strategies like repressive, empowering, and welfarist were adopted to address trafficking for prostitution. Take for instance, legal positions on prostitution in India, where repressive strategies are being adapted to in order to control the situation. It has been seen that the Immoral Traffic (Prevention) Act, 1956, provides for the arrest and removal of persons involved in the trade from public places, the prevention of soliciting and closure of brothels; punishing the wrongdoer, including punishing pimps and brothel owners; and suppressing undesirable or dangerous behaviour including punishments for soliciting, seducing and indecent behaviour. Besides repressive strategies, the empowering strategies adopted by the Indian government such as the establishment of health clinics and provision of vocational training are not up to the mark. Moreover, the welfare strategies have been adopted to provide jobs, getting sex workers married, educating the children of prostitutes, supporting and assisting the victims by keeping them in state homes, providing them with vocational training and initiating awareness programmes. However, these programmes are usually either imposed on the prostitute or lack a sense of sustainability.

India needs to adopt and implement preventive strategies, which aim at understanding the root causes providing alternatives and raising awareness especially in the rural areas. Hence, in regard to trafficking for Commercial Sexual Exploitation for prostitution must be decriminalised and the Indian Penal Code must be used more effectively against any activity that violates the fundamental rights of women. It can be argue that, appropriate mechanisms must be established for effective investigation of cases of trafficking across state and international boundaries. Furthermore, I can say that, all individuals, whether or not in sex work, have the right to determine their future, have the right to be protected from exploitation and for this the State machinery have the duty to safeguard the health and work environment of the sex worker which needs to be improved. Besides, there must be severe penalisation of persons who knowingly use the services of individuals in slavery, or individuals being physically and sexually exploited especially women and children.

NOTES

1. Isabel Borges, "The Challenges of the Current Legal Regime to Trafficking in Women" 6 *The JBSIS 5* (2009).
2. United Nations Treaty Collection (UNTC), "The International Convention for the Suppression of the Traffic in Women and Children", 1921, Geneva, *available at:* https://www.treaties.un.org. *(Last visited on July 15, 2017)*
3. United Nations Human Rights, "Convention for the Suppression of the Traffic in Persons and of the Exploitation of the Prostitution of Others", 1949, Geneva, available at: https://www.*ohchr.org. (last visited on March 10, 2017)*
4. *Supra* note 3.
5. Thomas, Sarasau Esther, "Responses to Human Trafficking in Bangladesh, India, Nepal and Sri Lanka: Legal and Policy Review" 26 United Nations Office on Drugs and Crime: New Delhi, 2011, *available at:* http://www.unodc.org/.
6. *Supra* note 5.
7. United States, Trafficking in Persons Report 2011, (Department of State, 2011) *available at*: http://www.unhcr.org.
8. *Supra* note 7.
9. *Supra* notes 5 at 27.
10. Nair, P.M., *Trafficking Women and Children for Sexual Exploitation: Handbook for Law Enforcement Agencies in India* 3 (United Nations Office on Drugs and Crime: New Delhi, 2007).
11. *Supra* note 10 at 3.
12. *Supra* note 10 at 5.
13. *Supra* note 10 at 9.
14. *Supra* note 10 at 10-12.
15. Donna, J. Guy, *White Slavery and Mothers Alive and Dead: The Troubled Meeting of Sex, Gender, Public Health and Progress in Latin America* 70 (University of Nebraska Press, London, 2000).
16. *Supra* note 1 at 6-7.
17. Paul, Knepper, *The Invention of International Crime: A Global Issue in the Making 1881–1914* 98, (Palgrave Macmillan, London, 2010).
18. Magaly Rodríguez Garcia, "The League of Nations and the Moral Recruitment of Women" 57 *International Review of Social History* 97-128 (2012).

19. Georgios Papanicolaou, "The Sex Industry, Human Trafficking and the Global Prohibition Regime: A Cautionary Tale from Greece" 11, *Trends in Organised Crime* 379-409, (2008).
20. Ethan, A. Nadelmann, "Global Prohibition Regimes: The Evolution of Norms in International Society" 44, *International Organisation* 479-526, (1990).
21. Leila, J. Rupp, *Worlds of Women: The Making of an International Women's Movement* 211-212, (Princeton University Press, NJ, 1997).
22. Jo Doezema, Who Gets to Choose? Coercion, Consent, and the UN Trafficking Protocol 10 *Gender and Development* 20-27 (2002).
23. League of Nations, Report of the Special Body of Experts on Traffic in Women and Children, (Geneva, 1927).
24. U.N. Department of International Economic & Social Affairs, Study on Traffic in Persons and Prostitutions, 1959.
25. *Supra* note 23.
26. H. Wilson, Human Merchandise: A Study of the International Traffic in Women 38 *JILI* 49 (1928).
27. *Supra* note 24 at 53
28. League of Nations, *International Conventions for Suppression of the Traffic in Women of Full Age* (Geneva, 1933).
29. *Supra* note 27.
30. Joyce Outshoorn (ed.), *The Politics of Prostitution: Women's Movements, Democratic States and the Globalisation of Sex Commerce* 1-20, (Cambridge University Press, UK, 2004).
31. Nora, V. Demleitner, "Forced Prostitution: Naming an International Offense" 18 *FILJ* 171-172 (2000).
32. *Supra* note 29
33. Mary Ann Glendon, *A World Made New: Eleanor Roosevelt and the Universal Declaration of Human Rights* 16-17, (Random House, London, 2001).
34. Gordon Brown (ed.), *The Universal Declaration of Human Rights in the 21st Century: A Living Document in a Changing World* 140-145, (Open Book Publishers, UK, 2016).
35. *Supra* note 3
36. Laura Reanda, "Prostitution as a Human Rights Question: Problems and Prospects of United Nations Action" 13 *Human Rights Quarterly* 202-228 (1991).
37. *Supra* note 3.
38. *Supra* note 3.
39. *Supra* note 3.
40. *Supra* note 3.
41. *Supra* note 3.
42. *Supra* note 3.
43. *Supra* note 3.
44. *Supra* note 3.

45. James C. Hathaway, "The Human Rights Quagmire of Human Trafficking" 49 *JILI*21 (2008).
46. *Supra* note 45 at 22.
47. Egon Schwelb, "International Conventions on Human Rights" 9, *The International and Comparative Law Quarterly* 668 (1960).
48. Supra note 47 at 668-669.
49. Suzanne Miers, *Slavery in the Twentieth Century: Evolution of a Global Problem* 127-128, (Altamira Press, New York, 2003).
50. *Supra* note 49 at 129.
51. *Supra* note 3.
52. *Supra* note 3.
53. Joyce, A. C. Gutteridge, "Supplementary Slavery Convention, 1956" 6 The *International and Comparative Law Quarterly* 449-271 (1957).
54. Hugo, Fischer, "The Suppression of Slavery in International Law: II" 3 *The International Law Quarterly* 503-522, (1950).
55. *Supra* note 54 at 504-508.
56. *Supra* note 54 at 509.
57. *Supra* note 53 at 466-467.
58. Jean Allain, *The Slavery Conventions* 358 (Lieden and Boston: Martinus Nijhoff Publishers, 2008).
59. *Supra* note 58.
60. Marley S. Weiss, "Human Trafficking and Forced Labor: A Primer" 31 *Journal of Labor & Employment Law* 1-52 (2015).
61. *Supra* note at 60.
62. International Standard on Forced Labour, ILO, *available at*: http://www.ilo.org. (last visited on March 5, 2017).
63. Supra note 60 at 40-45.
64. *Supra* note 62.
65. *Supra* note 62.
66. UNITED NATIONS: "CEDAW 19 *International Legal Materials*" 33-45(1980).
67. Sindiso Ngaba, "CEDAW: Eliminating Discrimination against Women" *Agenda: Empowering Women for Gender Equity* 81-95 (1995).
68. Kwong-leung Tang, "Internationalizing Women's Struggle against Discrimination: The UN Women's Convention and the Optional Protocol" 34, *The British Journal of Social Work* 1173-1188 (2004).
69. *Supra* note 66 at 43.
70. Valerie A. Dormady, "Status of the Convention on the Elimination of All Forms of Discrimination Against Women (CEDAW) in 1998 33, *International Legal Developments in Review* 637-643 (1999).
71. United Nations Human Rights: Office of the High Commissioner, "Committee on the Elimination of Discrimination Against Women", 1992, Geneva, *available at:* https://www.ohchr. org. (Last visited on March 10, 2017)

72. *Supra* note 71.
73. *Supra* note 71.
74. Kapstein, Ethan B, The New Global Slave Trade 85 *Foreign Affairs* 103- 115 (2006).
75. Reanda, Laura, "Prostitution as a human rights question: Problems and prospects of United Nations action" 13 *Human Rights Quarterly* 202-228 (1991).
76. Joffres, Christine., Mills, Edward, Joffres, Michel, Khanna, Tinku, Walia, Harleen, & Grund, David, "Sexual Slavery without borders: trafficking for commercial sexual exploitation in India" 7 *International Journal for Equity in Health* 7-22 (2008).
77. *Supra* note 76.
78. *Supra* note 71.
79. Laura Gomez-Mera, "The Global Governance of Trafficking in Persons: Toward a Transnational Regime Complex" 3 *Journal of Human Trafficking* 303-326 (2017).
80. J.N. Pandey, *The Constitutional Law of India* 300 (Central Law Agency, Allahabad, 45th edition, 2008).
81. Ratanlal&Dhirajlal, *Law of Crimes: A Commentary on the Indian Penal Code, 1860*, 1751, (Bharat Law House, New Delhi, 24th edn., 1998).
82. *Supra* note 80.
83. *Supra* note 80.
84. *Supra* note 80.
85. Kesar Mal v. Emperor AIR 1932 Lahore 555.
86. Ramesh v. State of Maharashtra AIR 1962 SC 1908.
87. Meena & Ors v. State (Delhi Admin.) 43 (1991) Delhi Law Times 527.
88. *Supra* note 86.
89. *Supra* note 80 at 1755 -1756.
90. The Criminal Law (Amendment) Act, 2013, (Act 45 of 1860) s. 370.
91. *Supra* note 89.
92. *Supra* note 80 at 1755 -1756.
93. The Indian Penal Code, 1860 (Act 45 of 1860), s. 372.
94. Gazette of India, Statement of Objects and Reasons Appended to Bill No. 9 of 1924 (19240.
95. Juvenile Justice (Care and Protection of Children) Act, 2015 (Act 2 of 2016), s.2.
96. *Supra* note 94.
97. Suppression of Immoral Traffic in Women and Girls Act, 1956 (Act 104 of 1956).
98. *Supra* note 96.
99. The Immoral Traffic (Prevention) Act, 1978 (Act 46 of 1978).
100. Ashok K Jain, *Socio-Economic Offences* 48-51 (Ascent Publications, Delhi, 2nd edn., 2017).
101. *Supra* note 99.

102. Shama Bai v. State of Uttar Pradesh, AIR 1959 Allahabad 57, V 46 C 22.
103. The Constitution of India, art.19.
104. Razia v. State of Uttar Pradesh, AIR 1957 All 340.
105. *Supra* note 98.
106. *Supra* note 98.
107. *Supra* note 98.
108. *Supra* note 98.
109. The Immoral Traffic (Prevention) Act, 1986 (Act 44 of 1986).
110. *Supra* note 108.
111. AIR 1996 Mysore 10.
112. AIR 1969 Gujarat 43.
113. AIR 1971 Kerala 166.
114. AIR 1989 Madras 671.
115. *Supra* note 96 at 5.
116. *Supra* note 96 at 6.
117. *Supra* note 96.
118. *Supra* note 96.
119. *Supra* note 96.
120. *Supra* note 96 at 7.
121. Ashok K Jain, *Socio-Economic Offences* 62-67 (Ascent Publications, Delhi, 2nd edn., 2017).
122. The Immoral Trafficking Prevention Act (104 of 1956) s 2 (h).
123. *Supra* note 121 at s.8.
124. AIR 1966 Mad 312.
125. *Supra* note 121 at s.9.
126. *Supra* note 120 at 72-73.
127. *Supra* note 120 at 75-76.
128. *Supra* note 121.
129. *Supra* note 121 at s. 18.
129. *Supra* note 121 at s. 19.
130. *Supra* note 121 at s. 20.
131. *Supra* note 120 at 64.
132. AIR 1997 SC 3021.
133. AIR 1969 Calcutta 544
134. AIR 1990 SC 1412.
135. The Immoral Traffic (Prevention) Act, 1956 (Act 104 of 1956).
136. *Supra* note 135.
137. *Supra* note 135.

138. Annexure-I – Code of conduct for police in India
139. The Code of Criminal Procedure, 1973 (Act 2 of 1974), s. 2(o) (l).
140. Sunil Kumar V. State of M.P AIR 1997 SC 940.
141. Madhusudan Singh V. State of Bihar AIR 1995 SC 1437.
142. State of U. P V. R.K. Srivastava (Criminal Appeal No. 323 of 1988, dated 11-8-1989 (SC).
143. B. Bhadriah V., State of Andhra Pradesh AIR 1995 SC 564
144. AIR 1978 SC 1025.
145. Section 162 Cr.P.C.
146. Section 13, Immoral Traffic Prevention Act, 1956.
147. Section 13, Immoral Traffic Prevention Act, 1956.
148. (1965) 67 Pun LR 965 (967), 1980 Cri LJ 28 (29) (Goa).
149. AIR 1964 Punj 436 (438), 1964 (2) Cri LJ 455.
150. 1973 Mad LW (Cri) 23 (23, 24).
151. 1974 Cri LJ 1337 (1340).
152. 1971 Cri LJ 952, AIR 1962 Mad 31 (35).
153. Editorial, "Trafficking of Persons (Prevention, Protection and Rehabilitation) Bill 2018", *The Economics Times*, 28 February, 2018.
154. *Supra* note 153.
155. *Supra* note 153.
156. *Supra* note 153.
157. Annexure – II for Schedule.
158. *Supra* note 149.
159. 1973 All Cri R 321 (323).
160. AIR 1959 All 206 (208) (DB).
161. (1991) 2 Cri LC 6 (9) (DB) (Bom).
162. 1963 All LJ 894 (898, 900 to 902).
163. Jean D'Cunha, "Prostitution Laws: Ideological Dimensions and Enforcement Practices" 27 *Economic and Political Weekly* 34- 44 (1992).
164. *Supra* note 155 at 34-35.
165. *Supra* note 155 at 34-35.
166. Anuja Agrawal, "Situating the Law on Prostitution/Sex Work in India" 2 *Indian Sociological Society* 3-20 (2018).
167. *Supra* note 158 at 5-6.
168. *Supra* note 158 at 5-6.
169. *Supra* note 158 at 5-6.
170. Savita Bhatt, *Women and Human Rights* 197-198 (Altar Publishing House, New Delhi, 2010).
171. *Supra* note 155 at 34.

172. Pravin Patkar, Preeti Patkar & Monica Sakrani, *Trafficking and Commercial Sexual Exploitation – International Conventions, Laws and Policy* 10 -18 (Anti Traffciking Centre (Prerna), Mumbai, 2003).
173. *Supra* note 163 at 20.
174. UN Convention, *Convention for the Suppression of the Traffic in Persons and of the Exploitation of the Prostitution of Others* (UN, 1949).
175. Global Alliance Against Traffic in Women, *Public Perceptions and Responses to Human Trafficking* (GAATW, Bangkok, 2019).
176. *Supra* note 159 at 81.
177. Prabha Kotiswaran, "Born unto Brothels: Toward a Legal Ethnography of Sex Work in an Indian Red-Light Area" 33 *Law & Social Inquiry* 579-629 (2008).
178. Martha C Nussbaum, *Sex and Social Justice* 280-288 (Oxford University Press, New York, 1999).
179. *Supra* note 169 at 288-297.
180. *Supra* note 155 at 34.
181. *Supra* note 155 at 34-35.
182. *Supra* note 155 at 42-43.

Chapter - 5

Immoral Trafficking for Commercial Sexual Exploitation among Women of Bedia Community of Agra District: Empirical Study and Analysis of Data

Agra was developed in 1475 by Badal Singh and it was mentioned in "Mahabharata" as "Agraban". It was considered to be twin city of Mathura but when Sikandar Lodhi chooses Agra as his capital then this city received further prominence in this region. But in 1526, Babar defeated Ibrahim Lodhi in "First Battle of Panipat" subsequently he captured Agra and he put the foundation of Mughal Empire in India. Agra is known for Taj Mahal across world and it is among the "Seven Wonder of the World". Besides Taj Mahal, this city has many other monuments which are symbols of Mughal architecture. During the regime of Akbar, Jahangir and Shahajahan, this city was on peak and became a prominent centre for commerce, arts, culture, learning etc. While in 16th and 17th century, Agra witness the zenith of Mughal architecture and during this period Taj Mahal built by Shahajahan as a symbol of love. Nowadays, Agra is well known tourist and commerce centre, annually lakhs of foreign as well domestic tourist used to visit this city. Take for instance, most of the foreign heads of the government or state who visited India, their visit only completed with the visits to this city. Moreover, Agra is known for leather industry and a famous sweet i.e. "Petha".

For the sake of clarity and precision, I shall divide the present chapter into three parts. In part I, I will analyse the data for this study which was collected from courts, police stations, state home and "victims of commercial sexual exploitation" as well as women of Badia community. The facts and figures collected from the courts and police stations in Agra district are covered in this part i.e. law enforcement in Agra district. In part II, I will examine the interactions with the inmates, and officials of the state home in Agra district. Part III, covers the facts related to women of Bedia community indulged in prostitution.

5.1. Law Enforcement in Agra District

Table 5.1: Magnitude of crimes against women in Agra (2002-2006)

S.N.	Year	Agra Urban	Agra Rural	Registered Total Crime
1.	2014	507	329	836
2.	2015	513	233	746
3.	2016	289	214	503
4.	2017	163	108	271
5.	2018	547	178	722

Source: D.I.G., Office, Agra Division.

Table 5.1 shows that crime statistics from 2014 to 2018, there has been an increasing trend of crimes against woman in urban area while decreasing trend in rural areas. Further it is found that in the urban areas crime trend is increasing then decreasing then again increasing. It is also noted that total number of registered crimes against women was lowest in 2017 i.e. 271 cases out of them 163 cases registered from urban areas while 108 cases registered from rural areas.

Table 5.2: Crime Against Women in Agra District, 2014 -2018

S.N.	Type of Crime	2014	2015	2016	2017	2018
1.	IT (P) Act	3	4	4	5	4
2.	Kidnapping & Abduction	106	94	72	103	85
3.	Outraging Modesty	106	83	55	85	88
4.	Rape	57	33	29	36	39
5.	Murder	10	15	10	14	8
6.	Suicide	28	36	26	31	31
7.	Torture for Dowry	306	326	163	271	217

8.	Obscene acts	114	82	55	80	177
9.	Chain Snatching	33	40	32	46	35
10.	Dowry Death	59	49	53	72	38
	Total	**822**	**762**	**499**	**743**	**722**

Source: D.I.G., Office, Agra Division.

Table 5.2 shows that in 2016, total crime against women was lowest (499) while in 2014; the crime against women was highest (822). However, the data shows a trend of decreasing in number of dowry death cases from 2014 to 2018 and at the same time an increase was reported in incidences of chain snatching and acts of obscenity. Further the crimes under IT(P) Act was almost constant between this period.

The data collected from the courts in Agra revealed certain trends relating to the areas and police stations where cases were filed, the use of specific sections of the IT(P)Act, and the orders issued under these sections. The offences recorded were most often under "Sections 3 (keeping a brothel or allowing premises to be used as a brothel), 4 (living on the earning of prostitution), 5 (procuring, inducing or taking a person for prostitution), 6 (detaining a person in premises where prostitution is carried out) and 8 (soliciting or seducing for the purpose of prostitution)".[1]

The police stations from where cases under the IT (P) Act were filed between 2014 and 2018 in the courts whose records were examined during this study are mentioned in Table 5.3.

Table 5.3: Police Station Wise Breakup of Cases Examined in the Courts in Agra

S.N.	Police Stations	Number of Cases
1.	Chatta	6
2.	Jagdishpura	1
3.	Kotwali	1
4.	Sadar	1
5.	Sikandara	4
6.	Shahganj	1
7.	Tajganj	5
8.	Fatehabad	1
	Total	**20**

Source: Field Survey.

Table 5.3 shows that the highest number of cases was reported from Chatta (6) followed by Tajganj (5) and Sikandara (4) police station respectively. The distribution of cases over a wide range of police stations allowed the study of the patterns and nature of cases specific to some areas and also allowed the comparison of cases from different areas. Specific observations have been made from the files read at the Chatta, Sikandra, Kotwali & Tajganj police stations in addition to the files read in the courts. Statistics collected from courts corresponding to the Chatta, Sikndra, Kotwali & Tajganj police stations in the Agra reflected that a majority of cases were filed from Chatta, Sikandra, & Tajganj police stations and by the Special Cell.

Figure 5.1: Section-wise Breakup of Cases

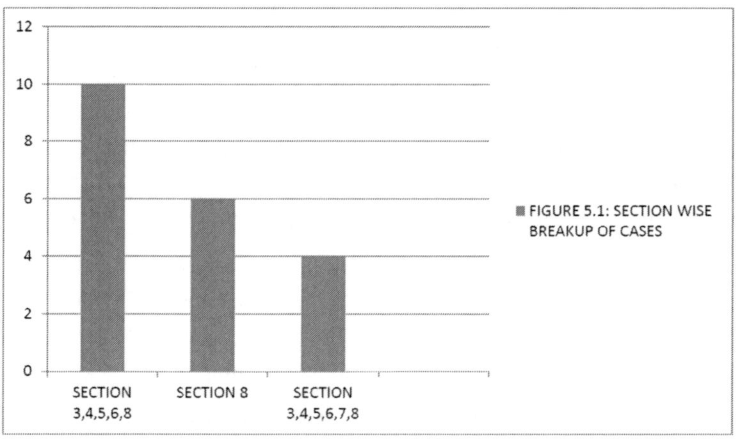

Source: Field Survey.

A majority of the cases from Agra districts was filed using Sections 4 and 8 of the Act. Maximum cases were filed under Sections 4, 5 and 8 of the Act. These sections pertain to "punishment for living on the earnings of prostitution procuring, inducing or taking persons for prostitution and seducing or soliciting for prostitution".[2] According to some lawyers interviewed, the Act has been used in a limited manner. Only Sections 3, 4, 5, 6, 7 and 8 have been used, while "Section 9 (seduction of a person in custody)" and Section 18 ("closure of brothel and eviction of offenders from the premises") have not. One lawyer pointed out that Section 3 (keeping a "brothel or allowing premises to be used as a brothel") could be implemented effectively only if supplemented with Section 18. Most of these cases relate to brothels in areas not commonly recognised as red-light areas. These brothels were run in residential flats, houses, hotels, and so on.

The police often act on a tip-off. They make phone calls to the agency managing the call girls or pay the manager or the co-worker of a sex worker, posing as prospective clients. In such cases, the sex workers are charged under Section 8, while the managers, pimps or brothel owners are charged under Section 4 or 5, or both. Such raids are common in non red-light areas, but not in red-light areas, as data collected from the Tajganj police station show. The Procedure to be followed by the police is laid down under Section 15 of the ITPA. It is vital to note the widespread use of Section 8 by the police, makes the accused persons mostly female. Also, the interpretation of the section by the judiciary and the police literally criminalises prostitution. This is borne out amply by the judgement of a first class magistrate, according to whom the main components of the section are:

1. There must be a woman who is either by way of words or by making wilful exposure of her person or by using gestures attracts the attention of a person for the purpose of prostitution.
2. That woman must be sitting or standing in a public place or must be in the sight of the public person in general.
3. She must be doing the aforesaid actions, i.e., the seducing or soliciting for the purpose of prostitution and for the purpose of earning her livelihood.

Figure 5.2 shows that 75% of arrest occurred in the red light areas, 5% of arrest made from bus stops and rest of arrest occurred from hotels, guest houses, flats and houses. Moreover, most of the arrests under Section 8 occur in red light areas but this area comes under a develop market and residential place. This too reflects the fact that most cases under Section 7 relate to women caught for 'soliciting in public places'. The view of most lawyers interviewed was that the IT(P) Act is targeted primarily at regulating sex work. They felt that the aim of the legislation is to eliminate the sex trade and to reform sex workers. Only two of those interviewed said that the legislation could be used to deal with trafficking in addition to sex work.

Figure 5.2: Localities Where Offences Occur

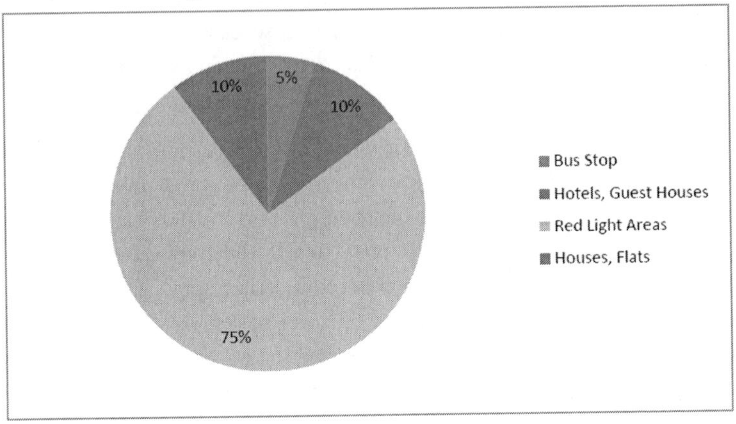

Source: Field Survey.

Figure 5.3: Distribution of the Sections Used in Orders Passed

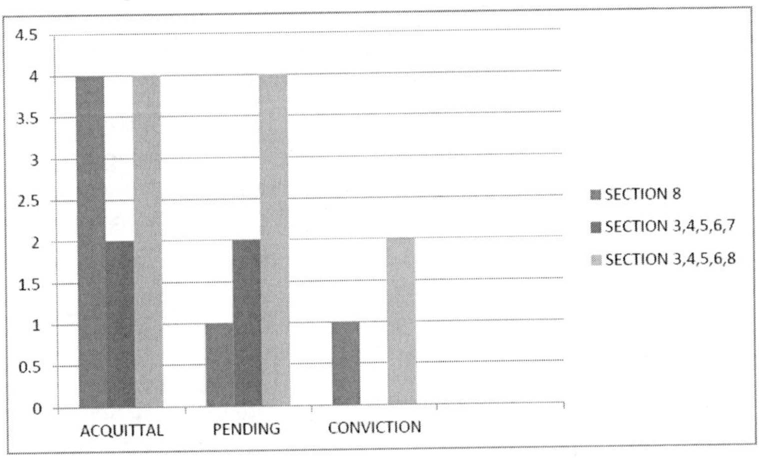

Source: Field Survey.

This graph shows that the distribution of the sections used in orders passed in relation to cases filed from the Agra district. The majority of the 10 acquittals and 3 convictions were under Sections 4,5,8 of the 20 case files examined, 6 were registered under Section 8 of the Act and 10 under Sections 3,4,5 and 6 of the Act. Section 7 of the Act was used in 4 cases. There were 3 convictions, of which 1 was only under Section 8 of the Act that stipulates "punishment on first conviction as imprisonment for a term which may extend to six months, or fine up to Rs 500 or both. And on second conviction as imprisonment extending to one year and fine up to Rs 500". There is a gender bias in this section as shown by the fact that if the offender be a man, the punishment is imprisonment for a period of not less than seven days and up to three months. There were 3 convictions under Sections 3, 4, 5, 6 and 8. In most of the cases the accused were convicted but released on account of the imprisonment undergone during the course of the trials. Not a single accused as per the cases examined was ordered as Proclaimed Offenders (PO) under 82 and 83 of the Cr.PC., 1973.

As per the provisions of the sections, a proclaimed "offender is a person against whom a warrant has been issued and who, a court has reason to believe (whether after taking evidence or not) is absconding or concealing himself so that such warrant cannot be executed. Under such circumstances, the court can publish a written proclamation requiring the person to appear at a specific place at a specific time not less than 30 days from the date of publishing such a proclamation". One of the accused was discharged because there was not sufficient ground for proceeding against them under section 227, Cr PC. The accused was also discharged under section 249 Cr.P.C., 1973 in certain cases where the complainant was absent on the day fixed for the hearing in a cognisable offence. The Magistrate in his discretion may before the framing of the charge discharge the accused. There were 10 acquittals for the reason that follows:

1. Untrustworthy witness: This was the case, especially, in the context of the Chatta police station. The same decoy customer was a witness in more than one case. In a particular instance the court observed that the decoy customer was a witness in over two other cases and he was said to be known to the Inspector of the particular police station.
2. Witness turning hostile: Public witnesses and decoy customers often turned hostile. In a particular case, a woman witness deposed that she was not a witness to the offence. There were cases where the witnesses were not sure as to who the decoy customer was. In cases where the witness or the complainant was the rescued woman, they did not return after being

repatriated to the place of occurrence of offence to attend to their cases or court hearings. The absence of the prosecutrix was the main cause for the failure of cases prior to 2004.

3. Lack of corroboration: In a few cases the public witnesses were not able to corroborate that the signed currency notes given by the decoy customer to the accused for the purpose of carrying out raids were the same as the ones given by the police during those raids.
4. Witness untraceable: In several cases, the public witness was not traceable and therefore, could not be examined. In a particular case from the South district the prosecution took four years and could examine only two witnesses, both of whom were from the police.
5. Discrepancy in evidence: The statements of public witnesses and the police being vastly different was another reason for acquittal. According to the police, a major problem faced by them is that defence lawyers confuse the police constables during cross-examination.
6. Procedural problems: Often cases fall through because the police fail to follow the provisions under IT (P) Act and CrPC. In cases where the decoy customer is from the police, the evidence doesn't stand because he is likely to be in favour of the prosecution. The court, in a particular judgement[3] wherein the decoy customer had sexual intercourse with the prostitutes, stated that the conduct of the investigation was very reprehensible and that 'instead of suppressing immoral traffic the investigation encouraged it'. It ordered that the charges against the girls be quashed.
7. Failure to include a public representative in the raid party is one of the procedural lapses. In some cases, the police clearly stated that 'nobody from the adjacent house was called to be a witness because we were in a hurry. Despite that fact that there were women staffs in the hotel, they were not asked to join the raid, in some cases.
8. Eyewitness: In some cases, the prosecution evidence was closed because they were unable to examine the eyewitness, despite several attempts.

9. Absence of SPO: In some cases, examined, the reason for acquittal was that the Special Police Officer was not present during the raid. As per section 13(2) of the Act, all offences of the Act are to be dealt with by a Special Police Officer (SPO) not below the rank of an Inspector of Police. In other cases, the officer conducting the raid was said to have been authorised by an SPO, but the prosecution was unable to produce such orders in court. In cases where the officer conducting the raid was not an SPO but authorised by the SPO to conduct the raid without warrant then the raid could be legal but in some cases the prosecution was not able to produce such orders in court. According to the Act Section 14 arrest without warrant may be made only by the SPO or an officer not below the rank of a Sub Inspector, by authorising him with a written order unless the circumstances did not permit the time for such an order.
10. Absence of women officer/constable: by the courts the absence of a woman constable or officer in the raid team made the raid illegal. According to section 15 (6A) of the Act, "the officer making a search under this section, shall be accompanied by at least two women police officers, and where any woman or girl removed under sub section 4 is required to be interrogated, it shall be done by a woman police officer and if no woman police officer available, the interrogation shall be done only in the presence of a lady member of a recognised welfare institution or organisation."

In other words, 80% of cases selected at random were filed under Section 8. In 30% cases section 8 was used by itself while in the remaining 70% cases it was used with other sections. This goes against the main purpose of the Act, which is to prevent the exploitation of women by procurers, pimps, traffickers, brothel owners and so on. Given that section 8 of the Act does not pertain to the trafficking of persons, these figures suggest that a majority of cases filed under the I.T. (P). Act only serve to criminalize the sex workers position. Police raids or arrests made under Section 8 were found to be predominantly of two types:

First, the police receive information about women soliciting at a particular place or the name or number of an agency or person who provides girls for prostitution. In the former situation, the police reach the spot with a bogus customer who approaches the sex worker who is soliciting for clients. The bogus customer strikes a deal and pays the sex worker some money. The currency notes used in the transaction are signed by the S.P.O. beforehand. In the latter case, the police call the agency or person as a prospective client, set up a time and place for meeting the sex worker, and proceed as described before. After the deal between the bogus customer and sex worker is struck, the police wait until the deal is struck between the manager and the bogus customer, before making arrests. The accused in these cases are always women sex workers, and pimps and managers, if they are involved. The cases are registered either solely under Section 8, or under Sections 8 and 4, or under Sections 3, 4, 5, 6, 8 Section 7 is rarely used.

Second, cases of this type were found only in files pertaining to the Kashmiri Bazar police station. The police are usually informed by a complainant (passerby, usually non-police) that while crossing Kashmiri Bazar, they came across some women from the *kothas* who used dirty words and vulgar actions to solicit for clients on the streets. In such cases, the police go back to the spot with the complainant, ask him to walk past the kothas and if they witness something similar to the act described, they arrest the women under Section 8.

It is to be noted that all the cases filed under Section 8 at the Chatta police station state the place of occurrence to be Kashmiri Bazar. In both first and second raids, the police or complainant accuses the women of vulgarity, on the basis of actions such as, 'taking a deep breath while standing at the bus stop' or 'pulling the complainant by his arm towards the kotha or saying that 'she would make him forget his wife. Additionally, most of these cases are based on a 'trap witness. According to "Section 133 of the Indian Evidence Act, 1872, an accomplice shall be a competent witness against an accused person; and a conviction is not illegal merely because it proceeds upon the uncorroborated testimony of an accomplice". "Section 114 (b) states that an accomplice is unworthy of credit, unless he is corroborated in material particulars". "The evidence of a trap witness can be admissible if it satisfies two conditions. First, the statement of the approver (trap witness) has to be credible. Second, the corroboration of the approvers evidence has to be of such a nature as to connect the (other) accused with the crime. In cases where the person is only an accomplice by implication or in a secondary sense, his evidence does not require the same amount of corroboration as that of the person who is an actual participator with the principal offender".

In some cases, in the Sikandra, Chatta and Tajganj police stations, the decoy customer, who was asked to only make the deal, was found in a semi-dressed state with the sex worker, who too was in a semi -dressed state, when the raid took place. This raises the question of the role and limitations of decoy customers. Are they merely police accomplices by implication or real accomplices in the offence? Arrests have also been made in case of sexual intercourse between consenting adults in private rooms, since IT (P) Act makes soliciting in a public place illegal. It appears that these arrests primarily serve the purpose of satisfying the voyeuristic appetite of the police personnel involved in the operations and only exploit and abuse the 'accused' further.

A total of 6 cases were read under Section 8 of the Act from the Sikandra, Chatta and Tajganj polish stations of Agra districts. Of these, 4 cases occurred in Kashmiri Bazar brothels, which are within the jurisdiction of the Chatta Police Station. Not a single case examined was filed under Section 9 of the Act, which deals with 'seduction of a person in custody'. The rank of the Investigating Officer was consistently and clearly mentioned only in the files of the courts in the Agra district. In the 20 cases examined from Agra district the Investigating Officer was of the rank of an Inspector in 85 % of the cases, and of the rank of Sub Inspector in the rest.

The observations about witness lists is based on the data collected from the court files examined Ideally, a 'raid party must include female police personnel, and arrest must be made in the presence of public witnesses, a medical professional and some residents of the area. However, in the cases read during the research, on an average, the ratio of police personnel to non-police witnesses was 8:2. In many cases, there was only one public witness, and in some cases, there was no public witness at all.

The police remand letters sent by the Station House Officer (SHO) to the courts reflect a considerable bias against the sex worker, who is considered a morally deprived individual. This is reflected in statements which describe such persons as 'a habitual sex worker who operates in a residential area where respectable citizens reside, or 'has left her husband and is now living with co-accused as his concubine... she is a very dangerous lady who is spoiling the life of well settled families. They also show a lack of understanding of legislation. They have statements, such as 'the accused and the co-accused procured beautiful and young girls in the illegal trade of prostitution and indulged in nefarious activities of illegal prostitution. But these statements are not linked with the use of the appropriate sections.

While examining the cases in Agra the researcher found that the police did not make use of the appropriate sections while filing the charges in the F.I.R. In a particular case registered at the Chatta police station, the police claimed that the accused 'was doing the business of prostitution and buying and selling girls yet failed to use the relevant IPC sections, such as 366, 366A, 366B. In a case registered against a pimp, manager/owner and two sex workers at Chatta police station, the police used Sections 4, 5, 8 of the IT(P) Act. Though the police stated that the accused had been arrested in similar cases earlier and was facing trial and that the two main accused were 'notorious criminal and have been arrested by the crime branch for committing similar offences, and are making their livelihood on illegal trafficking of women, they failed to use the relevant IPC sections. None of the four accused was convicted. Two of them died, one was discharged and one became a proclaimed offender.

Table 5.4: Time Taken by Courts for Orders in Agra District

S.N.	Number of Years	Sections 3,4,5,6	Section 8	Sections 3,4,5,6,7	Sections 3,4,5,6,8	Sections 3,4,5,7,8
1.	0 to 5 Years	0	1	0	4	2
2.	5 to 10 Years	0	3	0	2	0
3.	10 to 15 Years	0	1	0	0	0
4.	15 to 20 Years	0	0	0	0	0
5.	Above 20 Years	0	0	0	0	0

Source: Field Survey.

Table 5.4 shows that one of the cases filed under section 8 of the Act was pending for 10 years and another filed under sections 3, 4, 5, 6, 8 of the Act for more than 10 years at the time of the research. Presently the Act does not provide any guidelines for the completion of the cases under a specified time period. In the cases from four polish stations of Agra district, the maximum numbers of accused were under sec 8 or when sec 8 is used with other sections. This is illustrated in the table below:

Table 5.5: Number of Accused per Case under Various Sections in Agra District

S.N.	Number of Accused Per Case	Sections 3,4,5,6	Section 8	Sections 3,4,5,6,7	Sections 3,4,5,6,8	Sections 3,4,5,6,7,8
1.	0 to 3	0	0	0	1	0
2.	4 to 7	0	0	0	4	2
3.	8 to 11	0	0	0	3	2
4.	12 to 15	0	6	0	2	0
5.	16 to 19	0	0	0	0	0
6.	20 onwards	0	0	0	0	0

Source: Field Survey.

Table 5.5 shows that the maximum numbers of accused are arrested under Section 8. Out of a total of 20 accused in cases from the Agra district, 70% were female and 30% were male.

Table 5.6: Cases Registered from 2014 -2018 under IT (P) Act in Various Sections

S.N.	Year	Section 8	Sections 3,4,5,6,8	Sections 3,4,5,6,7,8	Total Cases
1	2014	2	1	0	3
2	2015	1	2	1	4
3	2016	1	2	1	4
4	2017	2	1	2	5
5	2018	0	4	0	4
	Total	**6**	**10**	**4**	**20**

Source: Field Survey.

Table 5.6 shows that there has been an increase in the number of cases registered in the Agra during 2014 to 2018. It has been found that the cases under Sections 3,4,5,6 & 8 are 50% which significantly greater in number than those under Section 3, 4, 5 and 7 of the IT (P) Act i.e. 20%.

Broadly the cases can be categorised under two heads namely; cases that are exclusively under Section 8 and cases under Sections 3, 4, 5, 6 & 7. Usually Sections 3,4,5,6 IT (P) Act are coupled with certain sections of the IPC. These are Sections 109, 323, 342, 354, 363, 365, 366, 372, 376, 415, 506, 34 and 120B. While examining the cases in Agra the researcher found that the police did not make use of the appropriate sections while filing the charges in the F.I.R. In a particular case registered at the Chatta police station, the police claimed that the accused 'was doing the business of prostitution and buying and selling girls yet failed to use the relevant IPC sections, such as 366, 366A, 366B. Even not in a single case the police fail to use appropriate IPC sections, which should be coupled with IT (P) Act.

Cases under Section 8

As a researcher, I have examined 6 cases registered under section 8 during 2014 to 2018 out of these cases, 1 ended in convictions and 2 in acquittal. The status of the rest was unknown as on 17/11/2018. After analysis, I found that these cases follow a general pattern; first, the complainants are always male and who were residents of Kashmiri Bazar, Sikandra and Basai or employed there or are passers-by. The statement of the complainant is usually to the effect that a woman standing at the place of offence harassed or abused him and that the police should take the necessary legal action against her. All the case files mention that the accused was later arrested at the place of occurrence of the offence when the complainant, accompanied by the police went back to the site and the accused behaved in the manner described by the complainant in front of the police. The consideration usually mentioned for sexual services offered by the accused ranges from Rs 200 to Rs 500.

Interestingly in none of the cases resulting in conviction did the witness list include a public witness or the panchnama in the case file. The accused were all women and most of them pleaded guilty. The statement confessing guilt was usually to the effect that the accused

used to sing and dance in the kotha and that lack of customers and the fact that being uneducated she had no other means of sustaining herself and her family had forced her into prostitution. The accused usually pleads guilty and asks forgiveness.

Another characteristic feature of these cases is the brief period of investigation. The time taken for the police to take these cases to the court and for the court to try them is very short. The investigation by the police in 60% of the cases is completed within a period of 15 days. Interestingly, a few cases were submitted in court on the same day or the day after they were reported. The reason the police contends is that they caught the accused red-handed and the accused confessed guilt.

Highlights

1. The complainants are always men and the accused always women.
2. The place of occurrence of offence and the residence of the accused is the same.
3. The statement of the complainant follows a pattern.
4. The complainants are passersby, employed at Chatta, Sikandra, kotwali or residents of surrounding areas.
5. The witnesses are the complainant and the police. There is an absence of independent corroboration.
6. The convictions are mostly based on the confessional statements of the accused. It is not clear whether these women are told that they are not obliged under law to make any statement and that they have a right to remain silent and that any statement made in front of the magistrate is admissible as evidence against them.
7. The accused mostly site poverty as the cause for choosing prostitution as a means of earning a livelihood.
8. 60% of the cases were investigated within a period of 15 days.
9. The usual punishment in most of the cases is imprisonment for 5 days and fine of Rs 500.

Prostitution is not a criminal offence under the IT (P) Act and its main objective is to prevent trafficking of persons for the purpose of prostitution. However, as indicated by the cases researched, women sex workers seem to be the prime target of the IT (P) Act in reality. Moreover, cases of soliciting are primarily filed from red-light areas, showing a bias against these women. Not a single of the cases researched was against a male, though there are many men offering sexual services in this area, as stated by some medical practitioners from Kashmiri Bazar.

Cases under Sections 3, 4, 5, 6 and IPC

Out of the 26 cases registered at the various police stations in Agra during the period of research. However, as a researcher I could investigate only 20 of the cases out of them 10 cases, i.e. 50% were under Sections 3,4,5,6 & 8. The police usually take cognizance of such cases on receiving a complaint from a public person or on their own. They then form a 'police party and plan a rescue operation'. The police party raids the brothel and takes into custody children and those who appear to be minors and those who express their willingness to come out of the flesh trade. They also arrest or detain those persons who are accused of maintaining the brothel, living on the earnings of the prostitution of others, procuring a person for the purpose of prostitution or detaining someone at such premises. The statements of the rescued persons are recorded and presented before the First-Class Magistrate at the civil court accompanied by a request for an order to the state home to take the rescued persons into protective custody. A medical examination of those rescued is carried out by a registered medical practitioner as per the procedure established under Section 15 (5A) of the Act. Those who are above 18 are sent to the Protective Home and minors are placed under the protective custody of the Observation Home for Girls (OHG).

The girls are brought to court whenever necessary for recording their statements under Section 164 of the CrPC or for a decision on their custody. The usual procedure is to send minors back to their native village if they are willing to go, after a social inquiry about their family environment conducted by the probation officer. In cases where the court orders for the detention of the person in protective custody under

Section 17 of the IT (P)A, she/he is provided with vocational training or education as the case may be, considering his /her best interests.

Demographic Details

Only women and girls are rescued under IT (P) Act and most of them are trafficked from West Bengal, followed by Nepal and Andhra Pradesh. Persons trafficked from these areas account for 70% of all those trafficked from within India. Other states from where persons are trafficked are Uttar Pradesh, Karnataka, Bihar, Rajasthan, Tamil Nadu and Assam. However, women and girls from Nepal account for 14% of the total number of cases reported under this category.

To be more specific, the cases examined for this study show that 33% and 6% of those trafficked are from 24 Parganas and Kolkata (West Bengal) respectively and 10% from Chittoor (Andhra Pradesh). Those trafficked from Bihar are mostly from Muzaffarpur. The other areas with a high incidence of such cases are Azamgarh (Uttar Pradesh), Anantapuram and Nellore (Andhra Pradesh), Barpeta (Assam), Hugli, Nadiya, Sakada, Lal Bazar and Howrah (West Bengal), Latur (Maharashtra) and Nepal. These areas have been represented as 'others in Figure 5.5.

Figure 5.4: Origin of Trafficking Victims

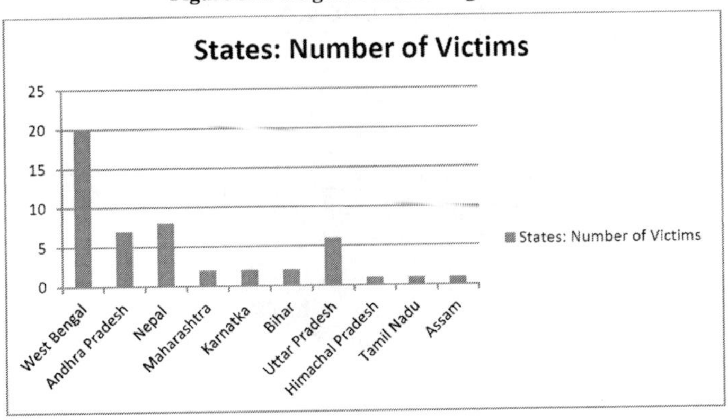

Source: Field Survey.

Figure 5.5: Districts to which Trafficking Victims Belong

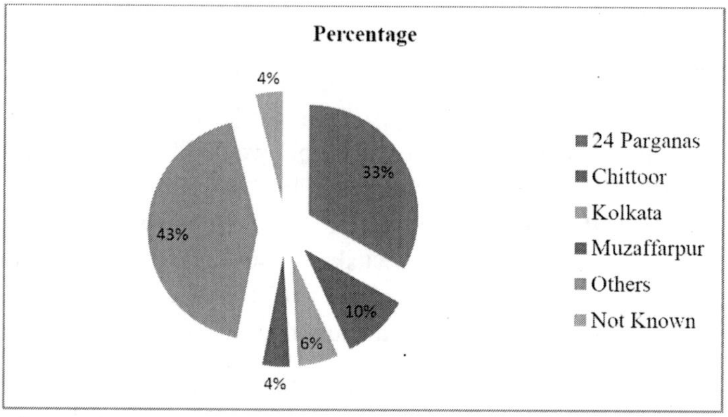

Source: Field Survey.

According to police records, 33% of the girls fall within the age group of 1-16 and this group come under the category of 'children as per Section 2 (aa) of the IT (P) Act and 18% are between 17 and 18, minors under Section 2 (b). Most of the women rescued are within the age group of 19-25 and are majors under section 2 (ca).

Figure 5.6: Age of Trafficking Victims

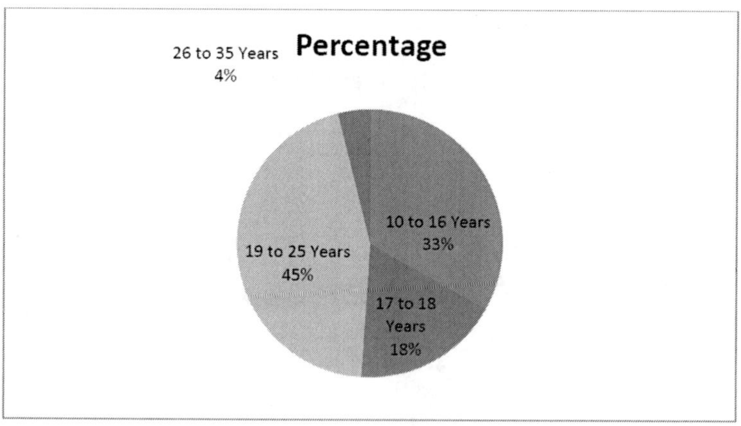

Source: Field Survey.

The age reported in the files is that mentioned by the victims. In most cases there was no medical certificate to corroborate this. Eleven of those rescued were married, and 13 unmarried, while the marital status of 27 was not known. The place of occurrence of offence in these cases is always recorded as the kothas in Kashmiri Bazar and Sikandra. There seems to be no effort to include the transit areas, places of origin or the places where the victims are detained immediately after arrival at Agra as places of occurrence of offences. There is no attempt on the part of the police to trace all the actors in the process of trafficking. Their targets are the brothel owners, managers and pimps, who are the last link in the chain.

The victims of trafficking come from an economically backward background. They are mostly lured with prospects of lucrative jobs in cities like New Delhi and Kolkata. Traffickers usually target those who are vulnerable not only by virtue of their economic status, but also difficult circumstances like widowhood, desertion by spouse, proposed forced marriage and a tragedy in the family. Most of the girls trafficked from West Bengal are first brought to Kolkata from their native villages. Similarly, girls from Nepal are first persuaded to shift to Kathmandu. Then they are tricked into traveling to Delhi with excuses like non-availability of jobs in Kolkota, better options in Delhi and so on. When persuasion does not work, threats are used or chemicals administered. Railway stations situated in and around the native place of the trafficked are crucial hunting grounds for the traffickers.

In Andhra Pradesh, it is women or girls who are already in the sex trade, who lure others from their own village or neighbouring villages. Sometimes they befriend the victims' family and bring her to Delhi, Bombay, Indore, Jaipur and Agra with the help of others involved in the racket. In some cases, relatives act as traffickers. In others, the victims are duped with the promise of marriage or under the illusion that they are being taken to metropolitan cities to look after children. Immediately after they arrive in metropolitan cities, the girls are most often kept under cover in lodges and hotels. These hotels and lodges and rural Agra like Dauki, Fatehabad and Shamshabad and border area of Uttar Pradesh with Madhya Pradesh and Rajasthan are business points for the sale and purchase of men, women and children for commercial sexual exploitation.

From these locations women and girls are sold to 'Kothas for prices ranging between Rs 20, 000 and Rs 100,000. They are beaten and starved by the 'Kotha owners' until they succumb to the demands of the owners. Managers and other sex workers in the 'kotha' also use threats and physical violence to force them into prostitution. They turn up the volumes of TVs, and so on, to drown the cries of the victims. They also give the girls instructions on how to answer the police and hide them in basements and other places at the time of police raids and rescue operations.

Usually, the traffickers or procurers sexually abuse the girls before selling them off. Figure 5.7 shows the relationship between the trafficker and the trafficked. In 70% of the cases, the trafficker is unknown to the trafficked while in 18%, the trafficker is a family friend or someone from the native or neighbouring villages and in 4% he/she is a distant relative.

In none of the 51 cases read was there any mention of the initial trafficker in the list of accused, even though the trafficked person could have identified the trafficker in at least a few of the cases. In all the cases read, the accused were the brothel owners, managers, pimps and other helpers in the brothel.

Figure 5.7: Relationship between Traffickers and Victims

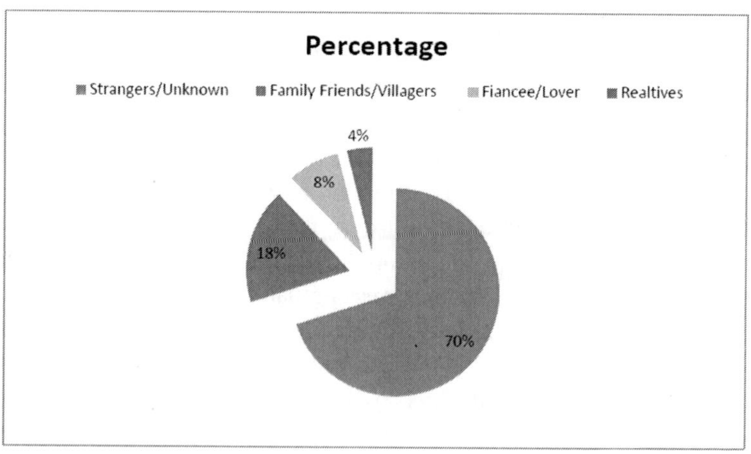

Source: Field Survey.

The period of investigation in this category of cases is quite long. In 20 (39%) cases out of 51 the police investigation lasted between 3 and 6 months. In 15 cases, the investigation took 61 to 90 days. In 7 cases (14%) the investigation was completed within 60 days, while in 6 cases investigation went on beyond 6 months.

Figure 5.8: Period of Investigations

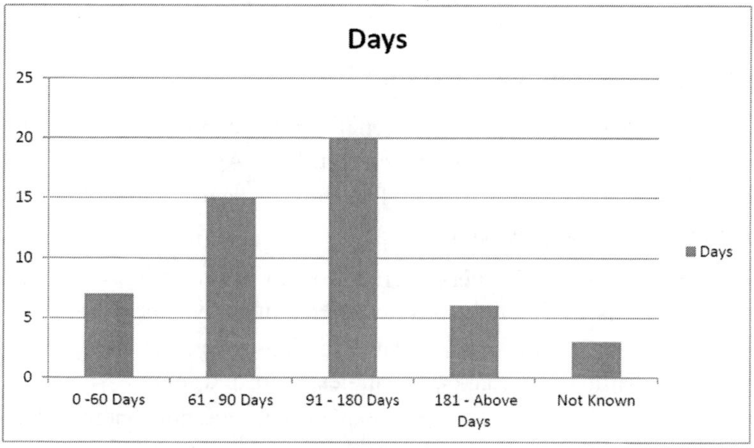

Source: Field Survey.

The reasons for the delay in trial and the poor rate of conviction, inferred from the comments made in the public prosecutor's memo, were as follows:

1. Witnesses turning hostile
2. Lack of evidence
3. Most of the sections used against the accused not having evidentiary proof
4. No evidence to establish the ownership of the place in question
5. Accusations of rape are leveled in the statements not matching the FIR
6. Technical failures like failure to enclose a photocopy of the statement of the witnesses, incomplete MLC, failure to name officers who took the prosecutrix for medical examination and absence of witness list and signature of the investigating officer on the FIR

7. Prosecutrix not being traceable or not appearing in the court
8. Discrepancy in the statement of the accused under sections 161 and 164 of Cr.P.C
9. Inherent defects in the complaint like the status of the SPO
10. Misjoinder of charges the same case for charges involving the trafficking of a number of persons weakens the case
11. Accusation of rape not corroborated by the medical examination report

Medical Examination (Section 15)

Under Section 15, persons taken into custody must be put through a medical examination. The police station in Agra has a prescribed format under section 15 of IT(P)A for medical examination that includes the following details:

1. Consent of the Person: The woman has to indicate whether she is willing to be physically examined by a male doctor.
2. Identification marks: This section mentions the persons identification marks, like moles, scars and so on.
3. Personal history: The personal history does not contain details regarding the personal health and hygiene of the person. Instead what is noted down are the details of her stay at the brothel or the profession in terms of time; whether she would like to continue in or leave the profession; whether she has accepted the job willingly; and so on. This section also has a column stating the persons marital status, the number of children she has (if any) their age- group, and so on.
4. Physical examination: The physical examination consists of details as to the built of the person (averagely built/well built), mental status (normal/ abnormal), height, weight and age. It is in this section that the medical examiner gives his opinion regarding the persons age.
5. Details of private parts: This section covers details regarding the womans private parts, including the pubic hair, auxiliary hair, breasts, and hymen etc. The emphasis is on whether these parts are those of a mature adult or not etc.

Highlights

1. Only women and girls are trafficked as per the cases registered.
2. In 78% of the cases the persons trafficked are from West Bengal, Uttar Pradesh and Nepal.
3. 47% of the persons rescued under the Act are under 18.
4. In 70% of the cases the traffickers are strangers to the persons trafficked.
5. The rate of conviction under these cases is very negligible.
6. The period of investigation in this category of cases is very long as compared to cases under Section 8.
7. Though aimed at all those involved in the process of trafficking, the law enforcement agency does not charge all the actors involved. All the accused in these cases are kotha owners, managers and other agents related to the final trafficking destination.
8. Despite the fact that those trafficked are from certain parts in and outside the country, there is no evidence of any sustained effort for inter-state coordination for curbing trafficking.
9. The statements of the girls show that they have been illegally detained in the brothel for one year/two years which illustrates the ineffectiveness of the process of raid and rescue prescribed by the Act.
10. No investigation is carried out to identify areas that are used as spots for the sale and purchase of women and girls.
11. The technical failures in the records leading to the acquittal and discharge of the accused shows that the law enforcement agency has to re-look at its training, methods of functioning and its overall perception with regard to the IT (P) Act.

5.2. Interactions at State Homes

While my field survey I have interacted about 50 inmates of the state home in Agra. The interactions ranged from brief conversations to detailed ones spread over many days. The level of interaction obviously depended on the willingness of the respondents to speak with me. Moreover, the narratives of respondents from the state home have been analyzed under the following ways:

1. Pre-trafficking social context of the respondent and the nature of violence faced by the respondent at their native area
2. Incidents associated with trafficking or Incidents associated with migration to the red-light area
3. Initial period of being forced to prostitute or, the period subsequent to migration.
4. The period of relative independence, if spoken of by the respondent
5. Interface of the individual with the state authorities.

1. Pre-trafficking Social Context

The reasons that led to the displacement of the respondents from their native areas were both economic and social. A vast majority of the respondents were from economically deprived backgrounds. Many belonged to families of landless agricultural labourers. Those who came from families, which owned land, had suffered due to crop failure and indebtedness as a consequence. Respondents from an urban setting had been working as domestic helps or in factories or living as dependents of factory workers. In most cases, friends, relatives or neighbours had promised to help them find work in the city as domestic helps or factory hands. The desire to supplement the family income made most of the respondents migrate willingly. In some cases, the respondents were from families headed by females and the initiative to travel to the city to earn a living and send money home was entirely volitional. The persons supported by the respondents in their native place were usually their parents and children.

A significant proportion of the respondents had been victims of gender-based violence, in their natal and marital homes. In fact, gender-based violence was a contributory factor leading to voluntary migration in most cases. The perpetrators of violence were fathers, brothers, stepmothers, and other relatives in the natal home and members of the marital home. In the natal home, violence was often faced because the respondent was regarded as a burden who ought to live with her husband's family. In such cases, the respondent had returned from the marital home due to violence or the death of the husband. A large number of respondents spoke of violence faced in the marital home, where they were battered, ill-treated and even raped at the instigation of the spouse. Several respondents were deserted by the spouse, and left with no place to go, with little support from the natal family. Three respondents said that their families had married them to significantly older men or to men who were already married, who later sold them. Respondents often spoke of abusive fathers who were violent towards them and their mothers.

In some cases, gender-based violence was coupled with economic difficulty, when a father married a second time, leading to near starvation conditions. Sweety had a violent childhood, with an abusive father. Her father regularly cheated on her mother making his childrens childhood and his wife married life miserable. Sweety herself was married at a very young age and was battered by her husband. After her children were born, her husband deserted her and went to Bangladesh. Following this, six years ago, a woman from her village brought her to the city under the pretext of getting her a good job. Sweety was, however, sold to a brothel keeper. After being sold, she was never made to live in confinement, but the initial months of her stay in Agra were difficult nonetheless. After the initial months, Sweety started sending money home to her mother and children.

Five years after coming to Agra, Sweety got married again. Before the marriage, her second husband insisted that she leave prostitution but Sweety refused, saying that she had children to feed and that her work should not be interfered with. For the entire period of her stay in Agra, Sweety maintained close links with her home and regularly sent money. Sometimes, she managed to make a trip home. On her last visit, her first husband came to her house and demanded that she accompany him to Bangladesh. A violent argument ensued after which Sweety came back to Agra. After her return to Agra, Sweety was arrested in a raid and was brought to the home for adults. When asked whether she wanted to stay on in Agra or be sent home she told the police that she wanted to stay on in the city.

Sima was married for two years and three months pregnant, when she lost her husband in an accident and moved to her stepmother's and brothers' home. Sima was severely abused by her brothers, particularly after the birth of her child. She was taunted and constantly reminded that she was a burden on the family. The beatings from her brothers were brutal and resulted in permanently slurred speech. Simas stepmother colluded with a neighbour to send her to the city. She was paid by the neighbour who transported Sima. Despite the abuse she had suffered at the hands of her brother, Sima had not anticipated what lay in store for her. Her life in the brothel was replete with the most severe abuse. She was confined, raped and beaten.

Sima managed to leave the brothel during a raid and was brought to the home for adults. The one place where she could go from there was her village, where she knew she would be beaten. At one point during her stay in the home, she was to be escorted to her village by the police, but she changed her mind. She reasoned that life would be safer in the home than at the brothel or at home. A few months later, Sima changed her mind again. She asked to be escorted to her village, to be with her child.

Runa came from a family of twenty-four, including siblings, half siblings, parents and stepmothers. Her violent and alcoholic father severely abused her, her mother, and her siblings. Also, making ends meet was very difficult with so many mouths to feed. A neighbour employed in a city came to meet her family one-day. She asked Runa whether she wanted to work in the city with her. She told Runa specifically that she would have to do work of the kind that exists in a husband-wife relationship. Runa found it odd, but was not entirely unaware of what the work would involve. She decided to accompany her neighbour to the city since the need for money was very pressing.

When they reached the city, her neighbour took Runa to her place of work. The neighbour exchanged money with the brothel owner and Runa began to work there. Runa was brought out of the brothel in a raid. She was brought to the home for minors, where she was asked to leave prostitution. She was told that she would be allowed to leave the home only if she did so. Runa told them that she would leave the profession, as long as she was allowed to go to her village. In the days after the raid Runa, like many others, was asked to implicate the people who had brought her to the city. She, however, did not wish to make any such statements. She only wanted to be free and to earn again.

2. Incidents associated with migration

Though the circumstances under which migration took place and the ways in which the trafficker lured the respondents differed, most traffickers posed as understanding, compassionate persons who claimed that they could help the respondents. In some cases, the trafficker posed only as an empathetic co-passenger but in other cases stated specifically that they could help the respondent find employment in a city.

In a majority of cases the respondent was willing to travel with the trafficker. In several cases the traffickers were elderly women or couples, people least likely to appear threatening. Some respondents said that they faced violence at the hands of the trafficker only when they were no longer in a position to seek help from a third party to go back home.

In many cases, however the respondent faced no violence at the hand of the transporter whose sole concern was to sell the victim to the brothel keeper. Several respondents mentioned being drugged by the trafficker after being induced to travel with them. This was more the case with those who were kidnapped and trafficked against their wish.

In very few cases, the actual incident of migration is one where the individual has given some nature of informed consent to the fact of migration to the city. This can be seen in Reshma's case where a neighbour offered to take her to the city and told her that she will have to do work akin to the type which exists in a spousal relationship. Reshma states that she was somewhat foxed about the nature of work but decided to accompany her neighbour.

A significant proportion of the inmates had been trafficked by relatives. In Rimas case, her second husband brought her to the brothel, while she was under the illusion that she was going to her marital home. Cases of the victim having given some sort of informed consent (as in the case of Runa) were rare.

3. Period subsequent to migration

The period immediately after migration was when most respondents suffered the greatest amount of violence. Beatings at the hands of the madam and rape by brothel managers were the order of the day in the initial period. Many respondents were almost enslaved during this period, with no access to or interaction with the outside world. Respondents said that they were battered even when they interacted with others working in the brothel. Many said that constables working in the area often knew of their plight, but did nothing to help them. The violence generally decreased as the respondent grew to accept the work, since the brothel owners were only interested in the money the respondent could earn for them.

As a general rule, the older respondents did not speak of being battered in the initial phase. Some even said that they were allowed to keep a part of their earnings from the very beginning, which was not the case with the younger respondents. Wherever the brothel management felt assured that the respondent would earn, at least, the amount paid for purchasing her without making an attempt to leave, they generally did not resort to violence. Most respondents described the following phases of evolution in the life of a sex worker in a brothel.

Phase I: This is when the victim is unwilling to be in prostitution. The person at this point is abused and unhappy. The incidence of physical battery is high and the movements of the individual are entirely controlled by the madam.

Phase II: This is when the individual acquires some right over her earnings and attains a degree of independence. Increasing right over her earnings makes the individual willing to engage in sex work. It is at this point that the brothel owner is viewed as a support system and the individual starts trusting the brothel management. She is no longer forced to take clients by the madam and can keep the tip given by the client Since the management no longer fears that the individual might try to escape, she is trusted by the brothel owner and allowed to go out with clients and other people. Towards the beginning of this phase, the individual might still be living under a madam, with the madam taking a substantial amount of her earnings. At a later point however, she might rent a room and have access to all her earnings except the rent for the room. She can then send money home on a regular basis and might even visit her native place.

Phase III: When it becomes difficult to take clients, a sex worker may start to run a brothel and employ young girls to work for her. She may start living on the earnings of younger prostitutes, recently trafficked or otherwise. A former victim of trafficking may eventually become a trafficker herself. Alternatively, however, the individual might also become a destitute with no access to her earlier source of livelihood and no other means of earning.

4. Interface with the police

The emotions harboured towards the police by the inmates of home in Agra are those of antagonism and mistrust. All the respondents have been victims of police corruption. They look upon the police as people to be feared, as those in a position to exploit their vulnerability rather than as people to whom to turn to seek protection by legal means. In a discussion about the raids in Agra, the respondents reasoned that the aim of the raids could not be nabbing traffickers, since the police know exactly when traffickers bring new girls to the brothels. They take a certain amount of money from the madams who keep unwilling girls in their brothels and do nothing to help the girls. Suman stated that the personnel involved in the raids used to come up to the brothels, to find out if there were any new girls. She said bitterly that the same police personnel are now being hailed as champions of the cause of trafficked girls and women.

Ncha is onc of many inmatcs who cxprcssly stated that she had seen police officers involved in the 'rescue operations taking bribes in the past from the madams. She claimed that the officers even demanded free sex. She also said that she could not recover her belongings (including money) from the brothel after the raid when she went back to the brothel to collect her belongings; she stated that the police had informed the madam beforehand about her visit. This, according to the other respondents, is a regular practice.

Several inmates and women in prostitution said they did not see any point in making statements to the police, as the police are the integral part of the problem. Some inmates in, especially those in the home for minors, however, had a more favourable opinion of the police. Some of them were grateful that they had been able to come out of the brothel with the help of the police.

5. Interface with State Home authorities

Within the State Home, the researcher came across respondents who were glad to have been brought out of the brothels and those who had not wanted to be brought to the State Home at all. The inmates of the first category, though not always minors, were usually those who had been in the red-light area for a relatively short period of time. Those who wanted to continue with their current work were usually in the age group of 20 to 35 years.

The purported reason for the raids in Agra was to rescue minor victims of CSE and to nab traffickers who had brought them there and local criminals involved in trafficking. According to the statistics provided by the Probation Officer at the Protective Home for Girls, approximately 24 girls were brought to the Protective Home between 1/11/2015 and 1/7/2018. A total of 20 girls were brought to the Home from 2015 till November 2018. At the point of data collection, no attempt had been made to communicate the reason behind the raids to the individuals rescued in the raids. Had the legal position been clarified to the inmates it might have helped them to make better- informed statements to the police and to the State Home authorities. Urmilas story is a case in point. She was booked for offences under Sections 3, 4, 5 and 6 of the IT (P) Act two years before she was removed from Sikandra and Kashmiri Bazar in a rescue operation. Though she was brought out of the brothel as a victim of trafficking and housed at the Home, she said that she did not know whether she could make a statement against her original traffickers without drawing herself further into legal problems. She said that there had been no attempt on the part of the authorities at the Home to tell her why she was there. She said further, that it was only at the Home that she had understood that she could still make a statement against her trafficker, which her counsel in the previous case had warned her against.

The apparent apathy of the authorities at the Protective Home could be attributed to the fact that the inmate-to-staff ratio at the Home is far larger than that prescribed in the Act. Nonetheless, it does seem that adequate importance is not given to the right of the inmates to information concerning their lives, even though the aim of the operation is to provide justice to victims of abuse. The adverse impact of the lack of information was seen in several cases where respondents believed their stay at the Home implied that cases had been lodged against them during the course of the raids. The fact that those rescued in Agra were housed in the remand section of the Home, meant for 'children in conflict with the law, only reinforced this idea. Most inmates were unaware of the fact that they were being detained to nab the people who had trafficked them.

The inmates also said that they had not been informed of the results of their bone age tests. For a lot of the inmates, the possibility of attaining freedom was hinged on the results of these tests. The lack of understanding shown towards the inmates is evident in other cases too. Reshma, for example was taken to Civil Court to testify against a madam in the same vehicle as the accused. She was also kept in the same lockup as the accused while she was waiting for her case to be heard. She asked to be shifted to another lock-up after the accused threatened to kick her in the stomach. The Superintendent of the Protective Home stated that inmates and accused were taken to court in the same vehicle. No logical reason could be found for keeping the victims and accused in the same lock-up. Such acts fly in the face of all the concern expressed by the State for the welfare of trafficked persons. From a sample of 14 case files read at the Home for minors, Agra, 10 cases were filed under sections 3, 4, 5, 6 IT (P) Act. Four cases used section 7 IT (P) Act. The final status of the cases was not available.

From the group of persons withdrawn from red light areas under the above cases, 4 were from West Bengal, 1 from Gujarat, 3 from Karnataka, 2 from Maharashtra and 4 were from Nepal. From information available from age verification tests in 10 cases, 3 were between 15-16 years of age, 4 were between 16 - 17 and 3 were between 17-18 years of age.

Environment in the Shelter Home: The State Home aim to be institution that provides protective custody to victims of abuse. The environment in these homes should be such as to instill a sense of wellbeing in the inmates and make them look upon such an institution as a place that provides support. Most inmates in Agra said that they were made to feel like criminals. At the Protective Home, Agra, the respondents were housed in the remand section. They were allowed to move out of their room only for a sewing class or duty in the kitchen. Food was served to them in the corridor outside their dormitory, which was sealed off by a gate, preventing them from moving out into the rest of the compound. The inmates of the Home in Agra, had a larger space to move around in, but they were locked into their room from 7:30 pm to 6 am and again after lunch. In the entire Home, the rooms of the inmates had a television that they could watch for a certain number of hours in the morning and the evenings.

Interaction with the Authorities: Though it would be wrong to label all the State Home as being antagonistic and hostile towards inmates, it cannot be denied that many in positions of authority are apathetic in their dealings with the inmates. Several respondents at the Home, Agra, for example, were told that they would have to stay at the Home for four years, but they were not told why. A respondent from the Home, a mother of three children, was at one point advised to give her children up for adoption. Given her position of disempowerment and vulnerability, the suggestion was possibly entirely unnecessary. Given the number of beneficiaries at the state home, it is virtually impossible for the Welfare Officers to engage in effective case work exercises with the inmates. At the State Home in Agra, counselling was done by personnel working at the State Home themselves. It is important to note, however, that the interactions of the respondents with the staff at the homes in Agra positive. Two of the teachers at the Home were especially spirited and supportive. The inmates of the Home for Minors did not express any hostility towards the personnel working at the Home. This was the only Home where creative initiatives, such as theatre classes, had been tried.

Training facilities: The facilities for imparting training to inmates were limited to needlework and knitting. Many inmates expressed the wish to learn a skill that might help them to earn a living. Some wanted to attain basic literacy. Others said they would like to learn to read and write in their vernacular. But these options were not open to them.

Living conditions: In the Home the inmates lived in clean surroundings. They cooked their own meals and were allowed only one helping of food. The medical facilities in Agra were minimal. Inmates of the Home in Agra were taken to a doctor if they felt unwell. However, if they happened to feel unwell at night, they would have to wait for the doctor to come the next morning.

Options available to the inmates: Women brought to the Home from brothels have the following options before them:

1. Going to native home with police escort: According to the statistics available at the Protective Home, Agra, 16 women were sent with police escorts to their native homes. No information was available as to the outcome of such initiatives. Ten girls from the Home were sent to their native place with police escorts. Interactions with the inmates and State Home authorities revealed that the presence of a police escort in uniform and a written statement saying that the girls had been rescued from brothels created problems in such repatriation efforts. Several families did not accept the girls when they learnt that they had been rescued from brothels. Several respondents said that they had been visiting their home or sending money on the pretext that they were working in factories or as domestic helps before they were escorted back home by the police. They said if the State really wants to rehabilitate them within their native homes they should send them with escorts in civil clothes and their relatives should not be told that they had been rescued from a red-light area. Alternatively, they should be allowed to go home on their own.
2. Going home with NGO escort: According to the statistics available, 16 women from the Nari Niketan were sent to their native place with NGOs.
3. Being released without escort: According to the statistics of the Home, 12 inmates were released from court and allowed to leave independent of escorts between 2014 and 2018. Such

cases are on the decline since only two girls were released in 2016 –2017 and one in 2017 – 2018. These are alarming statistics as the girls in the Protective Home are adults and have the right to choose where they wish to go. At Home for majors, the two options given to the inmates are that they can be escorted to their native place or helped to find other work. Several inmates chose the latter to be able to return to sex work.

4. Going home with family/parents: Six women from Home were restored to their family/parents. During interaction with the inmates we found that State Home staff, especially in Agra, was very strict regarding visitors under the order of the court. It was stated that the girls were not being allowed to meet their parents. During a brief discussion with brothel owners it came to light that when they went to visit the girls they were not allowed to do so and were humiliated. The girls said that the authorities asked parents to show ration cards or family photographs before allowing them to meet the girls.
5. Being transferred to another institution: According to the Home statistics, two girls were shifted to the Home from the observation home for girls as they were above 20. The reason given was that the girls were above 20 years of age.

Figure 5.9: Status of Cases at State Home, 2014-2018

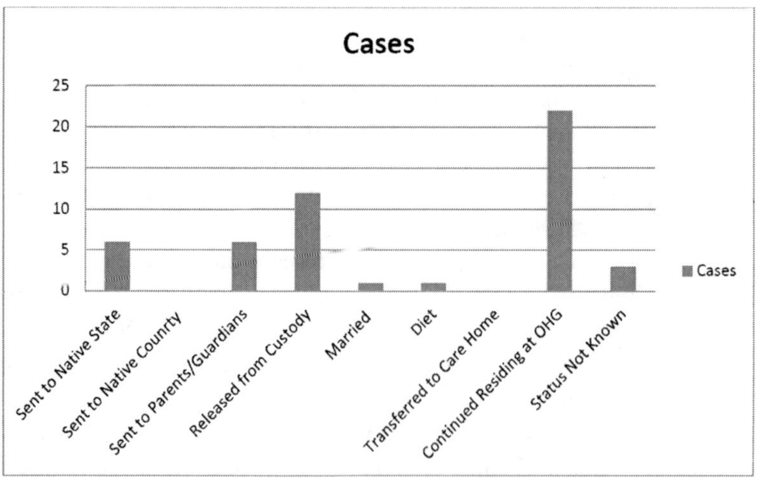

Source: Field Survey.

5.3. Findings of the Study Regarding Women (CSW's) in the Bedia Dominated and Red-Light Area of Agra District

Table 5.6: Information about the family chief & CSW

S.N.	Information About Family Heads & CSW	Community (N-50)		CSW (N-80)	
		Yes %	No/ NR%	Yes %	No/ NR%
1.	Any female involved in CSW in your family	84	16	69	31
2.	Will you indulge your female in CSW	76	24	38	62
3.	Your female should adopt other profession	84	16	85	15
4.	Do you know any family who left this profession	4	96	10	90
5.	Do your daughter get share in property as your son	82	18	69	31
6.	Do you aware about reservation in jobs	60	40	15	85
7.	Have you heard about IT (P) Act	8	92	10	90
8.	Have you heard about HRs or FRs	44	66	69	31
9.	Do you think you are victim of HRs violation	28	74	60	40
10.	Have you heard about HIV/AIDS	44	66	70	30
11.	Do you think about HIV risk in this profession	20	80	60	40

Source: Field Survey.

Table 5.6 showed information of family chief (N-50) and CSWs (N-80). When asking about any female indulged in this profession in their family, 16% community and only 69% CSW respond yes. 76% family chief said that they indulged their females in this profession while 38% CSW were in opinion that they indulged their females (daughters) in this profession in future.

84% of chief of Bedia families and 85% of CSWs were in opinion that their females should adopt other profession if provided. While 82% of family chiefs and 69% of CSW says that their daughter gets equal inheritance right in their ancestral property as their son. Only 4% of family chief and 10% of CSWs know some family who left this profession. Moreover, 60% of family chief of Bedia community knew about their reservation in Government jobs but only few of them were in jobs due to lack of proper educational prevalence in their community.

Further, survey revealed that only 44% of community and 70% CSW knew about human rights and fundamental rights, but in-depth discussion it was found they heard about these rights regarding police torture, and administration attitude towards them. 28% community person & 60% CSWs were in opinion that they are victim of human rights violation. Another question was asked to the community persons of Bedia families and CSWs about HIV/AIDS and found that 44% community persons and 70% CSWs heard about HIV/AIDS, 20% & 60 simultaneously were in this opinion on that they can get HIV infection due to this profession.

Table 5.7: Reasons for Becoming Sex Worker

S.N.	Reasons for Becoming Sex Worker	Non-Bedia (N-40)		Bedia (N-40)	
		Number	%	Number	%
1.	Economic Hardship	16	40	8	20
2.	Cheated or Mislead	0	0	0	0
3.	Kidnapping/Abduction	0	0	0	0
4.	Personal Choice	2	5	0	0
5.	Ill Treatment by Parents	4	10	0	0
6.	Rejection in Love	4	10	0	0
7.	Mothers Profession	6	15	12	30
8.	Traditions/Social Custom	8	20	20	50
9.	Divorced	0	0	0	0

Source: Field Survey

Table 5.7 shows that the parental status of most of the prostitutes had their parents living who had sent them into the profession. There were also women in the profession who had either lost their parents or had come from broken homes. I have also collected data on the basis of Bedia and Non-Bedia women in this profession, which show that 80% of Bedia women introduced into the profession by their parents due to mother's profession or tradition/social custom. While only 35% women from non-Bedia category came in this profession due to this reason. It indicates that, 40% "women were introduced into the profession by their relatives or their family members due to poverty". While only 20% women from Bedia families entered into this profession due to poverty. No other cases were reported of CSWs entering into this profession such as cheated or misled, kidnapping / abduction, divorced etc. While only 2 out of 80 CSWs were from personal choice, 4 out of 80 were from ill treatment by parents and 4 out of 80 were due to rejection in love. The "highest number of prostitutes comes from families where prostitution had become normal trade and was getting training for their profession".

Table 5.8: Education Level and Marital Status of CSWs (N-80)

S.N.	Educational Level	%	Marital Status	%
1.	None	73	Unmarried	85
2.	Primary	18	Married	3
3.	Middle	9	Divorced/Disserted	5
4.	Higher	0	Widow	7

Source: Field Survey.

Table 5.8 shows that out of 80 cases 73% were illiterates, 18% were below primary school level and 9% were "middle school level". Thus, "most of these women are illiterate". The aim of education is to develop a social personality or behaviour and education is absolutely necessary for the development of human personality. Education is ultimately connected with public enlightenment and it can also provide sex education and social hygiene teaching. Further, the marital status of these women showed that the majority, i.e. 85% were unmarried. As against this, only 3% were married and only 5% of married had been deserted, divorced from their partner and 7% were widows.

Table 5.9: Entering Age in this Profession (N-80)

S.N.	Age of Entering in this Profession	Numbers	%
1.	Less than 16 Years	32	40
2.	16 to 20 Years	36	45
3.	21 to 25 Years	8	10
4.	26 to 30 Years	4	5
5.	Above	0	0

Source: Field Survey.

The Table 5.9 showing that, "highest numbers of prostitutes were in the age group of below 20 years and as many as 85% of the girl entered into the profession when they were in this age group"[4]. They have found the profession lucrative as schedule caste families were living in extreme poverty and were tools in the hands of exploiters.

These people have no means of livelihood though most of them worked as pimps or brokers or workers in unorganised sector. Their wages were miserable below the subsistence level and could hardly meet their living needs. Poor socio-economic conditions of these women prevented them from receiving education.

The highest percentage of case entered into this profession "in the age group of 16 to 20 years"[5]. With the advancement of age, the demand for prostitutes decreased. This is why more were brought to profession at the prime of their youth. The law of supply and demand works to the determent of aged prostitutes. Thus, this reason is more vital in trafficking for prostitution for minor girls leads to human rights violations in minor girls.

Table 5.10: Who is Responsible to Introduce in this Profession (N- 80)

S.N.	Who is Responsible	Number	%
1.	Male	28	35
2.	Female	40	50
3.	Themselves	12	15

Source: Field Survey.

In Table 5.10, data shows that 50% females were responsible to introduce these girls in this profession and only 15% CSWs (Women) are responsible themselves because it had become normal business of the family rather than 35% of male. This showed that women are more responsible to introduced minor girls in this profession.

Table 5.11: How Much Earning They Shared with You (N- 80)

S.N.	How much Earning they Share	Number	Percentage
1.	More than 50%	46	58
2.	25 to 50%	20	25
3.	Less than 25%	14	17

Source: Field Survey.

Table 5.11 was attempting to know about who run the brothels, treatment of brothel keepers and percentage of earnings paid to the brothel keepers. 56 CSW out of 80 discloses that brothel keeper were women and 24 out of 80 told that brothel keeper were other i.e. landlord of these property, where they paid a big amount to these owners.

It further revealed that 46 % women paid more than 50% of their earnings to brothel's keeper, 20 of them paid 25% to 50% of their earnings and remaining 14 paid less than 25% of their earning. The "highest number of prostitutes paid 50% of their income to brothel keepers"[6]. The money, which remained with them, was not sufficient to meet their needs. Some had to send some money to their home, they were hardly able to save any amount after meeting their manifold charges and these women were always in the grips of money tendered who most were the brothel keepers, touts and their exploiters.

Table 5.12: Attitude/Treatment of Brothel Keepers (N0-80)

S.N.	Attitude of Brothel Keepers	Number	%
1.	Bad	52	65
2.	No Boundation	16	20
3.	Others	12	15

Source: Field Survey.

Table 5.12 showed that "65% brothel keepers treated prostitutes badly, 20% treated them nicely" and 15% showed other reasons. Thus, highest numbers of women were treated badly by brothel keepers who were "interested only in earning money by adopting any means".

Table 5.13: Problems Faced by CSWs (N-80)

S.N.	Problem Faced by CSWs	Yes %	No%	NR%
1.	Clients Forced/Beat You	18	58	24
2.	Police Demands Money	61	7	30
3.	Torture by Pimps/Brothel Keepers	0	25	75

Source: Field Survey.

Table 5.13 describes about the problems faced by CSWs, in which 18% of women faced problems from client, they beaten women that forcibly used them without using condom. So, the danger of getting HIV infection is also high in these women. While survey, I also met many CSWs having HIV infection. 24% women didn't reply in this matter.

61% women accepted about police interference, and these policemen received money from these CSWs regularly, 30% do not replied on this issue. No CSWs was ready to disclose any torture by brothel keeper or pimps. But in our field observation I found the organizers and brothel madam kept full hold over their matter.

Table 5.14: Children of CSWs (N-80)

S.N.	Child of CSWs	Yes %	No %
1.	Do you have Children	21	79
2.	Child live with Mother	33	67
3.	Child live with Relatives	67	33
4.	Sent to Hostel	0	0

Source: Field Survey.

Table 5.14 exhibiting about children of CSWs and data explains that most of these women issueless and most of the children were born after entry into the professions and therefore incidence of illegitimate children was quite high. Only 21% CSW have children. Only 33% children lived with their mother among of these women and 67% children lived with their relatives.

Most of the women and maintained their ties with their families and they had sent their children to their parents or to other relatives. The "problem of keeping their children in this brothel was a hurdle in their profession". Thus 67% children of these women were with their relatives, and only 33% children were kept with themselves.

Finding of the Study Regarding Children of Bedia/CSWs (10-14 Years)

Table 5.15, 5.16 and 5.17 showed responses regarding education level, reasons of dropout and community responses toward these children belong to Bedia community & CSWs.

Table 5.15: Response Regarding Education (N-24)

S.N.	Response Regarding Education	Yes %	No %	DK/NR
1.	Do you go to School Regularly	33	67	0
2.	Drop before 6th Class	67	33	0
3.	Do you desire for further Education	75	17	8

Source: Field Survey.

Table 5.15 revealed that 67% children were illiterate, 67% drop-out before 6th class 75% children sowed their interest to further education.

Table 5.16: Reason for Dropout (N-16)

S.N.	Reason for Dropout	Yes %	%
1.	Poverty	25	65
2.	Not Interested	12	20
3.	Discriminate Behaviors of School Teachers and Schoolmates	38	15
4.	Parent not Allowed	19	
5.	School is Too Far	6	
6.	Education is not Proper	0	

Source: Field Survey.

Table 5.16 illustrate about the reasons for drop out of children of Bedia community where 12% children not interested which showed that they have not got proper environment in family and socialisation of these children were not in right direction. 38% children of these CSW and Bedia community said that they dropout from due to discriminate behaviour of schoolmates and teachers.

19% says that parents were not allowed them to get further education, while only 25% children drop-out due to poverty, which shows that parent of these children does not want to educate them properly because they ultimately become part of their business and income generation. This showed about the human rights violation within their family and by their parents.

Table 5.17: Responses Regarding Community Behaviour and Acceptance of Children (N-24)

S.N.	Community behaviors and Acceptance	Yes %	No %	NR %
1.	Are they friendly with You	38	12	50
2.	Are your parent discriminate you as a Girl	13	58	29
3.	Do you know your mothers Profession	8	21	71
4.	Will you adopt yours mothers Profession	12	25	67
5.	Other work or Job	67	8	25

Source: Filed Survey.

The Table 5.17 explains about the responses regarding behaviour and acceptance showed that 13% of girl children says that parents discriminate to be a girl, 8% of girls knew about their mother's profession, when asking about to adopt their mother's profession only 12% says yes, while 25% reply no and 67% not replied. While 67% girls want to do other jobs such as teachers, doctors etc.

The data also reveals that children of CSWs and Bedia community faces many problems in getting education and in society, negative responses of the society pulls them to indulged in this business. Thus, the indirect violation also always matters and children of these vulnerable sections not found themselves in the mainstream of the society.

NOTES

1. The Immoral Traffic (Prevention) Act, 1956 (Act 104 of 1956) s.3,4,5,6,8.
2. *Supra* note 1 at s.4.
3. AIR 1960 Bombay 289 (V 47 C 82) – State v. Gaya and others.
4. Source: Field Survey.
5. Source: Field Survey.
6. Source: Field Survey.

Chapter - 6

Way Forward to Address the Issue of Trafficking in India

"The fact that the rights to development and to life with dignity are fundamental human rights has to be driven home and appreciated not just by the legal and executive agencies but by the society as well".

Immoral trafficking for commercial sexual exploitation among women and children has been a serious violation of human rights and their dignity. In other words, trafficking for women is considered to be one of the biggest problems as well as hurdle in the inclusive development of our society. Moreover, today we are living in 21st century where human beings have been able to reach beyond 'Moon and Mars' but still, a large section of the society selling their body for their livelihood. This situation poses us to think that we will not able to achieve a real development without taking every deprived sections of the society into mainstream development. However, the situation is more serious when trafficking for prostitution is became as a traditional and cultural norm that practiced by certain communities like Bedias who are still practicing prostitution as their family business and have the tacit support of their family and community.

Furthermore, it can be argue that, the commercialisation of women's body is not only a serious crime but also an "abuse of womens dignity that results in physical, social, mental damage to millions of women every year". Martha Nussbaum, a feminist thinker who has rightly pointed out in her book *Sex and Social Justice*, "Human beings have a dignity that deserves respect from laws and institutions. But human dignity is frequently violated on grounds of sex or sexuality. Many women all over the world find themselves treated unequally with respect to bodily safety and integrity and in many cases this hardship is caused by their being women and in many cases laws and institutions perpetuate these inequalities".[1] For instance, the existing systems concerning "trafficking of women for commercial sexual exploitation" in the spheres of prevention, protection and prosecution are not sufficient to address this complex problem in a holistic and rights-based manner.

Besides, the conceptual understanding that regulates "anti-trafficking legislation" so far has equated "trafficking with prostitution". It has; therefore, limit the scope of tackling various forms of trafficking. Therefore, it unable to deal with the vulnerability of the victims and the process that put them in circumstances of "abuse as victims of commercial sexual exploitation (CSE)". Furthermore, it imposes the burden of abuse on the victims only and abstains from talking the abuser as well as perpetrator. It has been found that majority of the country's legislation dealing with trafficking are designed in such a way to address prostitution and not trafficking. Still trafficking is not considered a serious crime and considered it as a minor offence as it is equated with 'prostitution'.

Trafficking in recent time became one of the heinous illegal trades globally only after arms and drugs and India is not an exception to it. Today India became "a source, transit and destination for both" in country and cross border "trafficking" due to many reasons like geographical location, population, economy etc. Now the question Is not it unrealistic to expect them to make use of human rights? It is unrealistic to expect from a government while does not even acknowledge of trafficking and more importantly does nothing to stop selling of innocent girls instead agree to provide sex workers the facilities for insurance, of security measures and health services, etc. seems to be idealistic. Sex-workers do not even have ration cards or voter's identity cards. They must first establish their citizenship many of whom are disowned by India and other country. They do not have the basic necessities of life like food, shelter, health facilities, basic education and they cannot resist violence inflicted upon them every day. Studies have revealed that the trade is extending beyond traditional red-light areas.

In the larger context, recognizing prostitution as a profession will be legitimism of the commodification of women. The question of choice vis-à-vis prostitution is a western concept, while in India and other developing nations; the question of choice is a force. Trafficking and prostitution is a trade, which institutionalises exploitation. The women should definitely be provided with certain safeguards; health services, protection from police harassment, education for their children, etc. There is a need to organise them into groups to achieve this objective. But to bring them under a labour union or any association would legitimize prostitution. Ideologically, we have no problems with the demand for human rights but doubts as to how much sex workers will be able to exercise these rights in the extremely exploitative set up in which they work or a part of the nexus. In all probability, the vulnerable section of sex workers will end up in the clutches of the more powerful elements like brothel keeper and pimps.

Due of the absence of rights of any sort, sex workers are subject to exploitation from at least four different quarters; clients, pimps, brothel madams and the police. According to most sex workers, it is the police who are guilty of the worst excesses. Their harassment is particularly sanctioned by the law, notably through the medium of the "prevention of immoral traffic Act". Moreover, this act does not provide for the punishment of clients but goes overboard in making soliciting punishable with long prison terms and fines. Not surprisingly, the act has become a convenient excuse for the police and state officials to harass sex workers.

The arguments favouring legalisation of the profession are many. First it would give the sex workers a measure of "human dignity" which has been hitherto denied them. This does not just affect the sex workers, but also their offsprings who are often denied educational and other opportunities on account of the social stigma which attaches to the profession of their mothers. Very often, they have no other option than entering their mother's profession. "One way to do this, felt to float an autonomous board" runs by sex workers themselves. It could have representatives from the government, the people from legal community and medical professionals who would regulate the entry of girls and minimum age for those involved into the trade, formulates rules and issues licenses after a through screening.

Under this system, each sex worker will be self-employed and operate under a tri-partite system comprising the government, the landlord and sex workers in question. And all this can be done by some "Non-Governmental Organisations" dedicated to the welfare of the sex workers and their rights. "This step would put a check on girls being sold-off and minor girls joining the trade. It is important that a girl in question should have a say in the matter." After interacting with women from Bedia community and realised that most of these women even from Bedia families were particularly worried about the entry of minor trafficked forced girls into the trade. As their own children's efforts should be made to ensure a better and more dignified life for them so that they live their life by their own and free choice with enjoyment of their basic human rights. Furthermore, the rehabilitation of sex-workers children should be made in such a way in which education, vocational-training; crèche and boarding can provide to them so that they can be a responsible citizen in coming years.

Second, giving sex workers licenses should considerably reduce the risk of harassment from various agencies. As a preliminary step towards legalisation, regulatory body to be set up, which among others, would prevent the entry of children and teenagers into the profession and which further taken step to rehabilitates their children and teenagers by providing signified profession rather than in rescued home or protective homes. Flexible altitude that combines legalisation with rehabilitation can scale down the problem and perhaps eliminate it eventually. But this calls for an open mind. Moreover, "Without legal status, the social rehabilitation cannot be achieved". We are up against all "types or harassment and exploitation". These are "tremendous obstacles but we shall not flinch from our path of struggle". Since most of them were not born to be in this profession. They forced to choose this profession due to "poverty, desertion by husbands, torture by in-laws and kidnapping pushed them to this state, but they do not want to be socially outcast."

The National Commission for Women organised a seminar on problems of prostitution in New Delhi where prostitutes from various states and many social activists participated in the deliberations. In this seminar, among the major problems highlighted were, first, the government had not been taking care of their health and not protecting them from contact diseases. Second, their offspring are discriminated against and not treated at par with common children. Educational facilities are virtually absent as a result their upbringing has been seriously affected. Lastly inadequate housing, exploitation by house-owners, moneylenders, pimps, doctors and harassment by the police put prostitute through enormous hardship and insecurity.

As Chanakya has pointed out that, prostitutions is an invisible profession and if made visible, the existence of the neglected soul may be in peril. Truly, it is and old profession and rough estimate reveals that there are at least 2.5 million women engaged in this profession. Of late, the greater tolerance shown to the profession, attempts to uplift them and efforts at changing the nomenclature from "prostitutes" to sex workers have been significant trends. Legally, prostitution or more precisely prostitution for livelihood is not an offence. A woman is allowed to take up this profession if it is necessary for the existence. According to Sections 3 to 5 of the Immoral Traffic (Prevention) Act 1956, it is an offence to keep "a brothel or living on the earning of prostitution procuring a person or inducing a person to carry on prostitution".[2] However, minors or persons "below 18 years of age living on the earning of prostitution" are not liable for punishment.

Evidently, the law is aware of the socio-economic problems, which often force a woman to take up such an ignominious profession. The law has extended protection towards and dependents who have to live on the earning of prostitutes up to a point. "Under Section 7 of the Act[3], prostitution in or the vicinity of public places notified and within 200 meters of a place of worship"[4], educational institutions, hostel and hospitals in prohibited, if a person, being a keeper of the public place, knowingly allows a prostitute to run her trade in such places, he is "liable to be punished". "Section 20 of the Act" empowers a magistrate to issue a show cause notice to a prostitute or to ask her to vacate her premises if there is a complaint against her or in the "interests of the general public".

Though society had adopted a rigid attitude towards sex relationship outside wedlock, law has always adopted a more liberal and practical attitude towards it. In India from time immemorial it has been trying to keep the profession within reasonable limits and have framed rules with this view. In old Sanskrit literature particularly in Kautilayas Arthasastra we find the mention of these regulations. During modern times, an effort was made to pass Acts, India Police Act 1861, Section 268 of IPC amended in two section 366A and 366 B in order to give effect to "International Convention of Suppression of Immoral Traffic Act 1956" is a comprehensive legislation passed so far to eradicate this social evil. The act was based largely on the recommendations of the "Report of Advisory Committee on Social and Moral Hygiene appointed by the Central Social Welfare Board". The Act deals with all aspects of prostitutes, prostitution and their rehabilitation and the Act has given a deathblow to organised prostitution and has given wide power to the State Government to deal with the evil.

Therefore, we need to think in a holistic approach "to deal the problem of immoral trafficking and human rights violation" among women and children of such communities like Bedia and other. Since it has been observed that, economic viability of the women among the Bedias continues to determine their status in the community. In fact, they are held in high esteem till the time they are economically productive. However, putting it clearly, the female sex in this community has been reduced to objects or commodities with a mere monetary value which needs to be address so that they each woman in the Bedia community can live their life in a dignified manner. However, another alarming truth was revealed while interacting to Mr. 'Y' whose daughter is pursuing the hereditary occupation and he realised that it is demeaning for a woman to prostitute; he was motivated by urge to have "a male progeny to carry on the family lineage", and put his daughter into prostitution. How are daughters being in prostitution could help him in this regard was explained by stinting that, if she were to be married she would go into another family. Now as a prostitute, her children will have this family name and his lineage would continue. His daughter, coincidentally, has a son. So, the purpose of putting her into prostitution has been served. Moreover, the problems in the way of initiating change of attitudes towards the profession are obvious. The Bedias are so organised and the process of conditions so perfect, that prostitution is deeply imbedded in their lives. It has proved rather difficult to make breakthrough in bringing about any change in attitude among them. Such efforts have been made and some results also achieved, the former being quantitatively limited has not left any visible mark in the overall situation.

Moreover, it can be argue that sincere and persistent efforts of individuals and organisations working in this field need a boost to create the kind of attitudinal change that is necessary. But their activities have not with stiff resistance because the community interpreted their intervention as threat to their source income. Despite all these, one must draw inspiration from those sections of Bedias who welcome change, and launch consorted efforts to reach out the community and induce in them attitudinal change. Even at present some change is noticeable, though things are moving only because of the emphatic resistance from other section of the community who prefer to be the way they are rather than accept change for betterment. What is required is getting together people from government society and the Bedia community to prevent the tradition that has dehumanised women. Intervention of like agencies is anticipated to be more effective because they found to be more sensitive to the issue in question as compared to the local bodies (even the administration and public) for whom whole thing is an everyday affair, probably, not worthy of all hue and cry.

The primary data was collected by interviewing 231 persons falling under seven categories. These categories are: (a) police officials, (b) lawyers and public prosecutors, (c) personnel of welfare office and protective home, (d) inmates of protective home, (e) women commercial sex workers of Bedia Community, (f) persons of Bedia community and (g) children of Bedia/CSWs.

Police personnel of different ranks at the police station level were interviewed. Altogether, 10 interviews were conducted at police stations in Agra district. On the whole, 2 senior-level officers, 5 middle-rung officers and 3 lower-rung officers were interviewed.

The advocates interviewed were from the Civil courts in Agra. All in all, 10 interviews were conducted. All the lawyers were either public prosecutors or defence counsels in cases involving issues of trafficking for CSE and commercial sex work.

Information was gathered through focused "group discussions with women and girls who are" under protective custody in the state homes. The total number of inmates with whom the researcher interacted in the state home of Agra was 51 and 80 CSWs and 24 children were also interviewed from Bedia dominated red light areas of Agra district.

The data for this study was collected from courts, police stations, state home and "victims of commercial sexual exploitation" as well as women of Badia community. Of the total of 26 cases registered during 2014-2018 at various police stations in Agra district, a total of 20 cases were studied.

The study contains a review of the laws and an analysis of responses on laws related to trafficking and sexual/commercial sexual exploitation and implementation of those laws gathered from legal experts, judges, lawyers, and members of the law enforcement agencies. The study also contains case studies from exclusive interviews with victims, women of Badia community, survivors of trafficking and sexual exploitation and findings derived from focus group discussions within the relevant groups.

The data collected from the courts in Agra revealed certain trends relating to the areas and police stations where cases were filed, the use of specific sections of the IT (P) Act and the orders issued under these Sections.

The offences recorded were most often under Sections 3 ("keeping a brothel or allowing premises to be used as a brothel"), 4 ("living on the earning of prostitution"), 5 ("procuring, inducing or taking a person for prostitution"), 6 ("detaining a person in premises where prostitution is carried out") and 8 (soliciting or seducing for the purpose of prostitution).

The distribution of cases over a wide range of police stations allowed the study of the patterns and nature of cases specific to some areas and also allowed the comparison of cases from different areas. Specific observations have been made from the files read at the Chatta, Sikandra, Kotwali and Tajganj police stations in addition to the files read in the courts.

A majority of the cases from Agra districts was filed using Sections 4 and 8 of the Act. Maximum cases were filed under Sections 4, 5 and 8 of the Act. These sections pertain to "punishment for living on the earnings of prostitution procuring, inducing or taking persons for prostitution" and seducing or soliciting for prostitution. According to some lawyers interviewed, the Act has been used in a limited manner. Only Sections 3, 4, 5, 6, 7 and 8 have been used, while "Section 9 (seduction of a person in custody) and Section 18 (closure of brothel and eviction of offenders from the premises") have not used. One lawyer pointed out that "Section 3 (keeping a brothel or allowing premises to be used as a brothel") could be implemented effectively only if supplemented with Section 18.

Most of these cases relate to brothels in areas not commonly recognised as red-light areas. These brothels were run in residential flats, houses, hotels, and so on. Couples and others ran some by single women. Most, however, were run by a female brothel manager, assisted by a male. This is also reflected in the statistics relating to the accused in the cases revealing that 20%, 20 and 15% of the accused from the Chatta, Sikandra and Tajganj respectively, are females. Other cases related to women prostitutes who had managers.

The police often act on a tip-off. They make phone calls to the agency managing the call girls or pay the manager or the co-worker of a sex worker, posing as prospective clients. In such cases, the sex workers are charged under Section 8, while the managers, pimps or brothel owners are charged under Section 4 or 5, or both. Such raids are common in non-red-light areas, but not in red-light areas, as data collected from the Tajganj police station show. Most arrests under

Section 8 occur in red light areas but this area comes under a develop market and residential place. This too reflects the fact that most cases under Section 16 relate to women caught for 'soliciting' in public places. Moreover, the view of most lawyers interviewed was that the IT (P) Act is targeted primarily at regulating sex work. Even they felt that the aim of the legislation is to eliminate the sex trade and to reform sex workers. I observed that only two of those interviewed they said that, the legislation could be used to deal with trafficking in addition to sex work.

In addition to that, this chapter shows the distribution of the sections used in orders passed in relation to cases filed from the Agra district. The majority of the 10 acquittals and 3 convictions were under Sections 4, 5, 8 of the 20 case files examined, 6 were registered under

Section 8 of the Act and 10 under "Sections 3, 4, 5 and 6 of the Act. Section 7 of the Act" was used in 4 cases. Moreover, there were 3 convictions, out of which, 1 was only under Section 8 of the Act that stipulates "punishment on first conviction as imprisonment for a term which may extend to six months, or fine up to Rs. 500 or both. And on 2 convictions, stipulate imprisonment extending to one year and fine up to Rs 500". There is a gender bias in this section as shown by the fact that if the offender be a man, the "punishment is imprisonment for a period of not less than seven days and up to three months". However, it is to be noted that, not a single accused as per the cases examined was ordered as Proclaimed Offenders (PO) under 82 and 83 of the CrPC 1973. As per the provisions of the sections, a proclaimed "offender is a person against whom a warrant has been issued and who, a court 'has reason to believe (whether after taking evidence or not") is absconding or "concealing himself so that such warrant cannot be executed".

It may point out that, out of 20 cases, 10 cases (Section 3,4,5,6, & 8) + 6 cases (Section 8) + 4 cases (Section 3, 4, 5, 6, 7 & 8) + 0 case (Section 7& 8) =20. In other words, 80 % of cases selected at random were filed under Section 8. In 30% cases section 8 was used by itself while in the remaining 70% cases it was used with other sections. This goes against the main "purpose of the Act, which is to prevent the exploitation of women" by procurers, pimps, traffickers, brothel owners and so on. Given that section 8 of the Act does not pertain to the trafficking of persons, these figures suggest that a majority of cases filed under the IT (P) Act only serve to criminalise the sex workers position. Not a single case examined was filed under "Section 9 of the Act, which deals with seduction of a person in custody". The rank of the Investigating Officer was consistently and clearly mentioned only in the files of the courts in the Agra district. In the 20 cases examined from Agra district the Investigating Officer was of the rank of an Inspector in 85 % of the cases and of the rank of Sub Inspector in the rest.

The observations about witness lists is based on the data collected from the court files examined. Ideally, a raid party must include female police personnel, and arrest must be made in the presence of public witnesses, a medical professional and some residents of the area. However, in the cases read during the research, on an average, the ratio of police personnel to non-police witnesses was 8:2. In many cases, there was only one public witness, and in some cases, there was no public witness at all. The police remand letters sent by the station house officer (SHO) to the courts reflect a considerable bias against the sex worker, who is considered a morally depraved individual. They also show a lack of understanding of legislation. For example, while examining the cases during my field survey in Agra, I found that the police did not make use of the appropriate sections while filing the charges in the F.I.R. In a particular case registered at the Chatta police station, the police claimed that the accused was doing the business of prostitution and buying and selling girls yet failed to use the relevant IPC sections, such as 366, 366A, 366B. Study shows that one of the cases filed under section 8 of the Act was pending for 10 years and another filed under sections 3, 4, 5, 6, 8 of the Act for more than 10 years at the time of the research. Presently the Act does not provide any guidelines for the completion of the cases under a specified time period.

The maximum numbers of accused are arrested under Section 8. Out of a total of 20 accused in cases from the Agra district, 70% were female and 30% were male. The number of years from time of occurrence till order in cases under specific sections is stated in the table below for the cases examined in the courts. In the Agra district the average number of days taken for the decision, i.e. number of days between date of occurrence and the date of decision in the case is 2568 days, or a little over 7 years. The Study reveals that "there has been an increase in the number of cases registered in the Agra during 2014 – 2018". Also, the cases under Sections 3, 4, 5, 6 are (68%) significantly greater in number than those under Section 8 of the IT (P) Act.

Broadly the cases can be categorised under two heads namely; cases that are exclusively under Section 8 and cases under Sections 3, 4, 5 and 6. Usually Sections 3,4,5,6 IT (P) Act is coupled with certain sections of the "Indian Panel Code". These are Sections 109, 323, 342, 354, 363, 365, 366, 372, 376, 415, 506, 34 and 120B.

While examining the cases in Agra, as a researcher, I found that the police did not make use of the appropriate Sections while filing the charges in the F.I.R. In fact, these cases follow a general pattern. First, since the complainants are always male. Moreover, they were residents of Kashmiri Bazar, Sikandra and Basai or employed there or in its immediate vicinity or are passers-by.

The statement of the complainant is usually to the effect that a woman standing at the place of offence harassed/abused him and that the police should take the necessary legal action against her. All the case files mention that the accused was later "arrested at the place of occurrence of the offence" when the complainant, accompanied by the police went back to the site and the accused behaved in the manner described by the complainant in front of the police. The consideration usually mentioned for sexual services offered by the accused ranges from Rs 200 to Rs 500. The accused were all women and most of them pleaded guilty. The complainants are always men and the accused always women.

Only women and girls are rescued under this Act. Most of them are trafficked from West Bengal, followed by Nepal and Andhra Pradesh. Persons trafficked from these areas account for 70% of all those trafficked from within India.

The reasons that led to the displacement of the respondents from their native areas were both economic and social. A significant proportion of the respondents had been victims of gender-based violence, in their natal and marital homes. In fact, gender-based violence was a contributory factor leading to voluntary migration in most cases.

Though the circumstances under which migration took place and the ways in which the trafficker lured the respondents differed, most traffickers posed as understanding, compassionate persons who claimed that they could help the respondents. In some cases, the trafficker posed only as an empathetic co-passenger but in other cases stated specifically that they could help the respondent find employment in a city.

The period immediately after migration was when most respondents suffered the greatest amount of violence. Beatings at the hands of the madam and rape by brothel managers were the order of the day in the initial period. Many respondents were almost enslaved during this period, with no access to or interaction with the outside world. Respondents said that they were battered even when they interacted with others working in the brothel.

Within the State Home, the researcher came across respondents who were glad to have been brought out of the brothels and those who had not wanted to be brought to the State Home at all. The inmates of the first category, though not always minors, were usually those who had been in the red-light area "for a relatively short period of time". Those who wanted to continue with their current work were usually in the age group of 20 to 35 years.

Most inmates in Agra said that they were made to feel like criminals. At the Protective Home, Agra, the respondents were housed in the remand section. They were allowed to move out of their room only for a sewing class or duty in the kitchen. Food was served to them in the corridor outside their dormitory, which was sealed off by a gate, preventing them from moving out into the rest of the compound.

Though it would be wrong to label all the State Home as being antagonistic and hostile towards inmates, it cannot be denied that many in positions of authority are apathetic in their dealings with the inmates. Several respondents at the Home, Agra, for example, were told that they would have to stay at the Home for four years, but they were not told why.

Women (CSWs) in the Bedia Dominated and Red-Light Area of Agra District were interviewed and I have showed information of family chief (N-50) and CSWs (N-80). When asking about any female indulged in this profession in their family, 84% community and only 69% CSW respond yes. 76% family chief said that they indulged their females in this profession while 38% CSW were in opinion that they indulged their females (daughters) in this profession in future. 84% of chief of Bedia families and 85% of CSWs were in opinion that their females should adopt other profession if provided. 60% of family chief of Bedia community knew about their reservation in Government jobs but only few of them were in Govt. jobs due to lack of proper educational prevalence in their community. The study revealed that only 44% of community and 70% CSWs knew about human rights and fundamental rights, but in-depth discussion it was found they heard about these rights regarding police torture, and administration attitude towards them. 28% community person & 60% CSWs were in opinion that they are victim of human rights violation. Another question was asked to the community persons of Bedia families and CSWs about HIV/AIDS, the study showed that 44% community persons and 70% CSWs heard about HIV/AIDS, 20% & 60 simultaneously were in this opinion on that they can get HIV infection due to this profession.

As regards the parental status most of the prostitutes had their parents living who had sent them into the profession. I have also collected data on the basis of Bedia and non-Bedia women in this profession which show that 80% of Bedia women introduced into the profession by their parents due to mother's profession or tradition as well social custom. While only 35% women from non-Bedia category came in this profession due to this reason.

The chapter indicates that 40% women were introduced into the profession by their relatives or their family members due to poverty. While only 20% women from Bedia families entered into this profession due to poverty. No other cases were reported of CSWs entering into this profession such as cheated or misled, kidnapping/ abduction, divorced etc. While only 2 out of 80 CSWs were from personal choice, 4 out of 80 were from ill treatment by parents and 4 out of 80 were due to dejection in love. The highest number of victims comes from families where prostitution had become normal trade and was getting training for their profession.

The aim of education is to develop a social personality or behaviour and education is absolutely necessary for the development of human personality. Out of 80 cases 73% were illiterates, 18% were below primary school level and 18% were middle school level. Thus, most of these women are illiterate. Education is ultimately connected with public enlightenment. It can also provide sex guidance and social hygiene teaching.

The empirical data showed that, "the highest numbers of victims were in the age group of below 20 years" and as many as 85% of the girl entered into the profession when they were in this age group. Most of the women belong to Hindu religion and majority of them are from scheduled caste families. They have found the profession lucrative as schedule caste families were living in extreme poverty and were tools in the hands of exploiters. These people have no means of livelihood though most of them are workers in unorganised sector. Their wages were miserable below the subsistence level and could hardly meet their living needs. Poor socio-economic conditions of these women presented them from receiving education.

The highest percentage of case entered into this profession in the age group of 16 to 20 years. With the advancement of age, the demand for prostitutes decreased. This is why more were brought to profession at the prime of their youth. The law of supply and demand works to the determent of aged prostitutes. Thus, this reason is more vital in trafficking for prostitution for minor girls leads to human rights violations in minor girls. Moreover, an attempt was made to know that who run the brothels, treatment of brothel keepers and percentage of earnings paid to the brothel keepers. 56 CSWs out of 80 discloses that brothel keeper were women and 24 out of 80 told that brothel keeper was other i.e. landlord of these property, where they paid a big amount to these owners. It further revealed that 46 women paid more than 50% of their earnings to brothel keepers, 20 of them paid 25% to 50% of their earnings and remaining 14 paid less than 25% of their earning. The highest number of prostitutes paid 50% of their income to brothel keepers. The money, which remained with them, was not sufficient to meet their needs. Some had to send some money to their home, they were hardly able to save any amount after meeting their manifold charges and these women were always in the grips of money tenders who most were the brothel keepers, touts and their exploiters.

This chapter reveals that 65% brothel keepers treated prostitutes badly, 20% treated them nicely and 15% showed other reasons. Thus, highest numbers of women were treated badly by brothel keepers who were interested only in earning money by adopting any means.

This chapter also describes about the problems faced by CSWs, in which 18% of women faced problems from client, they beaten women that forcibly used them without using condom. So, the danger of getting HIV infection is also high in these women. While survey, I also met many CSWs having HIV infection. However, 24% women did not reply in this matter. As far as interference by police is concerned, 61% women accepted about police interference and these policemen received money from these CSWs regularly and 30% do not replied on this issue. More importantly, no CSWs were ready to disclose any torture by brothel keeper or pimps. However, in my field observation I found, the organizers and brothel madam kept full hold over their matter.

Moreover, the empirical data of the marital status of these women showed that the majorities, i.e. 85% were unmarried. As against this, only 3% were married and only 5% of married had been deserted, divorced from their partner and 7% were widows. Most of these women issueless and most of the children were born after entry into the professions and therefore incidence of illegitimate children was quite high. Only 23% CSW have children.

The empirical data revealed that 67% children were illiterate, 67% drop-out before 6th class and 75% children sowed their interest to further education. The reasons for drop out were 12% children not interested which showed that they have not got proper environment in family and socialisation of these children were not in right direction. 38% children of these CSWs and Bedia community said that they dropout from due to discriminate behaviour of schoolmates and teachers. 19% says that parents were not allowed them to get further education while only 25% children drop-out due to poverty which shows that parent of these children does not want to educate them properly because they ultimately become a part of their business and income generation. This showed about the human rights violation within their family and by their parents.

Empirical data of the responses regarding behavior and acceptance showed that 13% of girl children says that parents discriminate to be a girl, 8% of girls knew about their mother's profession, when asking about to adopt their mother's profession only 12% says yes, while 25% reply no and 67% not replied. 67% girls want to do other jobs such as teachers, doctors, etc. It further revealed that children of CSWs & Bedia community faces no discrimination between male and female children, moreover society encourage and appreciate them to indulge in this business.

After analysing my empirical data, I have observed certain changes in the following manner:

1. In early days, Bedia males were not allows to marry in their own caste but now they marry within their own caste.
2. Earlier they were living under tents and huts and were moving from one place to another place. More importantly, they were not recognised by the government. But now they live in their payment dwelling and recognised in the schedule list of the Government.
3. Community started giving education to their children.
4. With the passage of time, some of them have left the profession of prostitution and engaged themselves in reputed jobs.
5. Earlier they do not marry their daughter. Now they do who does not want to become prostitute.
6. As observed from Agra Commissionary, they had shifted their house from the cities to town and rural areas.

7. In earlier days there used to be big prostitution and several girls worked under one roof as prostitutes. Now the style of prostitution business is rapidly changing. Big position is reduced to small or independent dwellings and nowadays the females come at particular place and go back to their house and or early several of them worked as call girls and reached as per the appointment in hotel or in a fixed place.

This rapid change gave them two advantages; one, no police atrocities and second, alleviation of their respect. Such type the community profession is a big challenge for the Government as well as several organisations who have been working in protection human rights.

Last but not the least, I can argue that women of Bedia community have been indulging for "commercial sexual exploitation for prostitution" and today it becomes a major human rights problem and it needs to be address systematically and urgently. Since it "deprives women s right to live with dignity and self-respect" and even their "bodily integrity" and makes them to live like an animal. After my field survey, I reach at the opinion from view of human rights that the following difficulties becomes a major hurdle in protecting human rights of CSWs among Bedia community. These are as follows:

1. Because of involvement of huge political and criminal nexus, women have become a commodity in this game and even they are not in a position to demand for their dignity and struggle for their rights.
2. Identify red light areas in Agra division are now diminishing and no longer remain a concept for sexual and thus they are not able to come under one umbrella so they have no platform to come forward to demand for their rights.
3. This profession is now on going in their own independent dwelling or in their residential area or working as call girls.
4. The biggest drawback is that such type of activities carried by women and it is very sad that the government has no effective rehabilitation programmes for these girls and to rescued women.

5. It has been found that open read light areas are running behind the dhabas during the daytime where passers stopped for a while for this purpose and the nexus is further involving the women from nearby villages in this trade.
6. With this type of rapid changing trend of so called red light areas, posing a big threat and act as a big barrier in reducing HIV/AIDS transmission.

Therefore, in the prevailing climate my appeal to government and local body is to give thought to the pool in efforts to evolve effective remedial measures that may redeem womanhood from disgrace.

Furthermore, I would say that, trafficking of women has emerged as one of the major problems for India because of fragile social and economic conditions which forced many women to become victims of trafficking, prostitution and other forms of violence. It is in this sense, if there would be no legal support provided then it further aggravates the situation. However, there are laws against these sorts of crime have been enacted from time to time but due to pragmatic approach and lack of implementation due to various reasons make the laws unable to protect women from being victimized. As a result, trafficking within the territory and across the border is gradually increasing. Hence, in present situation the laws of the land related to trafficking and the process of its implementation should be reviewed to explore ways and means to improve the situation of women. It is in this sense, I have given some steps as a way forward (a) to improve trafficking laws, (b) to protect the traffic victims from exploitation, (c) to fight the problem of trafficking for commercial sexual exploitation. In order to address this issue, I am trying to formulating four set of pragmatic solutions to address this menace and these are namely; legislation, law enforcement, adjudication of cases and shelter homes

6.1. Legislations

1. The title of the Act should be changed to "The Traffic in Persons for Commercial Sexual Exploitation (Prevention) Act" in place of "The Immoral Traffic (Prevention) Act" because the word "immoral" put a negative impact on the mind of law enforcement agencies, judges, lawyers etc.

2. The present Act, do not provide the definition of "trafficking" therefore, the Act should be amended and provide a clear and wide definition of the word "trafficking" which help the investigation agencies, judiciary to reach into conclusion of the cases more promptly and the accused would not be able to take benefit of loop and wholes of the Act.
3. In Section 2(a), the sentence "for the mutual gain of two or more prostitutes" in the definitions of "brothel" should be deleted because it emphasizes on "commercial sexual work" rather than exploitation and implied consent.
4. In Section 2(f) the ambiguity in the definitions of "prostitution and prostitutes" should be removed because it causes a major hurdle in the implementation of the Act. As "prostitution" indicate to "commercial sexual exploitation" while "prostitute" indicates to a trafficker or brothel owner.
5. The definition of "public place" should be removed from the Act as given under "Section 2(h)" because the crimes of "trafficking and sexual exploitation" are crime irrespective of specific location where the crime is committed.
6. The jurisdiction of Section 3 needs to be widened to include "transit points used by traffickers at ant point of trafficking" because in the present Section only punishment given for "keeping a brothel or allowing premises to be used as a brothel".
7. Section 4 should be "amended to include an exclusion of the children and aged parents of sex workers". Therefore, the Section should read as "where any person over the age of 18 years, other than the dependents, children or age parents of the person, who knowingly live wholly or in part, on the earning of the prostitution of any other person shall be punishable".
8. Section 8 may be deleted because this Section is not compatible with the purpose of the Act and even not related to "trafficking" and mainly used to harass sex workers only. As the present Section is to deal with "seducing or soliciting for the purpose of prostitution".
9. Section 17 should be change to make compulsory the presence of regional language translator when the language of inmates in protective custody is different from language

of welfare officers and the rescued person always kept in protective homes and they never put in police lockup in any circumstances.

10. To refers directly to "trafficking", Section 18 may amend to read "a magistrate may receipt of information from the police or any one that any room, house, place referred to Section 7(2) is being run or used as a brothel by a trafficker or is being used for adding or abating trafficking".

The legislatures, while amending the Act, should keep in their mind to make the laws in such a way that it will help the victims to start a new life along with deterring and punishing traffickers.

6.2. Law Enforcement

11. The Union Public Service Commission conducted exams every year to recruit official for different branches including "Indian Revenue Services" which was further bifurcated into "Indian Revenue Services (Income Tax)" and "Indian Revenue Services (Custom and Indirect Taxes)" for better enforcement of laws. In the same way, "Indian Police Services" should be bifurcated into "Indian Police Service (Law & Order)" and "Indian Police Service (Investigations)". The rationale behind this suggestion is that when same officer is involved in arresting and investigation then the investigation may be doubtful because the pre-assumption of the officers and he could be biased and at the same time, the burden of work on the officers would be too high.
12. The different state government should also recruit officials for different purposes to make officials more efficient in their field and make them specialized.
13. The law enforcement agencies should be well trained and must have right and sufficient knowledge of law which would help the prosecution the case properly in the court and restrained the accused to get benefit of loop and whole in the investigation.
14. The law enforcement agencies should be trained in such a way that they should be sensitive and empathetic towards the victims instead of abusing them.

15. There should be recruitment of enough women officials in the police force especially in those departments which deals with the trafficking or prostitutions related issues.
16. There should be enough coordination between different agencies of different state as well as across nations.
17. There should be special courts and prosecutors to deal with trafficking cases preferably women in every district and the cases must be concluded in the time bound manner.
18. The strength of police force should be increase to many folds to tackle crime more effectively especially crime against women. The salary of police officials should be enough to maintain their family which would reduce corruption as well increases their efficiency at the same time their duty hours should be limited to eight hours only and in case of overtime they should be paid extra money. More importantly, they should provide with specialised training to make raids and arrest in red light areas.
19. The victims and accused should be transported and lodged separately and the female victims or accused should be searched by female only.
20. The law enforcement agencies should involve members of NGOs in the raid, rescue, counseling of the victims to make them safer and more comfortable.
21. While taking the victims to their native place, it should be making compulsory to accompany police personal in civil dress and they should be trained to be empathetic towards the victims and to convince victim's family to accept them.

6.4. The Adjudication of Cases

22. The law should be made for speedy conclusion of the cases in a time bound manner because most of the acquittal under IT (P) Act because of victims' absence as they turned back to their native place.
23. There should establish of special courts for the cases of trafficking as given under the Act because it is not implemented properly yet.
24. The Act should be amended to "introduce witness protection programmes".

25. The judges, prosecutors and other officials "should be trained and educated to sensitize towards the victims of trafficking".
26. The public prosecutors should be given proper facilities and salary to eradicate corruption so that they can facilitate fair justice to victims.

6.3. Shelter Homes

27. Counselors with special skills must be appointed for counseling the inmates of shelter homes to take them out from the trauma which they had faced and to start a fresh beginning with hope and new zeal.
28. There should be proper and clear instructions to the officials of shelter homes not to treat inmates of the homes as criminals, they should allow to move freely within the shelter home and help them to feel like home.
29. The "traffic victims" rescued in police operation and sent to shelter homes must be informed their rights, status, reasons for their custody.
30. The inmates of the shelter homes must be provided with proper opportunities to learn different skills to make them or life better and at the same time they should be provided with educational opportunities and also encouraged them for further education.
31. The state homes "rules and regulations" should be made public and NGOs and other social workers should be allow to visits shelter homes regularly and to provide counseling for career, legal rights etc.
32. The main motive of shelter homes should be to help the victims to restart their life a fresh and for that prepare them in advance.
33. The problem of "trafficking" exists in society for various reasons like poverty, unemployment, lack of education and awareness. Therefore, the Government should focus on these issues along with punishing the "traffickers".

Bibliography

1. **Primary Sources**

(I) Legislations

- Suppression of Immoral Trafficking Act, 1956 (104 of 1956), s. 2 (f).
- The Code of Criminal Procedure, 1973 (Act 2 of 1974).
- The Criminal Law (Amendment) Act, 2013 (Act 13 of 2013).
- The Immoral Traffic (Prevention) Act, 1956 (Act 104 of 1956).
- The India Evidence Act, 1872 (Act 1 of 1872).
- The Indian Panel (IPC) Code, 1860 (Act 45 of 1860).
- The Juvenile Justice (Care and Protection of Child of Children) Act, 2015 (Act 2 of 2016).
- The U.P., Police Manual, 1959, Volume I – Administration.
- The U.P., Police Manual, 1959, Volume III – Powers and Duties.

(II) Government of India Policies

- Government of India & UNICEF, Dealing with Child Victims of Trafficking and Commercial Sexual Exploitation (Ministry of Human Resource Development, 2008).
- Ministry of Women and Child Development, India Country Report to Prevent and Combat Trafficking and Commercial Sexual Exploitation of Children and Women (Government of India, 2017).
- Ministry of Women and Child Development & UNO on Drugs and Crime, India Country Report to Prevent and Combat Trafficking and Commercial Sexual Exploitation of Children and Women, (Government of India, New Delhi, 2008).
- National Commission for Women, Societal Violence on Women and Children in Prostitution, (Government of India, 1996).

(III) International Conventions

- Asia Foundations, "Human Trafficking in India: Dynamics, Current Efforts and Intervention Opportunities", (March, 2010).

- Asian Development Bank, "Combating trafficking of women and children in South Asia: Regional synthesis paper for Bangladesh, India and Nepal. Manila, (2002).
- CATW "Coalition Against Trafficking in Women", (2002).
- European Union, Report on Trafficking in Migrants (International Organisation for Migration (IOM), 2018).
- Trafficking in Women & Global Alliance Against Traffic in Women (1997).
- UNIFEM, '*Trade in Human Misery: Trafficking in Women and Children*', Asia Region.
- United Nations Office on Drugs and Crime, UN. GIFT United Nations Global Initiative to Fight Human Trafficking. India South Asia Regional Conference: Responding to Trafficking for Sexual Exploitation in South Asia. Vienna: United Nations Office on Drugs and Crime. (2007).
- United Nations, Recommended Principles and Guidelines on Human Rights and Human Trafficking. UNHCHR to the ECOSOC, (2002).
- United Nations, The Protocol to Prevent, Suppress and Punish Trafficking in Persons, Especially Women and Children (December, 2000).

2. Secondary Sources

(I) Books

- A.K. Prasad, *Devadasi System In Ancient India: A Study of Temple Dancing girls of South India* (H. K. Publishers, Delhi, 1990).
- A.L. Basham, *The Wonder That Was India* (Surjeet Publications, Delhi, 2007).
- A.S. Altekar, *The Position of Women In Hindu Civilisation* (Motilal Banarasidass Pubishers, Delhi, 2014).
- A.S. Mathur, & B.L. Gupta, *Prostitutes and Prostitution* (Ram Prasad & Sons, Agra 1965).
- Abraham, Shailaja, *Going Nowhere: Trafficking of Women & Children In International Sex Trade* (Dominant Publishers and Distributors, Delhi, 2001).
- Abraham, Shailaja, *Going Nowhere*: *Trafficking of Women and Children in International Sex Trade* (Dominant Publishers, New Delhi, 2001).
- *Abul Fazal* & H. Blochmann, (eds.) *Ain E Akbari* (Oriental Books Reprints, New Delhi, 1977).
- Antony, M. J, *Landmark Judgements on Bonded Labour* (Indian Social Institute, Delhi, 1997).

- Anuja Agrawal, *Chaste wives and prostitute sisters: Patriarchy and prostitution among the Bedias of India*, India (Taylor and Francis Group, Routledge, 2008).
- Anuja Agrawal, *Migrant women and work* (Sage Publication, New Delhi, 2012).
- Aronowitz A Alexis, *Human Trafficking, Human Misery: The Global Trade Human Beings* (Library of Congress, London, 2009).
- Arvind Sharma, *Women in Indian religions* (Oxford University Press, UK, 2002).
- Asha Rane, *Child Prostitution in Uttar Pradesh* (Unit for Child and Youth Research, Tata Institute of Social Sciences, Mumbai, 1998).
- Ashok K Jain, *Socio-Economic Offences* (Ascent Publications, Delhi, 2016).
- August Bebel, *Women in the Past, Present and Future* (San Francisco International Publishing Co., 1897).
- Avtar Singh, *Principle of the Law of Evidence* (Central Law Publication, Allahabad, 6th edn., 20070.
- B.P. Mazumadar, *Socio-Economic History of Northern India* (Firma K.L. Mukhophadhaya, Calcutta, 1960).
- Badauni, *Niccolao Manucci, Storia do Mogol* (London, 1906).
- Bebel, August, *Women in The Past, Present and Future* (Ams Press Inc., New York, 1976).
- Beotra, B. R, *The Suppression of Immoral Traffic in Women and Girls Act, 1956 (with State Rules).* (Law Book Co., India, 1981).
- Biswanath Joardar, *Prostitution in historical and modern perspectives* (Inter- India, New Delhi, 1984).
- Brajesh Rajak, Pornography *Law: Must Not Be Tolerated* (Universal Law Co., Delhi, 2011).
- C.K. Takwani, *Criminal Procedure* (Wadhwa & Company, Nagpur, 2nd edn., 2007).
- Captain William (ed.), Abdul Qadir Badauni *Muntakhabu-t- Tawarikh* (Nesolias and Munshi Ahmad Ali, Calcutta, 1865).
- Carolyn Sleightholme & Indrani Sinha, *Guilty Without Trial: Women in Sex Trade in Calcutta* (Rutgers University Press, UK, 1996).
- Chandra, Satish, *History of Medieval India* (Orient Black Swan, New Delhi, 2007).
- D. Madhu Joshi, *Women and Children in Prostitution: Human Rights Perspectives* (Uppal Publishing House, Delhi, 1997).
- Darga Quli Khan, *Muraqqa-i-Dehli* ed. Nurul Hasan Ansari, (Delhi, 1982).

- David L. Sills, *International Encyclopaedia of Social Sciences* (The Macmillan Co., NY, 1968).
- Denis Kincaid, *British Social Life in India* (Routledge & Kegan Paul Ltd., London, 1973).
- Dipangshu Chakraborty, *Atrocities On Indian Women* (A.P.H. Publishing Corporation, Delhi, 1999).
- Dipankar Gupta, *Caste in Question: Identity or Hierarchy?* (Sage Publications Ltd, New Delhi, 2004).
- Dubois Abbe, *Hindu Manners, Customs and Ceremonies* (Oxford University Press, London, 1924).
- Durgabal Deshmukh, *Prostitutes and Their Children* (Central Social Welfare Board, Delhi, 2017).
- E. Westemarg, *History of Human Marriage* (The Macmillan Company, New York, 1892).
- Elaine Pearson, *Human Rights and Trafficking in Persons: A Handbook* 38 (Global Alliance, Bangkok, 2000).
- Frazer James George, *The Golden Bough: A Study in Magic and Religion* (The Macmillan Company, New York, 1951).
- G. R. Madan, *Indian Social Problems (*Allied Publishers, Delhi, 2012).
- Ghosh, S. K. *The world of Prostitution* (A. P. H. Publication, New Delhi, 1996).
- Gracy Farnandes, *Raids, Rescue, Rehabilitation: The Story of Mumbai Brothel Raids of 1996-2000* (Concept Publication, Delhi, 2001).
- H.A.R. Gibb (tr.), *The travels of Ibn Batuta* (Cambridge, 1956).
- H.M. Elliot, *History of India as told by its own Historians: The Mohammedan Period* (Trubner and Company, London, 1872).
- I.H. Siddiqui (tr.), *Waqiat-i-Mushtaqi* (New Delhi, 1993).
- Indian Social Institute, *Trafficking in women and children in India* (Orient Longman, New Delhi, 2005).
- J.J. Meyar, *Sexual Life in Ancient India* (Life Span Publishers, Delhi, 2015.
- Jana, Dr. S & Banerjee, Bhaskar (edt.), *A Dream A Pledge A Fulfillment: Five Years' Stint at Sonagachi* (Published by All India Institute of Hygiene & Public Health, Calcutta, 1997).
- Janaki Nair, *Women and law in Colonial India: a social History* (National Law School of India University, Bangalore, 1996).
- John Drazazga, *Sex Crimes and Their Legal Aspects* (Charles C Thomas Publisher, USA, 1960).
- Joseph Gathi, *Child Prostitution in India* (Concept Building Company, New Delhi, 1998).

- Joseph Gathia, *Child prostitution in India* (Concept Publishers, New Delhi, 1999).
- K. Jamanadas, *Devadasis Ancient to Modern* (Kalpaz Publications, Delhi, 2007).
- K M Ashraf, *Life and Conditions of the People of Hindustan 1200-1500 AD* (Gyan Publishing House, Delhi, 2001).
- K. K. Mukherji & Deepa Das, *Prostitution in Metropolitan Cities of India, A Study by: Central Social Welfare Board* 16 (Samaj Bhavan, New Delhi, 1996).
- K.D. Gaur, *A Text Book on The Indian Panel* (Universal Law Publication Company, Delhi, 3rd edn., 2007).
- K.K. Mukherji, *Child Prostitution in India* (GNK, Ghaziabad, 1997).
- K.N. Chitnis, *Socio-Economic History of Medieval India* (Atlantic Publishers and Distributors, Delhi, 2005).
- Kakolee Chakraborthy, *Women as Devadasis: Origin and Growth of The Devadasi Profession* (Deep and Deep Publication, New Delhi, 2011).
- Kambale Uttam, *Devadasi ani Nagnapuja* (Marathi) (Lokvangmaya Gruh Pvt. Ltd. Bombay, 1988).
- Karamjit Kaur, *More Internet Date Rapes* (Straits Times, Singapore, 2001).
- L.K. Khurana, *Ancient India* (Laxmi Narayan Publication, Agra, 2001).
- Lakshmi Murthi, *Raided: How Anti-Trafficking Strategies Increases Sex Workers' Vulnerability* (Sampada Grameen Mahila Sanstha, SANGRAM, India, 2018).
- Lyakat Ali, *Law Relating to Child Labour* (Indian Social Institute, Delhi, 1997).
- Martha, C Nussbaum, *Sex and Social Justice* 4 (New York: Oxford University Press, 1999).
- Maryse Choisy, *Psychoanalysis of The Prostitute* (Philosophical Library, New Yark,1961).
- Mohammed Qasim Ferishta (eds.), *Tarikh-i Ferishta* (Nawal Kishore, Lucknow, 1323).
- Moti Chandra, *Studies in the cult of Mother Goddess in Ancient India* (Vikas Publications, Delhi, 2017).
- Moti Chandra, *The World of Courtesans* (Vikas Publishing House Pvt. Ltd, Delhi, 1973).
- Mukherji, Santosh Kumar, *Prostitution in India* (Inter India Publications, Delhi, 1986).
- Murdia Ratna, *The Jogin System Among Scheduled Caste Women: A study in Exploitation* (Unit of Research and Consultancy in Social

Policy & Social Welfare Administration, Tata Institute of Social Sciences, Bombay, 1990).

- N Jayapaln, *A History of Indian Culture* (Atlantic Publishers, Delhi, 2001).
- N.N. Bhattacharyya, *Ancient India Rituals and their Social Contents* (Mamnohar Publishers & Distributers, Delhi, 2005).
- Nagendra Kumar Singh, *Divine Prostitution* (A. P. H. Publishing Corporation, New Delhi, 1997).
- Nagendra Kumar Singh, *Divine Prostitution* (A.P.H. Publishing Corporation, New Delhi, 1997).
- Nandi, Ranendranath, *Religious institutions and cults in Deccan* (Motilal Banarasidas, Delhi, 1973).
- P. Kotiswaran, *Dangerous sex, invisible labor: Sex work and law in India* (Oxford University Press, Delhi, 2012).
- P. Levine, *Prostitution, race, and politics: Policing venereal disease in the British Empire* (Routledge, London, 2003).
- P. Thomas, *Indian Women Through the Ages* (Asia Publishing House, Bombay, 1964).
- P.C. Naik, *Prostitution under religious customs* (Bombay Vigilance Association, Bombay, 1928).
- P.D. Mathew, *Measures for Eradication of Child Labour; Fundamental Right to Primary Education: Landmark Judgements of the Supreme Court* (Indian Social Institute, 1997).
- P.M. Nair & S. Sankar, *Trafficking in Women and Children in India* (Orient Longman, New Delhi, 2005).
- P.M. Nair, *Trafficking Women and Children for Sexual Exploitation: Handbook for Law Enforcement Agencies in India (*United Nations Office on Drugs and Crime: New Delhi, 2007).
- Patkar, Pravin & Patkar, Priti, *Frequently Asked Questions: On Commercial Sexual Exploitation and Trafficking* (PRERANA, Bombay, 2012).
- Patkar, Pravin, Patkar, Priti & Sakhrani, Monica, *Trafficking and Commercial Sexual Exploitation: International Laws, Conventions and Policy* (Anti - Trafficking Centre, Prerana, Mumbai, 2008).
- Paulette, Lloyd & Beth, A. Simmons, *Framing for a New Transnational Legal Organization: The Case of Human Trafficking, Transnational Legal Orders* (University of Pennsylvania Carey Law School, USA, 2015).
- Poudel, Meena, *Traffic in Women: Violation of Women's Dignity and Fundamental Human Rights* (Asian Conference on Traffic in Women, December 11 – 13, Seoul, Korea, 2018).

- Prabha Chandra Tripathy, *Crime Against Working Women* (Vikas Publication, New Delhi, 2000).
- R. Shamasastry (ed.,), *Kautilya's Arthasastra* (The Government Press, Bangalore, 1915).
- R. Suryamoorthy, *Girl Children in Prostitution in Kerala* (Loyela College of Social Sciences, Trivendrum, 1997).
- R.P. Kangle, *The Kautilya Arthasastra* (Motilal Banarasidas Publishars, Delhi, 2014).
- Ram Ahuja, *Social Problems in India* (Rawat Publications, Delhi, 3rd edn., 2014).
- Ram Ahuja, *Violence Against Women* (Rawat Publications, Delhi, 1998).
- Rama Mehta, *Socio-Legal Status of Women in India* (Mittal Publication, Delhi, 1957).
- Rama Mehta, *Socio-Legal Status of Women in India* (Mittal Publication, Delhi, 1957).
- Ratanlal & Dhirajlal, *Law of Crimes: A Commentary on the Indian Penal Code 1860* (Bharat Law House, New Delhi, 27th edn., 2013).
- Richard A. ONeill, *International trafficking in women to the United States: a contemporary manifestation of slavery and organised crime* (Centre for the Study of Intelligence, Washington, 1999).
- Rozario, Rita, *Trafficking in Women and Children in India* (Uppal Publications House, New Delhi, 1988).
- S. Gokilvani, *Child Prostitution in Tamil Nadu* (Centre for Women Studies, Alagappa University, Karaikudi, 1998).
- S. N. Rampal, *Indian Women and Sex* (Printox, New Delhi, 1978).
- S. Shah, *Street corner secrets: Sex, work, and migration in the city of Mumbai*. (Duke University Press, Durham, 2014).
- S.C. Banarji & R. Banarji, *The Castaway of Indian Society* (Punthi Pustak, Calcutta, 1989).
- S.C. Misra & M. L. Rahman (ed.), Sikandar Ibn Mohammad, *Mirat-i-Sikandari* (Baroda, 1961).
- S.K. Ghosh, *The World of Prostitution* (A. P. H. Publishing Corporation, New Delhi, 1996).
- S.K. Kappor, *International Law and Human Rights* (Central Law Agency, Allahabad, 16th edn., 2007).
- S.N. Shailendra, *Ancient Indian History and Civilisation* (New Age International Publications, India, 2nd edn., 1999).
- S.N. Sinha & N. K. Basu, *The History of Marriage & Prostitution* (Khama Publishars, Delhi, 1992).

- S.N. Sinha & N.K. Bose, *History of Prostitution in Ancient India* (Shree Balaram Prakasani, Kolkata, 2003).
- S.N. Sinha & N.K. Basu, *The History of Marriage and Prostitution* (Khama Publishers, Delhi, 1992.
- Sahni, R, Shankar, VK, Apte, H., *Prostitution and Beyond: An analysis of sex work in India* (Sage Publications India Pvt. Ltd, India, 2008).
- Salla Sariola, *Gender and Sexuality in Selling Sex in Chennai* (Routledge, London, 2010).
- Sanghera, Jyoti and Kapur, Ratna, *An Assessment of laws and Policies for the Prevention and Control of Trafficking in Nepal* (The Asia Foundation & Population Council, 2000).
- Sarkar, S. C., *Some Aspects of the Earliest Social History of India* (Oxford University Press, London, 1928).
- Satish Chandra, *History of Medieval India* (Orient Black Swan, Delhi, 2014).
- Savita Bhatt, *Women and Human Rights* (Altar Publishing House, New Delhi, 2010).
- Sewell, Robert, *A Forgotten Empire* (London, 1924).
- Shashi Prabha Jain & Mamta Singh, *Violence Against Women* (Radha Publications, Delhi, 2001).
- Shimona Khanna & Ratna Kapur, *Memorandum on Reform of Laws Relating to Sexual Offences* (CFLR, New Delhi, 1998).
- Sinha S.N. & Basu N.K., *History of Prostitution in India* (Cosmo Publications, New Delhi, 1994).
- Sumati Karmakar, *Red Light Area: Social Environment of Sex Workers* (Dominant Publishers and Distributers, Delhi, 2001).
- Sundra, Raj M., *Prostitution in Madras: A Study in Historical Perspective* (Konark Publisher Pvt. Ltd., Delhi, 1993).
- Tara Beg Aali, *India's Women Power* (S. Chand & Co. Pvt. Ltd., Delhi, 1976).
- Trivadi, Harshad, *Scheduled Caste Women: Studies in Exploitation* (Concept Publishing Company, New Delhi, 1977).
- Umesh Kr. Singh, *Women Crime & Punishment in Ancient India, Earliest Times to 1200 A.D.* 113 (Janki Prakashan, Patna, 2017).
- V. Sadhu Desai, *Social Life in Maharashtra Under The Peshwas* (Popular Prakashan, Bombay, 1980).
- V.N. Shukla, *Constitution of India* (Eastern Book Company, Lucknow, 10th edn, 2001).
- W.H. Carey, *Good Old Days of Honorable John Company* (R. Combay and Co. Calcutta, 1906).

- Zia Ahmad Awan, '*Shattered Dreams and Living Nightmares*': *Situational Analysis on Trafficking of Children and Women in Pakistan* (Action Aid Pakistan, 2000).
- Zia Barani (ed.), *Tarikh-i- Firozshahi* (Sk. Abdur Rashid, Aligarh, 1957).

II. Articles

(a) Journals

- Adi Parva, Krishna Mohan Ganguli (trs.) *The Mahabharata* (1883-1896).
- Anandhi, S. "Representing Devasasis: Dasingal Mosavalai" 26 *Economic and Political Weekly* (1991).
- Anuja Agarwal, "Kinship and Trafficking the Case of the Bedia Community" 22 *Canadian Women Studies* (2003).
- Anuja Agrawal, "Situating the Law on Prostitution/Sex Work in India" 2 *Indian Sociological Society* (2018).
- Anuradha Patil, "Rehabilitation of Children of Prostitutes and Devdasi" *Institute of Social Service* (1999).
- Arun Kumar Acharya, "Impact of Cultural and Religious Practices of Prostitution on the Trafficking of Women in India" 14 *Trayectorias* (2011).
- Asha Bajpai, "Child Sexual Abuse: Need for Law Reforms" 57 *The Indian Journal of Social Work* (1996).
- Asha Bajpai, 'Sexual Harassment in University and College Campuses in Mumbai" 60 *The Indian Journal of Social Work* (1999).
- Asia Pacific-Coalition Against Trafficking in Women, "Every woman has a right: Not to be prostituted" 31 *Off our Backs* (2001).
- Bannerjee, G. R., "Prostitution Requires Prohibition" 19 *The Indian Journal of Social Work* (1958).
- Barse, Sheela, "Rights of The Girl Child" 2 *The Indian Journal of Social Work* (1991).
- Bashir, M. Uddin, "Human Trafficking in South Asia: Issues of Corruption and Human Security" 2 *International Journal of Social Work and Human Services Practice* (2014).
- Baxi, Pratiksha, "Rape, Retribution, State on Whose Bodies?" 35 *Economic and Political Weekly* (2000).
- Chatterjee, R., "Prostituted women and the British empire" 1 *Antyajaa: Indian Journal of Women and Social Change* (2016).
- Christine Joffres & Edward Mill, "Sexual Slavery without borders: trafficking for commercial sexual exploitation in India" 7 *International Journal for Equity in Health* (2008).

- Datar, Chhaya, "Reform or New Form of Patriachy? Devadasis in the Border Region of Maharasthra and Karnataka" 3 *The Indian Journal of Social Work* (1992).
- Divyendu Jha & Tanya Sharma, "Caste and Prostitution in India: Politics of Shame and of Exclusion" 4 *Anthropology* (2016).
- Farrior, Stephanie, "The International Law on Trafficking in Women and Children for Prostitution: Making It Live Up to Its Potential" 10 *Harvard Human Rights Journal* (1997).
- Fernandes, Gracy, "Commercial Sex Workers in India – Action Taken by the College of social work" 9 *Perspectives in Social Work* (1996).
- G. Kuppuram, "Chanakya on Prostitution (Based on Arthasastra)" 40 *Proceedings of the Indian History Congress* (1979).
- Gangoli, Geetanjali & Solanki, Gopika, "Reining Womens Sexuality through Law: Implications for Social Work Education" 59 *The Indian Journal of Social Work* (1998).
- Gangoli Geetanjali, "Prostitution, legalisation and decriminalisation - Recent debates" 7 *Economic and Political Weekly* (1998).
- Gary Lewis, "Protocol on Inter State Rescue and Post Rescue Activities Relating to Persons Trafficked for Commercial Sexual Exploitation" 3 *UNODC* (2007).
- Geoffrey May, "Prostitution" 12 *Encyclopaedia of Social Sciences* (1936).
- Hooja, Swarn Lata, "Prostitution in Rajasthan: Then and Now" 31 *The Indian Journal of Social Work* (1970).
- International Organisation for Migration, "Trafficking in Migrants" 23 *Quarterly Bulletin* (2001).
- Iyengar, Vijayashree R, "Child Sexual Abuse Problem and Intervention; Perspectives in Social Work" 10 *Journal for social issues and social work Intervention* (1995).
- J. Nair, "Devadasi, dharma and the state", 29 *Economic and Political Weekly* (1994).
- Jaamdar, Shiva, "Bringing Justice to Juveniles-extension of poverty alleviation programmes" *Economic and Political Weekly* (1995).
- Jahangir, Arasli, "The Rising Wind: Is the Caucasus Emerging as a Hub for Terrorism, Smuggling and Trafficking?" 6 *Connections* (2007).
- Jean D' Cunha, "Prostitution Laws: Ideological Dimensions and Enforcement Practices" 27 *Economic and Political Weekly* (1992).
- Joffres Christine Mills, "Sexual Slavery without borders: trafficking for commercial sexual exploitation in India" 7 *International Journal for Equity in Health* (2008).

- John, Salt & Jeremy Stein, "Migration as a Business: The Case of Trafficking" 35 *International Migration* (1997).
- Joshi, Aiko, "The Face of Human Trafficking" 13 *Hasting Women's Law Journal* (2009).
- Joshi Manisha, "A Cry for Justice" 49 *Social Welfare* (2002).
- Kannabiran, Kalpana, "Judiciary, Social Reform and Debate on Religious Prostitution in colonial India" 30 *Economic and Political Weekly* (1995).
- Kannabiran, Kalpana, "Judiciary Social Reform and Debate on Religious Prostitution in Colonial Indian" 3 *Economic and Political Weekly* (1995).
- Kapstein Ethan B., "The new global slave trade" 85 *Foreign Affair* (2006).
- Krithika Rajam, "How Devdasis went from having high social status to being sex slaves and child prostitutes" 2 *Human Rights Quarterly* (2013).
- Kuppuram, "Chanakya on prostitution" 40, *Proceedings on the Indian History Congress* (1979).
- Levine Philippa, "Rereading the 1890s: Venereal Diseases as Constitutional Crisis" *The Journal of Asian Studies* (1996).
- Levine Philippa, "A Multitude of Unchaste Women Prostitution in the British Empire" 4 *Journal of Women's History* (2004).
- Makonen, Getu, "Human Trafficking and Development: The Role of Microfinance" 23 *Transformation* (2006).
- Mamoria, C.B., "Prostitution in India" 17 *Indian Journal of Social Work* (1956).
- Mehta, Leena, "Social Profile of Child Sex Workers" 49 *Social Welfare* (2002).
- Migration Information Programme (IOM), Trafficking in women for Sexual Exploitation (Brussels, 1996).
- Nag Moni, "Anthropological perspectives on prostitution and AIDS in India" 36 *Economic and Political Weekly* (2001).
- Nag Moni, "Sexual Behaviour and AIDS in India: State of the Art" 5 *The Indian Journal of Social Work* (1994).
- Nair, Janaki, "The Devadasi, Dharma and the State" 28 *Economic and Political Weekly* (1994).
- P.C. Sahoo, "The Arthasastra on Prostitution" 71 *Bulletin of the Deccan College Post-Graduate and Research Institute* (2011).
- Pai-Patkar, Preeti, "Children of Prostitutes" 5 *Perspectives in Social Work - A Professional Journal for Social Issues and Social Work Intervention* (1990).

- Patnam, Visala and Bagul, Megha, "Teenage Sex Workers – Aspirations and Interests" 49 *Social Welfare* (2002).
- Pawar, M. S., "Prostitution and the Girl Child" 2 *The Indian Journal of Social Work* (1991).
- Petras James & Wongehaisuwan Tienchai, "Free Markets, AIDS and Child Prostitution" 28 *Economic and Political Weekly* (1993)
- Pivar David, "The Military Prostitution and Colonial People: India and the Philippines 1885 – 1917" *The Journal of Sex Research* (1981).
- Poonam Pradhan Saxena, "Immoral Trafficking in Women and Girls: Need for Tougher Laws and Sincere Implementation" 44 *Journal of the Indian Law Institute* (2002).
- Pravin Patkar & Pariti Patkar, PRERANA: Lightning the Lamp of Self Esteem of the Children of Sex Workers, (Mumbai, 1995).
- Ramsanehi, "Untitled article on Bedias- Bedia jati jangal se gaon mein baskar jarayam pesha se vaishyavriti ki ore tatha uske kuch niyam" 45 *Morena: Abhyudaya Ashram*, New Delhi (1998).
- Rao, Asha, Nag, Moni, Mishra, Kingshuk and Dey, Arati, "Sexual Behaviour Pattern of Truck Drivers and their helpers in relation to female sex workers" 5 *The Indian Journal of Social Work* (1994).
- Reanda Laura, "Prostitution as a human rights question: Problems and prospects of United Nations action" 13 *Human Rights Quarterly* (1991).
- Robinson, Laurie Nicole, "The globalisation of female child prostitution: A call for reintegration and recovery measures" 5 *Indiana Journal of Global Legal Studies* (1997).
- Russell & Hiralal, "Caste and Tribes of India" 19 *ASI* (1861).
- S. Shah, "In the business of kama: Prostitution in classical Sanskrit literature from seventh to the thirteenth centuries" 5 *The Medieval History Journal* (2002).
- S.S. Hameed & E. Tanner, *Human Trafficking in India: Dynamics, Current Efforts and Intervention Opportunities for the Asia Foundation* 2010, *available at:* http://asiafoundation. *org*.
- Salt, John & Stein, Jeremy, "Migration as a business: The Case of trafficking" *35 International Migration* (1997).
- Samarasinghe, Vidyamali and Barbara Burton, "Strategizing prevention: A critical review of local initiatives to prevent female sex trafficking" 17 *Development in Practice* (2007)
- Sanighdha, S., "The sex worker Predicament: A Silent Wail", *available at*: info@probono-india.in.
- Saraswati Raju Iyer & N. Radha, "Women Trafficking in India: A Critical Analysis" *4, Shanlax International Journal of Arts* (2016).

- Shadab Bano, "Women Performers and Prostitutes in Medieval India" 70 *Proceedings of the Indian History Congress* (2009).
- Sikka, K. D., "Prostitution: Indian Perspectives and Realities" XLV *The Indian Journal of Social Work* (1984).
- Sikka, K.D, "Prostitution: Indian Perspectives and Realities" 15 *The Indian Journal of Social Work* (1989).
- Sukumari Bhattacharji, "Economic Rights of Ancient Indian Women" 26 *Economic and Political Weekly* (1991).
- Sukumari Bhattacharji, "Prostitution in Ancient India" 15 *Social Scientist* (1987).
- Sukumari Bhattacharji, "Prostitution in ancient India" 15, *Social Scientist* (1987).
- Tulsing Solwani, "Prostituion in Indian Society: Issues, Trends and Rehabilitation", *available at*: https://www.ugc. ac.in.
- Tulsing Sonwani & K. Davis, "Prostitution in Indian Society: Issues, Trends and Rehabilitation" 5 (2013).
- Umesh Kumar Singh, "Immoral Trafficking of Girls and Women in Ancient India" 68 *Proceedings of the Indian History Congress* (2007).
- Usha Rana, Diwakar Sharma and Debarati Ghosh, "Prostitution in northern Central India: An ethnographical study of Bedia community" *International Journal of Anthropology and Ethnology* (2020).
- Usha Rana, Diwakar Sharma and Debarati Ghosh, "Prostitution in northern Central India: an ethnographical study of Bedia community" 7 *International Journal of Anthropology and Ethnology* (2020).
- Vetticattil, J., & Krishnan, S. "Study unearths reality of sex trade in India: low caste, poor women lured into prostitution- World" 4 (2002).
- Wendy Doniger, "The Kama Sutra: It Isn't All about Sex" 5 *The Kenyon Review* (2003).
- Y. B. Singh, "Roots of the Ganika-Culture of Early India" 74 *Annals of the Bhandarkar Oriental Research Institute* (1993).

(b) Magazines

- Trafficking in Migrants, Quarterly Bulletin, April 2001, Special Issue, International Organisation for Migration.
- Wadhwa, Soma, '*For Sale Childhood*, Outlook - The Weekly Newsmagazine, 1998.

(c) Newspaper

- Anita Katyal, "Murmurs at SAARC over Pact Against Trafficking", *Times of India*, 27 January 2013.
- Aslam Mohammad, "When Prostitution was a symbol of high culture in elite circles of 19th century", *Quartz India*, 21 June, 2014.

- Deshpande Swati, "Browsing Child Porn will land you in Jail", *Times of India*, 16 October, 2016.
- Digal, Santosh, "India, World Hub in Human Trafficking", *Asian News*, 15 January 2010.
- Gupta, Monobina, "In A Perfectly Normal Job", *The Telegraph*, 24 January, 2002.
- Iram Agha, "The Bedia girls wont dance no more", *The Times of India*, 26 December, 2015.
- Kaur, Karamjit, "More Internet Date Rapes", *Straits Times*, Singapore, 28th February 2001.
- Renu Sharma, "Trade in Human Misery Trafficking in Women and children", Asia Region, *Newsletter*, 12 December, 2004.

(d) Thesis/Project

- Asia Watch: Womens Rights Project, *Trafficking of Burmese Women and Girls in Brothels in Thailand* (1993) (Project, Human Rights Watch).
- Dr. S. R. Sarode, *Historical Study of Prostitution Trade in India: Past and Present*, (2015) (Project, UGC).
- Rooppreet, K. Sohal, *The Exploitative Nature of Prostitution and Sex Trafficking in India* (2013) (Unpublished Ph.D. thesis, Texas State University).

(e) Reports

- Government of India, India Country Report to Prevent and Combat Trafficking and Commercial Sexual Exploitation of Children and Women (Ministry of Women and Child Development, 2008).
- Government of India, India Country Report: Prevent and Combat Trafficking and Sexual Exploitation of Children and Women (Ministry of Women and Child Development, 2017).
- Government of India, National Crime Records Bureau, Crime in India, (Ministry of Home Affairs, 2000).
- Government of India, National Crime Records Bureau, Crime in India, (Ministry of Home Affairs, 2016).
- Government of India, National Crime Records Bureau, Crime in India, (Ministry of Home Affairs, 2018).
- Govt. of India and UNICEF, Report on the Six Regional Consultations on Sexual Exploitation and Trafficking of Children, (Department of Women and Child Development, 1996).
- Looking Back Thinking Forward - World Congress report on Child sexual abuse, 1996.
- Maharashta State Womens Council, Rescue Home for Indian Women, (Annual Report April 2000-March 2001).

- Maitreya, 'The role of sex workers in preventing sexual exploitation of children'.
- Malla, Sapna, Report on Focus Group Discussion with the Law Enforcement Agencies, (Kathmandu, Nepal, 1 July 2001).
- Malla, Sapna, Report on the Focus Group Discussion with the Victims of Trafficking in Persons, (FWLD, Kathmandu, Nepal, July 11, 2001).
- Society for Development, Research and Training (SFDRT), Report on the Strategy meeting of the 'Forum for advocacy of rights of people in prostitution and sex work, (New Delhi, 22-24 August 2000).
- UN Recommended Principles and Guidelines on Human Rights and Human Trafficking, (Report of the UNHCHR, ECOSOC, 20 May 2002).
- United States, Trafficking in Persons Report. (Department of State, 2011).
- United States, Victims of trafficking and Violence protection Act, 2000 – Trafficking in Persons Report, (US Department of State, July 2001).

(f) Webliography

- http://articles.timesofindia.indiatimes.com.
- http://asiafoundation.org
- http://www.asianews.
- http://www.unhcr.org.
- https://qz.com/india/.
- https://www.state.gov/reports/2018.
- https://www.ugc.ac.in.
- info@probono-india.in,
- www.captivedaughters.org.
- www.catwintemational.org
- www.indiatimes.com.

Index

E

F

G

H

I

J

K

L

M

N

O

P

R

S

U

V

W

Y